Pastor John

Pastor John

A Practical Interpretation of St. John's Gospel

Brian N. Tebbutt

Forewords by Christina Le Moignan and John Cox

WIPF & STOCK · Eugene, Oregon

PASTOR JOHN
A Practical Interpretation of St. John's Gospel

Wipf & Stock
An Imprint of Wipf and Stock Publishers
199 W. 8th Ave., Suite 3
Eugene, OR 97401

www.wipfandstock.com

PAPERBACK ISBN: 978-1-5326-9312-0
HARDCOVER ISBN: 978-1-5326-9313-7
EBOOK ISBN: 978-1-5326-9314-4

Manufactured in the U.S.A.   08/10/20

The Scripture quotations contained herein, where they are not the author's own translation, are taken from the Holy Bible, Revised Standard Version (RSV), copyright © 1946, 1952 by the Division of Christian Education of the National Council of the United Churches of Christ in the United States of America. Used by permission.

Permissions are hereby gratefully acknowledged for poetry quotations as listed below.

For Siegfried Sassoon, "The Power and the Glory," copyright © Siegfried Sassoon. Used by kind permission of the Estate of George Sassoon.

For Malcolm Guite, "John," from *Sounding the Seasons*, copyright © 2012 Malcolm Guite, pub-lished by Canterbury Press. Used by kind permission of Hymns Ancient and Modern, rights@ hymnsam.co.uk.

For Jack Clemo, "Wedding Eve" and "Broad Autumn," from *Selected Poems*. Used by permis-sion of Special Collections, University of Exeter, UK.

For Fred Kaan, "God! When human bonds are broken," copyright © 1989 Hope Publishing Company, Carol Stream, IL (U.S. and Canada); Stainer & Bell Ltd, London, www.stainer.co.uk (rest of world). Used by kind permission of the publishers. All rights reserved.

For Brian Wren, "As man and woman we were made," copyright © 1983 Hope Publishing Company, Carol Stream, IL (U.S. and Canada); Stainer & Bell Ltd, London, www.stainer.co.uk (rest of world). Used by kind permission of Hope Publishing Company. All rights reserved.

R. S. Thomas, from *Via Negativa*, *The Absence*, *Montrose*, *The Covenanters*, *The Fisherman*, *Chapel Deacon*, *The Woman*, *Ann Griffith*, copyright © Orion Publishing Group, London. Used by kind permission of Orion Publishing Group.

For George Mackay Brown, *The Collected Poems of George Mackay Brown*, copyright © the Estate of George Mackay Brown. Used by kind permission of the Estate of George Mackay Brown. John Murray Publishers, permissions@hodder.co.uk.

For Christine
Without whom this work would not have been possible

Contents

Foreword

by Christina Le Moignan

PASTOR JOHN IS A book that makes connections. The author's primary concern is that readers of John's gospel should be able to connect with what they read. They are offered twin approaches in making this connection. One is a *reader-response* approach to the text, in which the emphasis is on what readers personally find in the text as well as on the more detached analyses of academic writing. The other approach, coupled with the first, is a *psychodynamic* approach, which encourages readers to examine their own interior "feeling" responses to what they read, and to use the responses to grow in their own self-understanding and in faith. This growth is shown to involve connections between people's emotional being, their personal identity, and their spiritual lives.

Thus, whilst *Pastor John* recognises the relevance of the narrator's relationship with and pastoral concern for his own community, the primary focus is about the way in which John's gospel can be used pastorally today. Throughout this book, the fundamental question addressed is how, through our reading and sharing the gospel text, Jesus gives himself to us.

The author is a Methodist minister who has sixty years' experience in that role. As both preacher and pastor, he has consistently sought to connect biblical exegesis with pastoral care. He has also given particular emphasis in his ministry to developing group work; hence a connection made throughout this book between group study of a text and the personal development of its members, both individually and as a group.

Fruitful as all these connections are, they are not always easy to make. This book will make demands of its readers, not only in making intellectual links between ideas which may be new or unfamiliar, but in the more personal challenges of the self-examination which readers are invited to make. People are more than once exhorted to "have courage!" They will be well rewarded if they do. For the connection that this book most fundamentally has been written to facilitate is the one between its readers and the Christ whom Pastor John presents to us.

Foreword

by John Cox

PASTOR JOHN IS A refreshingly radical and challenging book that takes the reader on a journey through the turbulent waters of developmental and psychodynamic concepts, pastoral theology, and biblical scholarship, towards a sharing of personal and group experience.

Yet faint not! Brian Tebbutt, as an experienced Methodist minister, will convincingly guide you through these cross currents and help you meet Pastor John. His companions on this journey include the origins of Methodism, especially the class meetings and hymns of Charles Wesley, as well as the Clinical Theology of psychiatrist Frank Lake.

Other writers have trodden this path before, but few (except perhaps the Swiss doctor Paul Tournier) have so successfully navigated these swirling waters of the personal response to the text, as well as the processes of the sharing group experience—each with ethical and clinical dilemmas for the leader and the led. Here is an opportunity for personal growth.

Recent *rapprochement* between psychiatric practice, faith, and spirituality in multifaith societies (evidenced from mental health journals) is creating a more fertile soil where some of the seeds scattered from this book could take root.

Psychiatrists, psychotherapists, and those from psychology of religion and counseling fields who are curious about the reasons for faith in a secular world will find *Pastor John* a very useful guide. For those of faith and those of none, the book provides a valuable exploration of "bibliotherapy." I hope it will be read and studied by many inside and outside the church. They will be rewarded and enlightened—and may even taste the new wine!

Preface

THIS BOOK IS INTENDED to stimulate reflection on St. John's Gospel whilst at the same time facilitating reflection on oneself, in company. Both dimensions, a study of the Gospel and a study of self—that is, of our response to the text—go hand in hand, like a loving couple walking through life!

This book *could* be read by oneself alone, and it will bring, I hope, insight into the Gospel, and, with the discipline of honestly attending to the questions, will create personal insight and growth. But it is significant that the book has had its birth over many years in workshops, and this is reflected in the rolling format. It is not simply a commentary on John; it is a prompt, pointing to deep appreciation of the text *along with* an adventurous togetherness in Christian experience. Here is an invitation to a pilgrimage, solitary *and* shared, a journey with John and with each other. What is offered is a way of sharing faith in groups, with personal growth intrinsic to the experience.

The book is written for:

- people who want to ask questions about John and what it can mean to them;

- ministers, clergy, and lay people who care about both biblical reading and pastoral care;

- those who need material to help reading and interpreting John, *and*

- who wish also to extend development in pastoral care based on biblical insight;

- those who, in a Christian context, teach pastoral depth and need it in themselves, and are willing to value a psychodynamic approach to *both text and person.*

The book is intended both for the general user, and also for those who already know John well. But we start where we start. One member of a teaching class asked, "Who is this person Frayudd that everyone is writing about?" That is how she pronounced Freud! We *all* start where we are! The chapters provide a mixture of simple and more advanced material, so that readers and group members can take what they can out of each section.

So two themes surface, exegesis and pastoral insight, and they are not to be separated, but run together. They are two sides of the same coin. Neither stands alone from the other. Brave biblical interpretation and brave personal interrogation coalesce. My experience over very many years in varied church situations is that this approach deepens the fellowship, the *koinonia*, of the church substantially. Not only are skills of interpretation learned, but with them are also learned skills of self-awareness, of care for each other, and of group work. These constitute a solid foundation for the continuance of church life.

It is the word "psychodynamic" that unites the process. It, and the critical approach advocated, are explained in two rather lengthy introductions. They outline the possibilities of the methods suggested. They are essential because some readers will not be acquainted with a reader response approach, and some readers will not be acquainted with a psychodynamic approach to the "living text" of our lives. The content can be "drip fed" as the groups progress, at points of relevance. The chapter numbers correspond to the Gospel chapters. My experience is that many in church (and emphatically not just the academically minded) rejoice in acquaintance with literary theory, the text of John read afresh, and the newness of sharing experience and mutual care. We should never dumb down content or method. We can all be stretched.

Of key importance is the fact that the aim of the group work that, along with following the "story," makes up the *practical* substance of each workshop, is not discussion, but sharing, not "topic orientated" but "personality orientated."[1] The inner world of the text addresses the inner world of the reader; and the inner world of the reader addresses the inner world of the text. And this happens in the outer world of those gathered in the presence of Christ. The gift of "hovering attention" is offered mutually to each other in the space created by attention to the text, the skill of

---

1. Cox, *Structuring the Therapeutic Process*, 152.

the facilitator, and the goodwill and grace of each person. This is the work of the Holy Spirit.

The thematic focus throughout is answering the question, "How does Jesus give himself to us?"

The landscape of the Fourth Gospel is indeed like a landscape, with strong contours and outstanding features, and with an evanescent quality as the light changes, the cloud comes and goes, the mist hides, and the sun reveals. The road (the "way") stretches ahead. And there is the figure of our Lord, deep in the valleys, standing on the tops, sitting by, striding ahead. As we read, "once under way the story is dominated by the powerful presence of Jesus, who keeps introducing fresh variations on the single theme of life giving revelation." As character after character moves from incredulity to faith, they invite "a similar response from the readers of the Gospel." [2] Jesus is the figure we follow.

Sadly, it is impossible to read all the commentaries, books, and articles on John. And each one has its own point of view. My actual work is a shadow of the dream, but I hope focus can be made on the *attempt* at an achievement, and I hope the activities can be used to let John speak to you. Writing this book has been a bit like doing a giant jigsaw, dimly perceived at first with a picture in mind, but taking shape as the pieces were arranged and inserted, but with endless additions as the image became deeper and richer. Jane Campion writes, "A lot of time writing is spent wondering if you're a failure." True, but I still have hope that this humble effort will enable the enjoyment of John and lead to an awareness of the brilliance of John. I hope it will connect John's picture of Jesus with current life, promote understanding of the interconnections between reading it and the psyche, and facilitate flow between the person of Jesus and the personality of you the reader. This coalescence between who Jesus is and who we are is not new. As early as 1925 one could read, "The emphasis of the Fourth Gospel on the central place of personality is a welcome anticipation and encouragement of one of the healthiest tendencies in modern thinking. For John, the highest revelation is in the person of Jesus—in His words and works as part of himself." [3] I live in hope that what will be facilitated is an enrichment of language and of the exchange of feeling supportively in the human encounter, a "baptism"

2. Ashton, "John and the Johannine Literature," 259.
3. Jones, *New Testament in Modern Education.*

of emotion in shared Christian experience, and, finally, a connectedness between "emotional being, personal identity and 'spiritual life'"[4] so as to make for growth in person and group.

The aim is to encourage honest reading, honest speaking, and honest encounter, the three dimensions—seeing (a key Johannine word), that is, perceptively, the text, seeing oneself, and seeing the other. As Charles Elliott wrote, "We shall never encounter the text (or be encountered by the text) as long as we allow ourselves to be 'distorted', to tell our self-narrative the way it is not."[5]

One impossibility is to embrace the vast expanding universe of scholarship that represents John to us. I have tried to let notes in each chapter point to avenues of thought leading to fascinating worlds. They are as signposts only, in an attempt to convey the excitement of travel in Johannine space. The same applies to the other discipline of psychodynamic studies. How hard to do justice to either. The aim has also been to highlight language that enhances the affect, the feel of the text, so that it may permissibly be aligned with our own affect, our feeling.

We need therefore to be aware of the nature of the material we read.

> John's Gospel is a proclamation of faith in narrative form, paradoxically recounting Jesus' earthly career in order to persuade its readers to accept him as their Risen Lord. This means that it has to be read on two levels, first the story level and secondly the level of spiritual understanding. The riddles of the Gospel, its symbols and its ironies are all aimed at reinforcing this purposeful ambivalence.[6]

It is helpful, if one can, to make some sort of contact with the Greek, familiar to some and strange to others. One needs to be alert to John's repeatedly used nuanced words, sometimes only visible, or rather audible, in the Greek, and I have tried to signify them in italics—a clumsy device, but it highlights John's use of words for sequence and impact of thought. John's language has a rich teasing quality. To understand it a little helps to facilitate overcoming the difficulty of the way John combines theological statement with a sequential narrative.

Then also we need to embrace ourselves, and our own reactions to the text. We were once studying the story of the man in chapter 5 who

---

4. Whitfield, *Mastering E-Motions*, viii.

5. Elliott, *Memory*, 257.

6. Ashton, "John and the Johannine Literature," 261.

had been ill for thirty-eight years. One member of the group, who died a
year or two after my writing this, sitting in his wheelchair, said, "Perhaps
he was tired!" Many have been kind and patient and brave enough to
make this journey with me, and the contribution of their thought and
words, and of themselves, has been a perpetual grace.

It will be essential to have the Gospel of John in one hand whilst
reading, and to continually refer to the passages in John in order to make
the fullest sense of what is written.

The chapters represent workshops. The content of each is meant
to be used selectively. There is vastly more in each chapter than could
be used even in a whole day's workshop, let alone in a couple of hours'
session! Take your pick! The aim is to convey knowledge of John, the
excitement of John, the pleasure of sharing, and personal growth with the
reassuring sense of the presence of Christ.

Acknowledgements

I WISH TO EXPRESS deep appreciation and sincere thanks to so many who have in various ways contributed to my life and thus enabled this endeavor.

The members and community of churches where I have ministered who have bravely made this journey of exploration and personal involvement with me, in particular, Trinity at Bowes Methodists at Palmers Green/ Wood Green, North London; Cheltenham Methodists and Anglicans; Park Avenue Methodists, Northampton; many adherents to the pioneering experience in the Clinical Theology Association; those from churches of the main denominations all over the country through group experience in Methodism; the clients and team at the Oxford Christian Institute for counseling. Many of these committed persons have influenced me greatly, supported me faithfully, become lifetime friends, and have been willing to enter into deep personal relations with each other; and many, sadly for those who are left, now know the glory for which we searched.

Particularly warm thanks are due to Rev. Dr. Christina Le Moignan, who has served as a tutor at the Queen's College, Birmingham, and as chair of the Birmingham Methodist District; and she is a past president of the (UK) Methodist Conference. She has scrupulously surveyed my text and tested its sense, and then kindly written a foreword.

Particularly warm thanks are also due to Prof. John Cox, emeritus professor of psychiatry at Keele University, Staffordshire, former president of the Royal College of Psychiatrists (UK), and secretary general for the World Psychiatric Association (2002–8). He too has scrupulously surveyed my text and tested its sense, and then kindly written a foreword.

There are many individuals who have kept me on the road. John Churcher, Mike and Sue Collins, Hugh McCredie, Michael Newman, Neil Richardson, Chris Hughes Smith, Francis Young, and many, many more, all known by name! Thank you all!

Abbreviations

CTA	Clinical Theology Association.
H&P	*Hymns and Psalms: A Methodist and Ecumenical Hymn Book*, 1983
JBL	*Journal of Biblical Literature*
JSNT	*Journal for the Study of the New Testament*
JSOT	*Journal for the Study of the Old Testament*
MHB	*The Methodist Hymn Book*, 1933
NEB	New English Bible
NTS	*New Testament Studies*
SBL	Society of Biblical Literature
SCM	Student Christian Movement
STF	*Singing the Faith*, 2011

Introduction 1

What Language Shall I Borrow?[1]

May we study you and study ourselves, we pray.

THIS IS A BOOK with a practical pastoral approach based on a fresh study of St. John's Gospel. St. John's Gospel is like an art gallery. Each chapter is like a room that gives a new vision of an answer to the question, "How does Jesus give himself to us?" Each chapter is journeyed through from a narrative-critical and reader-response point of view, defined below. Of course, I try to honor all Johannine scholarship. The emphasis here is that part of the message of John is devoted to pastoral theology and to an answer to that key question. Side by side with this, and step by step through the Gospel, connections are made to the deep pastoral care of persons, and an understanding of human personality development. In particular, I shall be using a developed model deriving from Clinical Theology and the work of psychiatrist Dr. Frank Lake. Alignments with John are made in sequence, with particular insights based on a psychodynamic approach into the pain and distress that often grows in us. Models of understanding from pastoral counseling, psychotherapy, and literature are brought to bear as a spur to our own awareness and ministry to others. Bringing together text and therapeutic applications in this way puts us in touch with, and enables us to sense, how it is that Jesus Christ can enter and bring healing and peace, the abundant life that consists of abiding in him.

---

1. Paulus Gerhardt, "O sacred Head sore wounded," *MHB* 202, *H&P* 176, *STF* 280.

1. The Beginning

Many threads have woven the tapestry of this book over a long period of time. I was privileged to go on a Mid-Service Clergy Training Course at St. George's, Windsor Castle, UK, in January 1974. My field of interest and experience was group work. I tried to write up a paper on it, especially on the value and effectiveness of group work that is pastorally informed, both in the core and on the edge of church life. The course arranged for small groups to meet for reflection. The tutor presence in the group I was in was Canon Stephen Verney (as he then was). He was sometimes not there, though never an absence, for he was always in our mind in that he was caring for his first wife, who was in hospital dying of cancer. I happened to be the leader on a day when he returned from hospital. We were put in touch with what we suffer when we and our loved ones are ill, and especially of what the ravages of terminal illness mean, and of how distressing many interventions are, both to patient and relative. We were put in touch with the extremity of human suffering and existential threat. We tried to listen and empathize and be not quite inadequate, to be a presence for him out of our own half/mid maturity of ministry.

Indebted to him for his courage, faithfulness, and sensitivity, for the way his ministry and personal journey had a shared integrity, and impressed by the openness of his approach to and passionate conviction about ministry, I suggested him as the person to take the meditations or sermons in the Holy Communion services of the annual Clinical Theology Association Conference in 1974 or 1975. He led four meditations on John, though that is too quiescent a word—four stimuli, stirrings, connectings, provocations (in the narrow sense), expositions—with passion: John 2:1–11; 4:4–26; 8:56—9:10; 15:1–17. The theme was the new consciousness that comes to us with Christ. Something of his own vitality cum pain made the great Johannine words our own—water, life, truth, worship, seeing, abiding, believing. He was representing the truth we were looking for. It was fresh. I was hooked on St. John. *Here, text and human personality and faith could run together.* These talks were a foundation for his later book in 1985, *Water into Wine: An Introduction to John's Gospel.* I thank him for the beginning!

I was inspired to start preaching seriously on St. John's Gospel! I began my long series in January 1977. There are now more than fifty sermons in it and it is still being added to over forty years later! *There is no point at which the text is exhausted.* It renews itself and me all the time. I have hopes for its effects on the hearers. The main thrust was to make it come alive in a fresh way for my congregations.

This was meant to happen in two ways. I tried, and am still trying, to relate the content of the message about Christ to personal life. The conviction (and the experience for self and others) is that all that is within us, our interior being, must hear the Gospel. Sadly, so many sermons do not speak to what is actually happening inside us, or in our lives. It is meant to happen for us by allowing a fresh response to the text, free of some of the old traditional issues. The question is, for instance, not so much "Did it happen?" or "What does it (objectively) mean?" as "What is the impact of this narrative on me and how does it touch me?" Later, when the language developed, I discovered this approach was called narrative and reader-response criticism!

Then in 1980 my daughter started her A Level religious education course on St. John's Gospel! As we swapped testing quotes and questions across the family table, I learnt by heart, for the first time, the content of every chapter and the sequence of every episode and discourse. That was in my development a huge step forward. It is always hard to remember what is in the Gospels, in which one, and in which place! My appreciation grew of the sheer brilliance of the Gospel we have to which we give the name John. The long journey started in earnest to understand how it came to be and what it was saying and how it was saying it, and what it means to us now. That fascination remains. It "remains enigmatic and fascinating."[2]

2. Reading John

2a. Some Parameters I Am Using

Some parameters need to be made clear. I am using "John" for the end product, and also for the writer whose writing has notionally completed itself in the final product we now work with. We must, we can, "let John be John." The *narrative-critical* approach burst on the scene from literary theory with Alan Culpepper's *Anatomy of the Fourth Gospel: A Study in Literary Design* in 1983. The dominance of historical-critical scholarship gave way to a style of looking at texts as literature, "that is as forms of communication that affect those who receive or experience them . . .

---

2. Witkamp, *Some Specific Johannine Features*, 43.

narrative criticism treats these same texts as mirrors that invite audience participation in the creation of meaning . . . texts shape the way readers understand themselves and their own present circumstances."[3] We are in touch with "The world barely in front of the text."[4] The text's purpose is to lead "readers to 'see' the world as the evangelist sees it . . ." and it "is therefore a mirror in which readers can 'see' the world in which they live."[5] We may be looking *back* on the life of Jesus, but as with all factual and fictional historical reading, we enter the historical world as though we are contemporaries.

A church member said, "I love Jane Austen. I read it and I become part of the story." The implication is that it becomes part of me because I feel and behave differently; I am moulded, stirred, and affected (affect) by the story.

There are tools of the trade:

- the implied author, the perspective from which the work appears to have been written;

- the point of view;

- the implied reader, the expectations we have of the effect the text has on the readers who seem to be the target;

- the plot, the aim of conveying a meaning in the events;

- characters, who appear to be historical yet are intended to convey a message;

- style, which contains, for instance, repeated themes, symbolism, double meanings, or irony.

Narrative criticism does not displace historical criticism. John Ashton, who is very wary of the former, can still say, "There is no obvious reason why the two approaches should not be combined."[6]

Taking the language at face value is not exhaustive; there is always more to its significance than meets the eye. Sometimes in John it can be said "the language does not quite surface."[7] Wolfgang Iser in *The Reader*

---

3. Green, *Hearing the New Testament*, 240–41.

4. Bartlett, "Interpreting," 55–56.

5. Culpepper, *Anatomy*, 4–5.

6. Ashton, *Studying John*, 208.

7. Philip Brockbank cited by Cox and Theilgaard, *Mutative Metaphors*, 28; and *Shakespeare as Prompter*, 231.

Process asserts, "the 'unwritten' part of a text stimulates the reader's creative participation," and quotes Virginia Woolf on Jane Austen: "She stimulates us to supply what is not there."[8] We need "a state of readiness for catching similarities."[9] "The continuous implicit communication within the Fourth Gospel is a major source of both its power and its mystery. What seems clear and simple on the surface is never so simple for the perceptive reader because of the opacity and complexity of the gospel's sub-surface signals."[10] These tools (reader-response and psychodynamic approach) help as a means of assessing the text, and of accessing the impact of the text on the reader. The writer draws us into a world "created from materials drawn from life and history as well as imagination and reflection. The narrator speaks retrospectively, telling a story that is a sublime blend of historical tradition and faith."[11] "[O]ne of John's most remarkable traits: the unique artistry with which it controls multiple layers of symbolic or associative significance."[12]

2b. John's Purpose: What Was It?

What was the purpose of John's writing? Many answers have been given to that question. In the short 125-page introduction by Gerard Sloyan, *What Are They Saying About John?*, there are seventeen different references to the purpose of the Gospel, each with a legitimate slant! The approach in this work is that it was "pastoral." This is a pastoral gospel, or *the* Pastoral Gospel. What I mean by that is that it deals with, to put it crudely, what goes on inside people and groups. *In particular it answers the cry, "How does Jesus Christ come to me? How does he get inside me?" Or better, "How does he give himself to me?"* At the very start of faith and continuing all through in the faith, I want to know, how does he give himself to me? This surely is the simplest expectation of those drawing near, and hearing talk or reading of the "presence" of Christ in us, abiding with us, living with us, giving his life to us, giving his life for us. What does it all mean in experience? When I read in earlier writings about union with

---

8. Iser cited by Tompkins, *Reader Response Criticism*, 51.

9. Arieti cited by Cox and Theilgaard, *Mutative Metaphors*, 39.

10. Culpepper, *Anatomy*, 151.

11. Culpepper, *Anatomy*, 231.

12. Ridderbos, *Gospel of John*.

Jesus, how does it happen? How did Jesus give himself to them, the first Christians? How does he give himself to us?

The Gospel answers that pastoral-theological question through the way John tells the story. The relationship of Jesus, and of the message to individuals and to the group and to the Johannine community, is pre-eminent. "Only the *narrative mode* through which a *theological claim* is made . . . throughout, shows the glory of God revealed in the person of Jesus,"[13] and connects him to ourselves and enables a response to be made to him. The Gospel clearly is both individually and corporately focused; it responds to the community needs at the time or times of writing, and thus can be perceived as dealing with the group process, and at the same time the experience of the individual is also preferred, as the range of individual profiles makes clear. So my focus, whilst, I hope, not doing injustice to the vast wealth of Johannine scholarship, is on the pastoral impact by utilizing instincts and much experience about personality and pastoral care. "Only when the FG is used as a mirror held up to readers' lives, as the narrator intended, can there be interaction with the glory of Jesus it discloses."[14] It is literature, it is history and art, truth and "fiction," "all reconciled in the evangelist's deft performance. If these are reconciled *in* the hearers' lives and *with* their lives, John can speak to them."[15]

In the simplest terms, John indicates his own purpose in writing: "that you may believe, continue in believing" (present subjunctive) (John 20:31). There is a possible alternative reading, the aorist (past-tense) subjunctive, and it is still possible to think that John is writing for those who already have faith and that the phrase means to have a renewal, or "a new impulse in their faith."[16] *This is the desired response of reading, for the first time or for all time.* "Belief" is more than responding to "signs"; it is a change in relationship to Jesus, to each other, and to self. "Signs" may refer, not just to the Book of Signs, which is postulated as lying behind the Gospel, but to "the whole content of the Gospel, sign and word."[17] For that, it is refreshing to substitute for "belief" the word "*trust*." That means the impact of the text is so much more fresh. Trusting means, not "believe and then so-and-so will happen," but being in a relationship and

---

13. Sloyan, *John*, 57, italics original.

14. Sloyan, *John*, 53.

15. Sloyan, *John*, 53, italics original.

16. See Moloney, *Glory*, 179 and n. 84; Brown, *Gospel*, 2:1056; citing Schnacken-burg, *St. John*, 3:337–38.

17. Brown, *Gospel*, 2:1058.

in it trust grows. The paradox of *trust*, especially in small group work, is that one only learns to trust by trusting. It is always liminal, crossing a threshold. Trusting is not conditional, but always the experience of mutual gifts, and as such harmonizes with and is transformative of the dynamics of our internal world.

Look at how the whole ministry of Jesus is about crossing boundaries and thresholds:

- Chapter 2: social distress;

- Chapter 3: a search that is preconditioned;

- Chapter 4: sexual and racial and religious conventions;

- Chapter 5: thinking about the nature of illness and healing;

- Chapter 6: that which really nourishes;

- Chapters 7–8: deep-rooted racial memory;

- Chapter 9: institutional control of health;

- Chapter 10: he actually claims to be the "door";

- Chapter 11: death of a loved one;

- Chapter 13: relating to his own disciples;

- Chapters 12–20: his own death, the final barrier, the "long good night" into which he went with much transcending conversation, the passion and the glory;

- Chapters 20–21, where he created a new orientation to shocked disciples. Yet he was still reaching out to and into others, especially those who trusted him. We too are enabled to live liminally in a threshold-crossing fashion.

Philo of Alexandria, contemporary with Jesus, whose thought came from both Judaism and Plato, especially in the use of *logos*, wrote, "to his Word, his chief messenger, highest in age and honor, the Father of all has given the special prerogative, to stand on the border and separate the creature from the Creator."[18] For Christians the life of Jesus means exactly the opposite, not separation but unity, as John consistently witnesses to. Incarnation means exactly that. Jesus walks with us along the fault lines of our human experience.

---

18. Barrett, *New Testament Background*, 263.

Rather than "crossing" the boundary, Jesus lives *on* the boundary. Better still, he *is* the boundary, the "gate" through which we go back and forth (John 10:7, 9). It is through him and within him that we can move and live, travel the boundaries within ourselves and between others. In Christ! When we are dealing with our psychic nature, this is the John theme par excellence.

My thought is that there is chapter by chapter a revealing of the process, of going through "gates" with Christ, that occurs in us step by step as we move from distrust to trust, and from not having Christ to having him. When you hear, see these steps, you will respond, will be able to respond. You can respond. This is the way to respond, this is the way you will be enabled to respond. We can experience the gospel, and the Gospel, as the expression of energy that will work in a dynamic way within us and between us. It is the nature of the rich and laden narrative to achieve this. For instance, John's metaphors, misunderstandings, double meanings, and ironies prompt us to ask, make us ask, "What is going on here?" The invitation is the same—come higher, go deeper—here in this way Jesus gives himself to you. We search for the realities beneath the appearance, "to let the uncertain remain uncertain, but to learn how much and what we could honestly regard as true, believe that and live by it."[19]

Re-experiencing the text depends on our capacity for imagination so that what has been concretely located can now be relocated in contemporary experience.

3. Language

We need language to build an adequate picture of things.[20]

A large proportion of investment in studying John is spent on "hearing" the language. This means a moderate attempt to both translate and listen to the Greek. I have tried to help those with no knowledge of Greek by including pointers to Greek words. This is needed less as we move through the chapters because we become familiar with words that appear time and time again. Words are transliterated for two reasons: so that we can hear the similarities of sound in the original, and also so that we can see that different English words in the translation may in fact be

19. Words of J. A. Froude applied to George Eliot by Stephen Gill's introduction to *Adam Bede* (p. 14).

20. Taylor, *Sources of the Self*, 197.

the same Greek root. It means also having an intensely attentive ear for the nuances of John's language. The sight of the Greek word also makes connections to other places where John has used it, and thus illustrates the way themes weave in and out of the tapestry. His use of imagery and metaphor is fluid and allows the mingling of ideas. John is like a tapestry with colors and images and threads now surfacing and now hidden. Ronald Ferguson writes of the Orkney poet George Mackay Brown, "George was captivated by the notion of divine creativity in the weaving of tapestries, the threads of which were the raw materials of human life and history."[21] John's tapestry in addition weaves in the divine life. The "process of reading is to become attuned to the profusion of textual indicators which between them weave the meanings of the narrative . . . to decipher the inner story within the outer story."[22] Astonishingly, in the process we will weave ourselves into the tapestry!

In terms of making sense of language, there is an unavoidable fundamental problem. It is partly related to the life situation of the Johannine community, but it is also totally general.

> When sacred texts develop to express and define group identity in a context of conflict, they often crystallize these idealizations and projections and preserve them in written form. While these formulations may be appropriate in the formative stages of the religious community, it sets the stage for future distortions. As Paul Ricoeur has observed, something significant happens when communication moves from speech to text. In dialogue, it is possible to clarify ambiguity by direct reference to the surroundings. Once a communication moves into text, however, the direct referential context is lost, and the multiple significances inherent in written language make a variety of interpretations possible.[23]

The plain fact is, of course, that we can't hear the words as spoken. *There is no intonation in the New Testament!* Yet the way we communicate is by intonation. A distinguished scholar reading a passage in John containing direct speech was *already* interpreting the meaning because he read with his own intonation. It was loaded with his own view of the character. There is no other way! Every time the language is read aloud we add in our own view. So much of our faith is based, not on what the

21. Ferguson, *George Mackay Brown*, 72.

22. Knights, *Listening Reader*, 82.

23. Rollins and Kille, *Psychological Insight*, 138.

written words say, but on how we read them. When we want to read afresh, even in our own heads, we must try out all sorts of possibilities of varied tonal voice and emphasis. Every piece of speech was originally spoken in a particular way, *and we have no access to it*. We simply do not know *how* the words were said. (And, of course, there is the question of how far John represents what Jesus and others actually said, and how—and the intonation running in his head whilst writing!) When reading text, we have to start with our own ignorance, our own "not knowing."

Inscribed on a pavement slab outside a bookshop in Inveraray, Scotland, is, "In the river of words ideas are eddies spinning downstream." In John we could also reverse it—in the river of ideas, words are eddies spinning downstream! To sail the sea of Johannine faith is to launch into a sea of metaphors and images—staying, water, birth, seeing, witnessing, breath, spirit, light, dark. Words such as these appear to be simple comparisons, when in reality "the images metaphors embody may originate in layers of thought that are usually inaccessible to inspection." It is not only the words that are repeated over and over again, but the metaphorical sense reappears again and again. We do not experience the images solely with cold reason; "Figurative language springs from strong affect."[24] To refresh ourselves at St. John's well is to need to sense the imagery afresh.

Metaphors in common usage become faded. So, for example, the word "anatomy" in the title *Anatomy of the Fourth Gospel: A Study in Literary Design* might enter our minds as, say, just meaning "the parts of," or "the elements in," or "structure of," or, picking up the word "design," "the plan of." Whereas if the metaphor itself came alive for us, we would be "image-ining" flesh, blood, eyes, sinews, muscle, breath, heart, bone, movement, a living being, sickness, the wrong sort of growth, dying! John's metaphors are not used merely as illustrations of propositions; they do not simply refer to theological concepts. They are much too dense for that. They are poetic; in imagination we experience a reality beyond our formulations; such experience is authentic. Culturally we have to live with the anomaly of having concrete statements that we do not interpret literally—Jesus as "the Son of God," or "the Father," for instance. In getting into John, we continually have to live in the metaphor afresh, without retreating into the fundamentalism of previous eras or contemporary literalism. When everything seems so familiar, we find we have to live on the edge of language.

24. Knights, *Listening Reader*, 62.

This seeking of a deeper meaning is not unknown to biblical interpretation. From the earliest Christian times, the text was deemed to have two levels of meaning, a "literal" (*historia* in Greek) and a "spiritual" (*theoria*). The latter required insight into the symbolic, the hidden, even esoteric, meaning. "[T]he worldview of the early church led the early Christians to a more introverted attitude that directed their gaze into the world of the soul, which for them was a living reality . . . the early Christian commentators were natural depth psychologists."[25] "What is hidden beneath the literal meaning is not merely another and more hidden meaning, it is also a new and totally different reality . . . It is the divine life itself."[26] So this "interpretation" does involve us in looking back on an ancient text through very modern lenses, and through lenses, in particular, that are therapeutically attuned.

The art of interpretation is called hermeneutics, from the Greek word *hermeneuo*, "to interpret," as used by Jesus in Luke 24:27 as he interpreted the scriptures on the way to Emmaus. "Hermeneutics is not simply a task of making a meaning from the text that suits the needs of the readers, nor simply a task of unlocking some a priori meaning ensconced in the text. Rather, hermeneutics is a process in which a unique relationship between text and reader evolves."[27]

Speaking of the need to make the old prophetic faith rooted in old treasured texts credible for today, Walter Brueggemann wants the church's pastoral task to be committed to the hard work of recovering a style of discourse that makes real now, in concrete ways, the significance of the old message. This needs not just heroic work by a pastor, but "an entire community of . . . believers who trust its own way of speech."[28]

4. The Style of Bible Study Used in the Workshops

My aim in the workshop is both to present the best scholarship I can and also to wish for readers to be open with the biblical text, and to want it to lodge and abide in themselves. (I distinctly remember in Sunday school, at the age of seven, thinking to myself that Daniel could not possibly have survived in a den of lions! What was important was that I was

---

25. Sanford, *Mystical Christianity*, 2–3.

26. Thomas Merton, cited by Sanford, *Mystical Christianity*, 4.

27. Underwood, cited in Rollins and Kille, *Psychological Insight*, 70.

28. Brueggemann, *Texts That Linger*, 41.

not shocked or fazed by the thought of alternatives.) It means that to take part in a Bible study is to accept that there will be "traditional" as well as "liberal" or radical views of event and meaning. Discourse over a passage will contain different points of view. Attitudes will be not only cerebral but heartfelt, and even unconscious. So the aim is both to maximize scholarship (as well as I am able) and also to want others to be nourished, "enfaithed." Finding a way through the minefield of Johannine scholarship is as tricky as finding a way through the territory of the human personality! The academic is fascinating, and traditional methods of criticism valid and essential; whilst the personal is also fascinating, essential, and valid in its own way.

Practically all the workshops have been worked through generally, and particularly in a group over about fifteen years in the Enfield, London Circuit of the Methodist Church. I am deeply indebted to them and to all the groups I have worked with, all faithful and adventurous. I take a leadership role, using a table or lectern to set out notes and books with quotations. This could be called a "tutorial" role. But with pleasure, and I hope some skill, I recognize that the group (of which I also am a member!) has a life, an energy, a cohesion, and a fellowship (*koinonia*) and will settle the text down into itself, the group, and find it full of significance.

So the method of study includes both a traditional one, a historically based discussion utilising knowledge of the text through the familiar criticisms, and also a recontextualization through meaning felt in group sharing, through social interaction. These "social means" (John Wesley's term for sharing personal experience in caring groups) extend the traditional hermeneutic stances. Speech exchange patterns and the interaction of different "voices" in a group illustrate "subtle interpretative interaction" and suggest "a hermeneutic at work . . . that is not driven by a quest for knowledge, but rather by relational concerns; and by the hope that in their 'fellowship' and learning together they will discover insight."[29] The groups are indeed meant to do "Bible study," but in the context of personal activity. They are what we call "experiential" or "empirical." They look at a text and relate to it, to their inner world, to each other, and to the group process. They practice biblical interpretation in a faith community. "[A] social interactionist approach recontextualizes understanding of biblical interpretation."[30]

---

29. Todd, "Interaction of Talk and Text," 70.
30. Todd, "Interaction of Talk and Text," 74.

In analyzing speech exchange patterns and the interaction of different voices in the group that connect a passage to personal experience, Todd notes that the leader with a tutorial style "projects the possibility of a particular kind of response," but when he also "invites people to identify their own experience . . . the effect is striking."[31]

Sharing personal material and story is facilitated by the questions asked. They have the effect of contextualizing the passage in our own experience. When the right questions are asked, people are set free to relate to the passage in themselves. The questions are the key. "In the question lies the answer."[32] They will reflect the mind of the facilitator, but will also open the doors of opportunity, opportunity for the members to speak their mind, to open their minds to the text and to each other. Asking the right question is signally important.

Boxes are used as a simple device to separate sharing activity from the unfolding commentary. Inside the box are one or more questions designed carefully to encourage personal sharing. *They are not intended for discussion, but for sharing*, with the framework of experience suggested in the passage which is being studied acting as the holding background. Time must be given to this, for members of the group to enter in to the narrative, together with entering into themselves. Where more than one question is suggested, they should be taken one at a time for the fullest benefit, and used to journey step by step along the inward and the exterior road. The pertinence of the passage, experienced through the question, is for self-awareness and deeply personal sharing. Because we open the text, we are enabled to open ourselves.

---

31. Todd, "Interaction of Talk and Text," 76.

32. Moran, *Listening*, 105–30.

5. The Workshop Style: In Particular, the Nature of Sharing in Small Groups

The advantage of a workshop style is that it provides the opportunity for a variety of distinct yet interrelated elements. A session can include straight teaching, discussion, personal reflection, sharing in pairs or small groups or in the whole group, debriefing together, and activities. There is flexibility and openness, separateness and togetherness, hard work and humor, giving and receiving, waiting and watching, and above all mutuality. Members of the group can be pressed to the utmost of their learning capacity. They can also press for slowing down and for explication. The more we know about the text, the world behind and within, the better. This is the context in which we can search the world, our world in front of the text. Yet we must move beyond the cerebral to the affect. We bring our whole self to the text and experience it in community. Reading John is both an individual and corporate activity. As interpreters we live and work in a collegiate enterprise.

Our fellowship is foreshadowed by the intimate relationships portrayed in the text, between men and women, insiders and outsiders, searchers and believers, unbelievers and followers, and the leader. The trust (belief) of which we read is practiced by us. So the *golden thread* that holds the tapestry of interaction together is the practice and awareness of *personal sharing*. All the other elements are important in their turn and are given reality by the encounter between persons that is taking place. Sharing takes place throughout, but especially in response to the bidding, "Share how you feel . . ." So we need to be quite clear what it involves.

What is new in the experience is a "new way of being oneself and being with others"[33] and being prepared to entrust our joy and suffering to the other. We shall live (even if briefly) in liminality, on the border between, in the space between, parts of ourselves, and between ourselves and others. Others will hear that "I am." And I will hear them saying, "I am." This is what "I am." And that is a very Johannine expression!

Sharing is a distinct activity. It involves talking about oneself. It is *not* discussion of ideas. It is a specific discipline, easily learnt but hard to practice consistently, needing constant watchfulness over oneself, one's thought about oneself and the language to express it. That sounds pretty bleak, but it is the richest form of communication. It is vastly more than the cerebral communication of ideas, though precision in ideas is not

33. Levine. *Poesis*, 54.

discounted. It is full of affect. It is the royal road to truth and comfort in the truth.

I started my first "Care and Share Group" in 1973, long before banks became "listening" and co-ops (a series of grocery and bank cooperatives in the UK) became "caring-sharing"! Training in Clinical Theology Association workshops and growth groups alerted me to a different style of meeting. I was the minister of a large Methodist church of over five hundred members; I was attending a lot of meetings, but began to feel I was not "meeting" people. I was usefully busy, leading a hectic life, with much pastoral visiting, and realized that there was no way I could care for everyone. People had to care for each other and be trained for it. The more insight and skill they had, the better. So I began to offer pastoral training courses, and continued to do so throughout my ministry! The core of the training was a new way of talking and listening to each other.

I was due to lead a house group one night and simply had had no time to prepare a talk. I nervously asked the members to share how they felt about their relationship to the church at the moment. After a long silence, one person said, "Well, I'm scared." She had just been made president of the Young Wives Club, a large fellowship of fifty or so members, and she felt the weight of responsibility. After a long pause, one by one, each shared what they felt. Just that! It was a most moving occasion. *I realized the agenda was in the people.* It was my "conversion to a life of dialogue" (Buber). It was a different style of ministry—open, trusting, intimate, moving, real, creative of deep relationships, healing of felt inadequacies—which also trained people in their own style of deep pastoral care. If you can talk about yourself in a mutually caring group, you can listen to others, you are empowered to offer the ministry you have received and receive the ministry you have offered. It was a breakthrough.

6. The Need for a Model or Models

Our practice of reading and sharing will need a model or models so that we have understanding of what we read, say, hear, and feel. Models are keys to understanding that illuminate and give shape to what goes from us and comes into us. *They are maps, not the territory itself.* The first map, called "The Babylonian Map of the World," from about 500 BC, "presents an abstraction of terrestrial reality"; a map presents "an imaginative representation of an unknowable object (the world)."[34] Models draw elements out of a dimly perceived reality and through the imagination offer a synthesis, eclectic in a non-compulsive way, whereby we have tools for hewing meaning out of multifarious input and output. They will make sense of our journey through the stages of life, of the qualities a carer needs, of the nature of personal distress, of the development of personality, of the relationship between helper and the person being helped, and of the nature of the writing we read and of the way it abides in us.

In particular, what is useful is a dynamic model of personality. "What particularly distinguishes the term 'psychodynamic' is that the activity of the psyche is not confined to relating to people, or to objects outside of the self . . . Activity also takes place within the psyche, in relation to itself." So if I say, "I don't like half of what is inside myself," I am being both subject and object. I am observing myself. "We can just as easily love, hate of fear parts of ourselves as we can other people."[35] We understand the different elements in us when we realize the power of the connection between our infancy and childhood experience and the development of our personality. So my comments and analogies are meant not to be definitive, but suggestive, of viewpoints into text and person.

I am using the basic model created by a deeply committed Christian, Dr. Frank Lake (1914–1982), a former parasitologist and medical missionary, who faced the clamant needs of the human psyche and trained and practiced as a psychiatrist. He was a key pioneer of pastoral counseling in the UK. He developed what he called "Clinical Theology," the basic insights of which we use because they are invariably helpful. He founded the Clinical Theology Association in 1962 (now the Bridge Pastoral Foundation). His aim was to train people in the churches to exercise fine, skilled pastoral care to each other and in small groups. An understanding of personality, its strengths and weaknesses, was essential and was held in the Christian experience.

The approach was eclectic, or in today's terms, integrative, built on the foundational works of the key thinkers in the psychodynamic field, and particularly influenced by the Object Relations school.[36] Lake and

---

34. See Brotton, *History*, 2, 5.

35. Jacobs, *Psychodynamic Counselling*, 5.

36. Object Relations, in the psychodynamic field, focuses on relationships, initially that between the carer, usually mother, and child. We carry persons we have known inside us, and have an idea, an image, and entity within us, which is a representation of the people, of mother. That image is called an "object." We are not objectifying

helpers offered training seminars in pastoral care and counseling, which he began in 1958. His large tome of nearly 1,300 pages, *Clinical Theology*, was published in 1966. It was abridged in 1986 by Martin Yeomans, a Methodist minister, and a reader was produced in 1991 by Carol Christian—both excellent introductions. My brief summary and application is a million miles from the depth and extent of his insight. Frank Lake wanted a combined base for both thought and praxis, namely, theology rooted in the love and power of God, but also pastoral care rooted in a careful and adventurous observance of the sound practice of psychiatry, psychotherapy, and group work.[37]

One of the difficulties for some is that his mind and his writing and his practice slipped seamlessly across the two disciplines of therapy and theology. For others it brought a great healing and window opening reconciliation.[38] Others have since crossed disciplines with approbation; for

---

people; we live in a dual, fluid world of internal and external relating. If we focus on a particular feature of a person, that image in us is called a "part object." Then we have a limited view of the person. D. W. Winnicott developed the insight further, in his psychotherapeutic work with children, with the idea of the "transitional object," the child's comforter, a blanket or toy, and what that external object signifies in our inner world, the presence of mother, say, even when she is elsewhere. It helps us to bridge the gap of absence. It gives security when anxious. It facilitates the stage of separating and becoming more autonomous. In any caring relationship, the carer becomes, for a time, a transitional object. An awareness of our inner objects helps us to form less incomplete relationships. See Howard, *Psychodynamic Counselling*, 11–12, 48; Gomez, *Introduction*, 1–2, 92–93.

37. Frank Lake's reputation faltered for a time; for some because he was a Christian; for some because early on he used LSD to access early memory, even though once the connection with pathological conditions was known, he gave up using it as soon as did everyone else, psychiatrists at the Tavistock Clinic, for instance. His standing should remain high. His insights, theoretical and practical, are of such worth.

38 A classic study joining psychoanalysis, history, and faith is Erik H. Erikson, *Young Man Luther*, risking "that bit of impurity which is inherent in the hyphen of the psycho-historical as well as of all other hyphenated approaches" (13). Of particular importance is Ulanov, *Finding Space*. A useful study of writing across disciplines is found in Miller, "Crossing the Border'; and a useful reader is Rollins and Kille, *Psychological Insight into the Bible*. Of interest is Watts et al., *Psychology for Christian Ministry*; and Buckley, *Where the Waters Meet*; and Mace, ed., *Heart and Soul* re: philosophy; and Fiumara, *Other Side of Language*; and re: literature, D. R. Davis, *Scenes of Madness*; Knights, *Listening Reader*; re: opera, Cordingly, *Disordered Heroes in Opera*. In relation to faith, Verhagen et al., eds., *Psychiatry and Religion*; Wilber, *Marriage of Sense and Soul*. In relation to theology, Ghiloni, "On Writing Interdisciplinary Theology." In relation to art, psychiatry, and brain science, the works of Eric R. Kandel; and Jonah Lehrer, *Proust Was a Neuroscientist*. In relation to biblical criticism, Wayne G. Rollins in Glas, et al., eds., *Hearing Visions*. A searching example where the general

instance, Cox and Theilgaard crossing the disciplines of literature and therapy. Murray Cox was responsible for bringing William Shakespeare into Broadmoor, the secure psychiatric prison. We apply their words to our theme: "Definition becomes sharper when one discipline immerses itself in the other and thereby discovers its own nature with greater certainty." "[T]he topic of inter-disciplinary transfusion is relevant." A nice phrase is "the mingling of contraries." "Our intention is to show how each sphere has much that can nourish its neighbour, without either discipline being reduced or diluted in any way." The boundaries between disciplines are important but permeable, or even porous, certainly not watertight (a metaphor John could approve of). In contemplating the hope and heartache of the human condition intrapsychically (within the person), and interpsychically (between persons), in the light of theological conviction and psychodynamic insight, it can be argued that "both modes of descriptive language are necessary." "[P]roviding vital inter-disciplinary boundaries are strongly guarded, each has much to give the other. So much so, that without their mutual gaze, both would be losers."[39] And Cox is quite precise in a Frank Lake memorial lecture delivered to the Clinical Theology Association: "We owe Frank Lake a very great deal, because he made us take seriously this interwovenness of things clinical and things theological." That was my note at the time, though it is not, I think, in the printed text of the lecture, *Transferring the Untransferable* (1993). There we do have: "Frank Lake was a tireless herald who kept high the banner which had clinical embroidered on one side and theology on the other . . . Woven into the very texture of the material is the paradox that feelings and attitudes which were presumed untransferable can, though the therapeutic action of grace and the graceful action of therapy, be transferred."[40] In our case, it is the disciplines of biblical study and psychodynamic insight that are blended in the "therapeutic" impact of the Fourth Gospel. To have a model that enables us to see into the text and to see into how we respond does *not* imply a denial of theological validity, but gives a whole new dimension of experience.

---

psychodynamic approach is sympathetic is Kalsched, *Trauma and the Soul*.

39. Cox and Theilgaard, *Shakespeare as Prompter*, 39, 51–52, 382–83.

40. Cox, *Transferring*, 15–16.

Introduction 2

Understanding People

Reading your word afresh, refresh our minds, we pray.

1. The Beginning

THE TITLE "UNDERSTANDING PEOPLE" is meant to carry two meanings, both valid and both relevant. It thus refers both to the vital importance of being an understanding person when caring for others, and also to the importance of having a volume of knowledge when we necessarily need to comprehend what is in a person. I need tools to understand people, and I need to be an understanding person.

That which has sustained and amplified the interest in and continually persuades of the relevance of this text, this "John," is twofold. Firstly, there is the sense of the worth of the text and the message it contains gained through the narrative-critical approach. Substantially this came on the scene from 1982 onwards. I had gone to theological college as the fifties ended, thinking, "Now I would discover what the Bible really is saying," and was still wondering about it years later, as much as I loved the intellectual search and what the other "criticisms"—historic, source, form, and redaction—were delivering in terms of meaning and applicability to the Christian life. Some of my tardiness was through having a hectically busy ministerial life, which was never going to properly keep up with the massive volume of work on John, let alone the complete explosion of all biblical studies from the early sixties till now. That part of the explosive and exciting development that did grab the imagination, the mind and the spirit, was the application of literary critical theory to the biblical writings in a new way. This has brought a sense and energy to the second half of my ministry by opening doors to new ways of sharing the Bible with people of different persuasions, by keeping the old difficulties in their appropriate place and allowing the text to speak and new response to be made.

Secondly, what was important was the ability and practice of paralleling pastoral insight; the opening of persons as the text became open. To link a response to each part of the text to what is happening in and to a person or group is priceless. This informs both our pastoral care and our preaching or teaching, and the learning of the text. The text is no longer irrelevant. It is made incarnate in people. Likewise, pastoral care, counseling, psychotherapy, and group work are grounded in gospel truth. They are no longer disconnected from Christian heritage or insight. Their categories of thought find reflection in the biblical themes, or rather we find reflections of biblical material in them.

It is necessary to look at the components of this style of study and relating in more detail. Many will be familiar with some elements but not all will be acquainted with all of the elements, or with this approach. Here is more explication.

We need some parameters. This is going to be a rather long second introduction because the workshops planned, and the insight into John and its relation to our faith and personality, need four areas of understanding and experience. Very humbly, we seek to fulfill the task set by Friedrich Schleiermacher (1768–1834), the founder of hermeneutics, "To understand the text at first as well as and then even better that its author,"[1] but also to understand ourselves. "In the final analysis, the reader provides the hermeneutical lenses that bring the texts into focus in particular ways."[2] The workshops outlined in the context of John's Gospel depend on:

i.   a knowledgeable awareness of John (see 2a);

ii.   a literary approach that combines reader-response criticism and psychodynamic criticism (see 2b, 3, and 4); and

iii. that combination requires a psychodynamic model (see 6) and

---

1. Cited by Ballard and Holmes, *Bible in Pastoral Practice*, 100.

2. Hodgson, *Theology*, 29.

iv. the practice of sharing as an intrinsic style of being together, with the outcome of personal growth and corporate cohesion and fellowship (see 5).

2. Reading John

2a. Reader-Response Criticism

"Reading" used to be virtually a sole concentration on the text in front of the reader. There was no occasion for the role of the interpreter to be relevant. It was what the writer intended and meant that was the focus. And New Testament theology was that which accurately derives from the understanding of the text, without considering who was doing the understanding and what that person brought of themselves to the act of interpretation. The focus on the reader is now stressed with more emphasis in the development called *reader-response criticism*, which describes the fact that *the reader makes sense* of the text, completes the text by filling in "gaps," brings interpretation to the text, and does not merely get it from the text. "Reading is a balancing act between, on the one hand, believing that each text has only one correct interpretation and, on the other, projecting ourselves into the text . . ."[3] "material that we are unaware of projecting. In a number of senses, we shall be projecting our very selves; and again that has to be interpreted at both the level of the individual and of the community."[4] We bring our memories and the way we symbolize things to the text.

A pause while we briefly consider how this issue is at the core of Christian belief itself. It lies at the heart of how we understand God; not only the nature of God, but the nature of how we come to a sense of what God is like. When we wrestle with the nature of projection, we will see that we create God in our own image. We do make the God we want. Stay with that (threatening) thought for a moment!

John Drury has written a moving account of the life of George Herbert, the aristocratic, intellectual, troubled, deeply "spiritual," devoted poet and minister. He assesses how subsequent writers have perceived him. One is Helen Vendler, the "most subtly sympathetic of Herbert's readers nowadays." She writes that "Love," in the poem "Love III" ("Love

---

3. Green, *Hearing*, 267–68.
4. Elliott, *Memory*, 255.

bade me welcome: yet my soul drew back"—to the end—"You must sit down, says Love, and taste my meat / So I did sit and eat"), "is the God Herbert created in his own best self-image—light, graceful, witty, not above a turn of phrase, and yet considerate, careful for the comfort of his guest, affectionate firm, and above all generous."[5] Then Drury adds, "A Christian reader might well, and more correctly from the historical point of view, put Vendler's perception the other way round: Herbert created, or rather constructed himself in life-long response to the Other who was there already, the God who according to the Bible 'is love.'"[6] Both attitudes are true.

We must note firmly that the reflection is not helped by setting the Christian as reader over against the non-Christian as reader. We both read in the same way. As readers we *all* project ourselves into the text and fashion God after our own image. But then we must recognize the genetic fallacy, namely, that just because we explain the origin of an idea does not mean that the idea is not true. Just because I want a God who as loving and comforting, for instance, does not mean that he does not exist and/or that he is not loving and kind! As Christians (or not), we live with the paradox: I do want God to really be as I want him/her to be, and I do want also to trust the human and Christian heritage as accurately describing him/her!

When we are aware that we are putting our own material into the text, then we are aware that the text is prompting us, is reading us; we see ourselves in the light of the text—it is a hermeneutic circle! It goes quite deep; Ricoeur wrote, "We must understand in order to believe, but we must believe in order to understand." (That is also especially true of trying to comprehend what the actual experience of group work or the psychodynamic encounter is.) It is "not a vicious circle (but) it is a living and stimulating circle."[7] We need not to go to extremes, and need to accept the value that there is in all critical approaches; "the alternatives are not mutually exclusive."[8] But we do need to recognize the reality that it is *we* who "complete" the text.

So reader-response criticism means reading with an awareness both of one's own response to a text and of the way in which one adds to, and

5. Cited in Drury, *Music at Midnight*, 320, Vendler, *Invisible Listeners*, 275.

6. Drury, *Music at Midnight*, 320.

7. Ricoeur, "Symbol Gives Rise to Thought," in Gunn, ed, *Literature and Religion*.

8. Ashton cited in Barton, *New Testament Background*, 260.

fills in, and completes the text. Though we are guided by a shared corpus of knowledge, the thought that there is an objective text and one "right" reading that we are searching for and will find if only we have enough cerebral knowledge falls away. "Understanding, Barth insisted, entails more than a scrutinizing of a text as a supposedly value-neutral 'object'. To understand Romans we ourselves must become the object of address. The text actively engages with the real reader, shedding light on the reader's own stance."[9] "[N]arrative criticism treats . . . texts as mirrors that invite participation in the creation of meaning. For the narrative critic, texts shape the way readers understand themselves and their own present circumstances."[10] This huge paradigm shift from natural science, with its analysis of events and causes and the quest for explanations, to the quest for meaning and understanding is a phenomenon experienced across the disciplines, including science, philosophy, literature, and, practically, a psychodynamic approach to psychotherapy and ministry.

Whereas it was thought that our observations and the language and sentences used to encapsulate them were trustingly objective, now it is realized "that the avoidance of subjectivity is not the way to get down to hard realities."[11] One part of this shift involves a new sensitivity to the power of language. In terms of psychotherapy or pastoral care, it means that the client is the expert in his or her own feelings and the facilitator is aware of his or hers. Accuracy of listening means that it is not a case of prescribing theories, but of reflective interpretation. The helper is not predictive or compelling, but a sharer in the human situation. It is the search for meaning that guides the dialogue *between the text and the reader, and also between the person talking and the person listening*, whether in a pair or a group.

Being open can be described as being "skeptical." Being skeptical is a positive, not a negative; the concern is to find the heart of relationship, not just the ideas that explain it "in the head." Knowledge is found in the questioning and answering, where what is of primary importance is not known previously, but is found when one shares in the process. The Greek *skepticos* means "thoughtful" or "paying attention to." Judgment is suspended so one can be tranquil or gentle in the encounter and can

9. Thiselton, *Biblical Theology*.

10. Mark Allan Powell cited in Green, *Hearing*, 241.

11. Kelly cited in Mace, *Heart and Soul*, 70.

rest in the relationship, however chaotic the pain, and able to rest in the possibility of peace. To "rest," or "abide," is a Johannine word.

The tangled knot is not straightened out by tugging the ends of the string but by patiently unravelling it. "To unravel a knot we do not need new knowledge or clever theories but patience and attention, two prime qualities in the practice of therapy" and pastoral care.[12] Unravelling the pain has to happen in the light of another's countenance. It takes all our grace, being with the one who is confused and suffers. Early on our "form of life" is shaped by experience, positive and negative, and held in language. "What goes on inwardly, too, only has meaning in the river of life."[13] Sharing involves risking old feeling to language, and language to new feeling, and allows the water to flow afresh, and in a new channel. The listener is both questioner and witness, stances not separated but held together. This is exactly the pattern of questioning and witnessing we see emphasised repeatedly in the Gospel, and which we practice in the sharing of our story.

Self-knowledge comes when reading a text. "I ought to be no more than a mirror, in which my reader can see his own thinking with all its deformities so that, helped in this way, he can put it right."[14] Transposing the metaphor, it is good when my listener can be a mirror; I can then read myself as I share my life text and note the reflection. As speaker or listener, an expression, a smile, conveys value to me; a nod indicates a presence; the sound of an escaping breath shows a sympathy; prolonged attention indicates empathy. As the speaker or listener, I am more than an inert mirror hanging on the wall. Another human being, needy or not, needs more than a narcissistic reflection. There must be a deeper dimension.

The moment of rich, healing, growth-giving encounter can occur in any meeting between two open, honest people. It is certainly a part of the ministering or therapeutic relationship. A client was receiving care by Dr. Frank Lake, including opportunity to go back into very early memories and experience of childhood, to express preverbal feelings.

> As I dared to look into the eyes of Dr. Lake, I dared to consent to allow the deeply buried unconscious material to surface. He used to say, "You could not say how you felt as the baby, but let yourself hear now how you feel as the baby, let me hear, and let

---

12. Heaton cited in Mace, *Heart and Soul*, 53.

13. Wittgenstein cited in Mace, *Heart and Soul*, 54.

14. Wittgenstein cited in Mace, *Heart and Soul*, 56.

God hear." The "Yes" to those primal feelings made me aware of God's presence, and a sense of divine acceptance. It was impossible to separate psychological and theological awareness. My image of God was influenced by Lake mirroring his own image of God.

In an I-Thou relationship not one but two realities are realized. *Both* persons engage in the process. So in the Gospel Jesus develops a complete (though unfinished) relationship with Nicodemus, the well woman, the pool man, the blind man,[15] and the rest—he is *real* with them. He shares his authenticity with them at great cost to himself. He listens and interprets and others are transformed. His interpretation is not only of the text (Luke 24), nor of previously held theories (John 7–8), but of his relationship with people and their attitude to him. If they let him, he becomes a mirror to them, as he reflects his Father.

O God . . .
To Thee through Jesus we draw near,
    Thy suffering well beloved Son,
In whom Thy smiling face we see,
    In whom Thou art well pleased with me.[16]

Charles Wesley had this extraordinary sense of intimacy with God or Jesus, expressed frequently in this image: "Jesus . . . / Strength of my failing flesh and heart; / O could I catch one smile from Thee, / And drop into eternity."[17] Sung a few days before he died! "And when thy smiling face appears . . ." "What is it keeps him from my view, / And makes me seek in vain? / If every earnest seeker finds / The smiling deity." Happy the man who is able "To see his smiling Lord." "I ask no other grace . . . My whole delight thy love to know, and see thy smiling face." "Show me in Christ Thy smiling face." "I long the smiling face to see, who freely dost forgive . . . the moment we believe." "To see the Saviour's smiling face." It was a profound image which sustained his spirituality. It reminds us of the face to face intimacy between Christ and us, and that that intimacy is reflected with the text, and between each other.

---

15. Chapter 3, 4, 5, and 9.

16. Charles Wesley, "O god of our forefathers, hear," *MHB*, 723, *H&P* 554.

17. *MHB*, verses 47 (verses printed following the hymns).

> Share what a smiling face does to you or for you, your own or another's!

The aim of creating caring relationship is to minimize self-deception in both helped and helper, either of the historical sort or that happening currently in the relationship. "Truth" and comfort must go together (John 14–16). The need to be discrete about self and other is genuine. Appropriate disclosure yields up the inner self to a listener who will be aware of a variety of mixed motives that may be operating. A certain wariness, even skepticism, is useful and *can be* contained in a warm relationship. In the moment of encounter, in the moments of sharing, both people experience "not knowing"—as all the interlocutors of Jesus do in John—before a painful, blissful moment of "knowing," of knowing self and other in a context of mutuality, along with a sense of a wider dimension.

The vehicle for such a delicate balance between text and reader, and person and person, is *language*. The infant attaches words to objects because he/she *trusts* the word of the adult who gives the information. Trust is the start; knowledge, understanding comes later. So in adult life the leap of trust enables the inner experience of the text and also of another person; and that allows the reflection back of knowledge of oneself. Understanding grows. Thereafter our language shapes our patterns of life which constitute our living, and which we express in words shared. John would have it that we give primacy to the Word, and because of the Word, trust follows. The two ideas are complementary. The Word was earthed in a human child born in a working-class home, who was loved and who trusted, so that words came to him. He later used them to give gifts to others.

In a real way we construct ourselves. "Our language defines and modulates us, how we describe our situation may imprison us or free us . . ."[18] Our language is formed by us and forms us, and in later life it is a great joy to have another hear the form of life that is ours and to allow us to re-form it, by finding new meaning in the language we use. We must revisit the context in which we were formed. It becomes in a fresh way a relevant context. Personal construct theory focuses on the context of our making, its benign and malign effect upon us; by our response to it we become the person we are. In a way, we "choose" our response to early encounters with parents and others. We choose, we

18. Brennan in Mace, *Heart and Soul*, 67.

to respond to Jesus, as every person in John does! We choose to follow Jesus—as the disciples did.

John noticeably gives every person a context—wedding, synagogue, pool, portico, neighbor, home, street, hill, garden, village, city, family, belief, tradition. Jesus himself is close to his roots, close to nature; his embodied existence is stressed; there is no alienation in his personality; subjectively he can say "I am" as, under his influence, a blind man also does. Every one of John's characters is a real person, with attributes, and above all with self-awareness. No person, not even a "Jew" or Pharisee or Roman, is to Jesus an "object." His objective is to be subjective to everyone, and to expect the same regard back from them. What freedom is given as one person listens to another! Mental distress freezes our response to others and ourselves. We are fixed in particular images of self or relationship to others. Creativity can emerge as one person meets with another, as one text and a reader meet. Perceptions change in the presence of another, careful enough to meet us mutually. Our symptoms are questions we are asking of the world.[19]

> I want to beg you . . . to be patient to all that is unresolved in your heart and try to love the questions themselves like locked rooms and like books that are written in a very foreign tongue. Do not now seek the answers, that cannot be given because you would not be able to live with them. And the point is, to live everything. Live the questions now. Perhaps you will then gradually, without noticing it, live along some distant day into the answer.[20]

It will take time, but living into the answers starts immediately. It did for John's characters, as it does for any person or client or disciple, being sensitively cared for in the Christian context. Making sense of our world is what we do as a person.

> Both Wittgenstein and Kelly [Personal Construct Theory] remind us that at some point "talk", that is, abstract discussion, explanation, theorising, have to come to an end, and we have to get down to the real conversation of daily living, the stories of our lives. This is a scary business, and Kelly provides us with some different ways of thinking about how and why we may find doing so difficult, by taking key psychological concepts and putting them in terms of the one "doing" them rather than the one

19. The man by the pool in chapter 5.
20. Rilke, *Letters to a Young Poet*, 1902–1926. There are various renderings.

perceiving (and often labelling) the process. In this way stress is
laid on actively elaborating the understanding of other people.[21]

What is in us—our personality distress, desire, fear, anxiety, anger
and so on—we reconstruct as life goes on according to the internal significance. What do the words I use signify? What *meaning* do I give to
them now? I was "blind"; now I "see." Jesus deals with what is in a person.
As we also do in our ministry of caring! An intermediate step, a pragmatic tool suggested by Kelly is to experiment with being what we want
to be, to try it out. So, for instance, to practice being kind, one begins to
feel and be kind. When John Wesley was searching for a lively faith, on
the boat as a missionary to Georgia he was told by the Moravian leader
Peter Bohler, "Preach faith until you have it." It is not being phoney, or
dishonest. It is really good "acting," acting "as if." It is part of reconstruct-
ing the self. Nicodemus held back, but then re-engaged; Peter stuck it out;
Mary remained mother when perhaps she did not feel like it; the blind
man persisted; Mary Magdalene had to learn not to touch and instead to
trust; Thomas how to touch and to trust; Jesus had to drink the cup. The
language that we use lives in our human context, and hence it is the vehicle and passenger of our change of gear. Reading, talking, and listening,
each of us is an authority on our own feelings, though we may not fully
know what each feeling signifies. That is where we need help and where
we grow. The living text, which we ourselves are, stimulated by the textual
word, shares its power in the words that happen between each other.[22]

Plurality of meanings is possible, and yet what the text means does
not become a matter of personal whim, for the reason that we work in a
community of interpretation; in microcosm, the group we are in at the
moment, or in macrocosm, the whole vast Christian tradition of study
and scholarship. However, we are still aware of our role as readers. "Meaning is actualized not by the author at the point of the text's conception but
by the reader at the point of the text's reception." "Readers must not only
respond but respond *responsibly*."[23] Reader-response criticism makes us
aware. "I must read myself as closely as I read the biblical text."[24] We bring

21. Brennan in Mace, *Heart and Soul*, 74–75.

22. For more analysis of these themes see Joady Brennan, "Picture This: Wittgenstein and Personal Construct Theory," in Mace, ed., *Heart and Soul*, 67–83. It was
Anton Boissen, the founder of Clinical Pastoral Education in the United States, who
used the phrase "Living Human Document."

23. Vanhoozer in Green, *Hearing the New Testament*, 259, 273, italics original.

24. Newheart, *Word and Soul*, xix.

ourselves *just as we* are to the reading of a text. We "unearth elements in our personal experience." We aim "for an exegesis of souls that parallels our exegesis of texts."[25] The combination of exegesis and psychodynamic insights brings life to the text and enlivens the reader.

2b. Psychodynamic Criticism

There is one form of criticism that overlaps with and gets some of its energy from both narrative and reader-response criticism, namely, *psychodynamic criticism* (a term preferred to "psychoanalytic criticism" because it is more general, and to "psychological criticism" because it is more focused). It gets its energy both from these two ways of reading, but also from outside, from psychodynamic models of life. The word "psychodynamic" refers to a broad position of insight (derived from Freud, Jung, and the whole therapeutic field developed from them) that senses that we are connected to our own history, that we defend against hurt by looking for safety, that we create a reaction pattern that becomes and is our presenting personality, and that there is retained depth to us, which we may call the unconscious.[26] A psychodynamic approach will not decide which interpretation is right, but combined with a reader-response approach we will be alerted to how *we* are reading the text. By reading the Bible, we learn what *we* are like. Psychodynamic criticism involves an awareness of a psychodynamic understanding, firstly, of the author, secondly, of the content and form of the text, and thirdly, of the reader of the text.

These two styles of criticism, reader response and psychodynamic, must be used together. The second is often shunned but in fact needs to be yoked to the first so that we can reflect on what we ourselves or other interpreters bring to the process of reading. The Bible reads us. As Gustav Mahler once said, "One does not compose; one is composed."

As we read, what is it that connects us with the text we are reading so as to produce interpretations, and interpretations that are often slanted in our own interests? The word "pastoral" means relating the text to ourselves so as to understand both ourselves and others, and how we relate to them, all with insight and care. The word "projection" involves the interpretation of the outside world and parts of ourselves, through the lens of our own positive or negative affect. It is the defense we most

---

25. Staley quoted in Newheart, *Word and Soul*, xx.
26. See, for instance, Jacobs, *Psychodynamic Counselling*, 4–6.

readily use, and is the engine of *transference*. "Transference" describes the content of the relationship between helper and helped when it reflects and is energized by earlier relationships and skews the current one. Projection is the key to the way we look at others. It is the key to the way we reflect on ourselves.

Projection is also the key to understanding how we interpret texts. By projection we read ourselves into a text. There is a world behind the text, and there is a world within the text (both being the traditional field of scholars), and we now realize *there is a world in front of the text*, of which we ourselves are the key part. Psychodynamic criticism is a discipline that encourages a new impression of the text. The text is seen to stand in relation to the reader and the reader in relation to the text.

It is absolutely essential (for reading texts and reading people) that we grasp the significance and power of projection. So here are two examples, both occurring in training sessions focussing on projection:

1. A role-play was set up with particular character roles suggested. The facilitator left the room and the group formed a line. He returned to choose who would play each part. He picked one person for the key role and the group was completely dismayed. For very personal reasons that all were aware of, she should not be performing that particular role. Some members were extremely angry and recriminations started against the leader. Eventually someone said, "Why on earth did you choose her? Completely inappropriate, you should have known." The leader replied, "Because she was number eleven!"

   Out of the room he had picked a number at random! And she was it. The internal agenda of the members and of the group as a whole, for good motives, had kicked in with a strong emotional splurge. Assumptions were made. Their feelings were projected onto the leader. Their emotion took over, when they could have asked the question *first*, but they didn't. They had made a judgment of another person based on their internal agenda. This was not manipulation because it was a training group and they could (should) easily have asked the question first! It was a moment of keen awareness.

Would it have occurred to you that there was an arbitrary reason why the person was chosen?

2. I read out a letter, a text, to a church training group. The writer was sharp in her concern about one or two issues in church life, where I had had a role. I told the group I had not replied to it. There was an immediate reaction. Assumptions were made. Our natural expectations are products of our own minds. "Shoulds" and "oughts," and "in my position," and courtesy, and "even if I felt I was being got at." Actually, then the group *was* getting at me. Then I showed them the letter: no address on the top, and no recognizable signature at the close. It was not possible to reply. Then their anger: "You should have told us!" Their projections had been put on me, and then they saw rather shamefacedly what they were doing.

This was not manipulation even if they felt it was, because the purpose was training, and they could (should) easily have *first* asked me why I chose not to reply.

Our internal agenda takes over and is projected onto others and our learning about ourselves depends on *withdrawing the projections.* That must be with people and with texts our "reader response"!

Would it have occurred to you that there was a logical reason why I had not replied?

We oscillate between a reading of the text and a reading of people, including, especially, myself the reader. The way we read ourselves into the text is through the mechanism of projection. It is a connective process. Projection describes our tendency to take affect-laden parts of ourselves (often unacceptable parts) and attribute them to another person, thing, or state of affairs. We point the finger. We condemn, dislike, accuse, or applaud the element in others which is actually part of ourselves. It is quite a normal process; we do it all the time.

This is the key to understanding how we interpret texts.

i. Writers and artists project their ideals, prejudices, all the "negatives" and all the "positives," into their text, because they project their personality into it. It is impossible to do otherwise. Sir Peter Scott, pioneer conservationist and artist of wildlife, particularly of birds, wrote, "when an artist sets out to paint three dimensional nature in two dimensions the process of interpretation has begun, and consciously or subconsciously some part of the artist's personality creeps in."[27] Hence, for instance, the puzzle of what "John" means by "the Jews." What of the nature of "John's" personality, or the personality of the community, has found its way into the text?

ii. Projection also enables us to understand the way characters in the text interact, and helps us to shape a view of the ways the writer portrays the actions and relationships he describes. We may begin to grasp how it is that Jesus incurs such vitriolic hatred. He is demonised.

iii. Recognizing projection is also essential when we wrestle with what we as readers read into the text and when we *face up to the learning process about ourselves as we read*.

Walter Wink, in his foreword to Rollins and Kille's *Psychological Insight into the Bible*, describes them as "developing a new kind of exegesis . . ."

> At their most profound level they [the authors] show us how to apply psychological insights *to ourselves* as a means of appropriating the text for the task of human transformation. The biblical text, clarified and illuminated by all the tools of critical analysis, now can probe *us*. The subject becomes object, as we ourselves become the focus of analysis . . . the text can now help us to discover the secrets of the unconscious that have been lost and languishing in the dark corners of our souls.[28]

John paints a broad canvas and in exploring it we will explore ourselves. It is the use of projection, in this third way particularly, that turns the Gospel into a practical text because it identifies the effect of the text on the reader and the effect of the reader on the text. John Wesley said he wrote for "practical believers." We must let the text do its practical work in us!

So two lenses are necessary for the text to become current, to surge into my consciousness of myself, and of my availability for others, and

---

27. Peter Scott in *Birds: The Royal Society for the Protection of Birds Magazine*, Autumn 1980, 45.

28. Rollins and Kille, *Psychological Insight*, xiv, italics original. And see for instance Theissen, *Psychological Aspects*, 81–114.

for it to be not merely a brilliant document from the past, but to become practical. The two lenses permit and aid intervisibility across "the ugly ditch" between past and present. *They are a psychodynamic reading of texts and a psychodynamic reading of people*, because *psychodynamic and reader-response readings are coupled.*

The pressing question of "How does the text get into us?" can be understood, at least in part, by the application of these models. They give a philosophy of, and commentary on, the free interaction at depth between people as we are and the text as it is. Wayne Rollins writes:

> [Whilst the Biblical material] is part of a historical, social, and literary process, it is also part of a psychological process in which unconscious as well as conscious factors are at work. Where are these factors at work? In every hand and soul that touches the tradition: in the biblical authors, in the communities they represent, in the stories and material they preserve, in biblical copyists, translators, and publishers, in biblical interpreters and preachers, in scholars . . . and in the biblical effects the Bible has worked and continues to work in individuals and entire cultures, for good and for ill.[29]

John is a pastoral gospel. It deals with what goes on inside people and groups.

3. Language

Opening up John's images is what we are trying to do. Images can be refreshed in many ways. Visually, for instance, for me the hot journey north from Jerusalem to Nablus enabled a visit to Sychar and the vertical well shaft. A monk draws running water from the depths, which one sips and which even today surprises and moves us; the situation, the legend, the memory of Jacob's place, the contrast with embattled peoples now, and the twin peaks of Mount Gerizim and Mount Ebal, sacred then to the Samaritans, are part of our experience now. Watching one's friends in the coach party, standing in peace, sitting in the shade in the pleasant garden, the scene and the memory of chapter 4's event and the "water" come alive. The metaphor is no longer faded but alive. We are living the metaphor. Of course, one may not be able to go there, and then it is attention to the literary device that is needed, and a recognition that as

29. Rollins, *Hearing Visions*, 284.

we recycle the text time and again, the metaphor loses its passion and becomes a cryptophor.

The word "metaphor" from the Greek means "to carry meaning across"; the word "cryptophor" means "to carry hidden meaning."[30] Our task with each other is to find, share, ingest, and celebrate the hidden meanings in the Gospel, and then relate them to personality and the hidden journeys that we are making. The task is to tally or parallel the development of our own psyche with the development of life in the Gospel, to hold Jesus near, knowing that he holds us. The possibility of such associative links is pregnant with significance. Coleridge's "secondary imagination" has free hand. The whole burden of Cox and Theilgaard's other key book, *Shakespeare as Prompter: The Amending Imagination and Therapeutic Process* (1994), is the prompting that is possible—nay, probable—between text and person and between person and person. We can apply to the resonances between "John" and our own inner self or psyche what Malcolm Pines (consultant psychotherapist at the Tavistock Clinic, London) asserts.

> Psychotherapists are rediscovering that psychotherapy is not primarily a precise technology of accurately used words, as tools of effective interpretations. The depths of the mind are reached and touched by simpler words that speak in images and metaphors, speak in a universal, timeless language . . . A language that touches the heart, the ancient seat of the emotions, that speaks to the soul, that aspect of the human being that nineteenth-century science thought to have eliminated, as bespeaks the suppression of that word in Strachey's translation of Freud, whereas in his native German Freud used the word frequently.

He points out that there are now many "maps of the mind" and that many are used "on journeys of meetings, of exploration, believing that to journey together in search of hidden meanings may result in the healing of hurt minds."[31] We may see Jesus as making those journeys with his disciples and the characters he meets, and see him as making such journeys with us as we make the same journey with John and at the same time also with each other. The phrase applied to Shakespeare, that he has a "relentless impulse to reach the depths of the psyche,"[32] we apply to John.

---

30. Cox and Theilgaard, *Mutative Metaphors*, 107.

31. Cox and Theilgaard, *Mutative Metaphors*, xxiii–xxiv.

32. Cox and Theilgaard, *Shakespeare as Prompter*, 206.

We are in good company. Bernard of Clairvaux (1090–1153), that lover of life and lover of God, said, "My curiosity has led me to explore my lowest depths as well, only to find the He went deeper yet. If I looked out from myself, I saw Him stretching farther than the farthest I could see; and if I looked within He was more inward still."[33]

Share with a partner how you feel about looking inward.

The depths of the psyche are reached by the aesthetic imperative, the impact of the power, the beauty, the impression of the story on us, and the inspiration that follows. The last word there, "inspiration," is of course a metaphor, a breathing into us of what we read and hear, see and feel, individually and corporately. And the indwelling (another metaphor) of spirit, *pneuma*, wind is a pressing Johannine theme. Partly this happens through the refreshing of faded metaphors. Light, for instance! Shakespeare highlights (a metaphor) Macbeth's "divided self in a divided world" in visual terms with the contrast between day and night, light and dark: "Now o'er the one half-world Nature seems dead, and wicked dreams abuse the curtain'd sleep." "Come seeling night . . . Light thickens and the crow / Makes wing to the rooky wood; / Good things of day begin to droop and drowse."[34] We *feel* his deadly dilemma. Compare how differently John describes Jesus the Word, the *Logos*: "In him life [*zoe*] was, and the life was the light [*phos*] of men, and the light in the darkness [*scotia*] shines, and the darkness did not overcome it" (1:4). What a vivid image; the battle between light and dark, and the light still shines! John's brilliance (a metaphor) is that we begin to *see* and then we *hear* Jesus saying, "I am the light of the world" (*ego eimi to phos tou kosmou*, 8:12).

Cox and Theilgaard take as a watchword a sentence from Gaston Bachelard (1884–1962), the French scientist, philosopher, poet: "But the image has touched the depths before it stirs the surface."[35] It is almost a Johannine image! When Jesus is present, we do not have to wait for years for the stirring of the waters (John 5:4 and in some texts v. 7). We look for

33. Cited by Cox and Theilgaard, *Mutative Metaphors*, 3.

34. Shakespeare, *Macbeth* 2.2.49; 3.2.45; Cox and Theilgaard, *Mutative Metaphors*, xix.

35. Cox and Theilgaard, *Mutative Metaphors* xiii.

a real encounter with each other because of the encounter we have with Jesus and with John's characters and language, with his point of view. We acclimatize ourselves to his rarefied atmosphere, learn a mutuality with each other and with John's language and thought. We feel and share the affect generated by it and we are changed in line with his purpose.

We are moved by the text. The impact of the "amending imagination" is in the direction of growth in faith, in the growing, developing process of life. There is a healing of spirit involved but we need, not a medical or pathological model, but a growth model. The prompting a precious text gives is that it gives core value, encouragement, and facilitating. We hear words in the text and, knowing all that has gone before in our literary growth, we greet them with "the listening landscape of prepared echoes."[36] John enhances our attentiveness however far we are journeying in the faith. *"[H]e makes us notice novel aspects of that with which we THOUGHT we were familiar."*[37]

The theatrical significance of prompting is a voice from the wings, when the mind goes blank, when speech fails. So we watch Jesus prompting "Are you a teacher of Israel?" "Give me a drink." "Do you want to be well?" "Do you believe in the Son of Man?" "Do you say this of your own accord?" "Mary." When we are telling our story, or listening to another's, there will often be times of "narrative failure," just as there is as a Christian pilgrim. Prompting enables discourse to begin again, and often at greater depth. So we reread the text and hear the message afresh. Maybe there is a vacuum in affect because we are stale, or there is a literal gap because we forget the words, or what has become concealed needs to be uncovered, yet whatever it is, between text and person, or person and person, new life is given; that which was not there before is called in to being. Energy is produced through proximity.[38]

4. The Style of Bible Study Used in the Workshops

Commonly one "story" will kick-start another. Todd writes, "The significance for a practice based understanding of hermeneutics is this: the offering of narratives of personal experience in response to a particular passage from the Bible is not occasioned by the group leader deploying

36. Cox and Theilgaard, *Shakespeare as Prompter*, 44.

37. Cox and Theilgaard, *Shakespeare as Prompter*, 95, original setting.

38. See Cox and Theilgaard, *Shakespeare as Prompter*, 89, 107–10, 172.

a narrative critical approach to the text." This is not a discounting of the narrative approach but a shift from working only in a "historical-critical register." "Rather the narrative response is consequential on an invitation to share experience. Further, the earlier historical response and the later narrative ones coexist . . ."[39] It is more than just prompting links with the Gospel; it is allowing conversation wherein the people come alive (often vulnerably) in a fresh way. There is an integration of text and personal story. Sitting in the shadow of the fig tree of the text, we are in touch with the living word and then with the living text. Indeed, *we* become the living text. And that is no solitary experience.

The discourse is composed of many voices—that of Jesus, of the text, of "John," of the characters, the canonical voices, and of what Todd calls the "lifeworld" voice of lifetime and current experience.[40] Some voices will be dissonant—like that, say, between a more literal interpretation and a more flexible one.

One of the members of the Enfield group mentioned in the preface had been a member of the church of which I had pastoral charge in the 1970s and was a convinced "conservative evangelical." We had begun to get across each other and I felt I was being pressured to secrete my "liberal" stance, and that I would only be accepted if I moved towards a "fundamentalist" one, an expectation I could not meet. (The labels, however rigid and limiting, still give a vivid picture of the possibility of conflict.) I remember meeting her and being straight with her, not about which interpretation was going to be "right" or to "win," but about the fact we were both seeking to live in Christ, to love each other and the same church, denominationally and locally, and that the only way to survive the possible abrasiveness was to practice tolerance openly. We became firm friends in Christ and maintained our difference without polarization. Now, years later, our different positions enrich the input. Person to person, we trust each other. When a tricky interpretation imposes, say, of the turning of water into wine, we smile wisely at each other. I love her and she loves me, in the sense of *agape*! The tension between what previously would be incompatible approaches is *held in the fellowship* because we are held in the shared text. We are not compelled to choose between different reading strategies.

---

39. Todd, "Interaction of Talk and Text," 77.
40. Todd, "Interaction of Talk and Text," 79.

Studying the Bible and having fellowship are intimately related. Difference is held in the fellowship. Such incipient reconciliation is possible because of two further features. Firstly, a reader-response approach through which we are aware of, and sensitive to, not only the way we receive the text, but to the way we add to it, complete it, write ourselves into it. And secondly, through a psychodynamic critical approach we understand through pastoral training and insight how psychodynamically we bring our distinct personalities to bear on the text, and on the living text of the person in front of us. The moves we make on the text as we seek meaning, and on each other as we seek relationship, and on the group process are part of the agenda we are now attuned to. The insight that is the product of this approach is really a form of knowing, of Johannine knowing. It is a whole way of being "in the know" adumbrated in the Gospel. In cooperation with studying the text, we are reading the living human document, the living text that we are.[41]

The purpose is plainly not just to study the text and let it speak, nor just to deepen pastoral awareness through the biblical influence, nor to try to attach one to the other (important as such intentions are), but to *experience the space between*.[42] The Gospel is a treasure house of psychological and spiritual insight, not in the sense that one can dip into it to find wisdom in one or the other, but in the sense of their complete integration.

The elements relating the relationship of the Bible to pastoral care that are relevant to these workshops on John are, in brief:

1. An act of imagination that goes beyond the bounds of the discussion of historical questions in relating self and group to what we read. Imaginative construal of the contents of the text becomes the text "reading" the community.

---

41. Anton Boisen, founder from 1925 onwards of Clinical Pastoral Education in the United States, used the phrase "Living Human Document."

42. Ever since the work of Donald Winnicott, the notion of "space between" is important. There is a border area, or space between, mother and infant. As separation looms it is filled with a comforter of some sort, called a "transitional object," the idea or image of which represents mother. It is in the space between ourselves and the other, or the world, or "God" that we create our symbols, or symbolizations of the world, images which become enshrined in words (our sense of what a text means), in play, culture, religion. This is known as "transitional space." Winnicott "opens for us the spaces we reconnoitre throughout our whole life, entering ever more deeply into contact with ultimate reality." Ulanov, *Finding Space*, 6. See *What Language Shall I Borrow*, n. 36.

2. Responsible recognition that we project into the text our own ideologies.

3. Accepting thus that our reading is contextual, and part of the context is constituted by our own needs.[43]

4. Taking the biblical material as authoritative in that it is the reference point for content and method of pastoral care, and (not "but") permissible openness of interpretation allows openness of self to the sense. "The use of the Bible should be consistent with good counselling principles,"[44] and also, the use of pastoral care/counseling/psychodynamic/psychotherapeutic styles should be consistent with good biblical interpretation.

5. Recognizing that there is a presence in the pastoral encounter of an energy, of grace, from a dimension beyond us. Kenneth Bragan, not writing ostensibly as a Christian but as a psychiatrist in retirement, looking back on the drive for health and wholeness, for self-worth, on a drive in patients that he had commonly experienced, wrote, "I would say that I am doubtful whether this is solely self-creation and not also the operation of grace that simply comes to one."[45]

6. It is possible to align biblical themes with life themes as a resource so as to encourage truth and comfort and reliability.

7. Through a combination of listening to self and others and to the biblical messages, there is a reality to the possibility of life change. The "disclosive role of the text" in no way diminishes the value of listening carefully to the human story as central to the pastoral engagement. "[H]ermeneutics is a process that interweaves written and oral processes."[46]

8. We are aiming at the nexus that connects a person in the life situation to the content of the biblical material. The hiddenness of a life overlaps with the hiddenness in the text; the "innerness" of the text is intertwined intrinsically with the inner world of the person. He/she hears words, only half understood, touching upon the half-understood inner psyche or upon its acting out. When psychodynamic

43. For example, Ballard and Holmes, *Bible in Pastoral Practice*, 16–18.

44. Ballard and Holmes, *Bible in Pastoral Practice*, 198.

45. Bragan, *Self and Spirit*, 109.

46. Ralph Underwood, "Winnicott's Squiggle Game and Biblical Interpretation," in Rollins and Kille, *Psychological Insight* 69–73.

ideas are repeated in the workshops, it is because, in relation to the text in hand or the fresh interactions between participants, a fresh application or insight links the inner world with the textual material. Each step forward is a new discovery.

9. There is a reciprocating influence: text to person, and person to text, and person to person. Our story weaves in and out of the written narrative of God's story. God's story in Jesus and his followers weaves in and out of ours, through the medium of text and shared experience.

10. The one whose turn it is to offer care embodies a self-emptying that reflects the vulnerability of God and allows an integration of human and divine story.

11. Understanding grows through moving through literal language to living in a world of metaphor. The Gospel of John works by this movement from the literal to the figurative. John's language and therefore his meaning slips, slides, and elides from what is seen to what is "seen," from the physical to the symbolic. "Literal thinking leaves a person spiritually in ignorance; psychological and spiritual truth is opened up only through symbolic thinking."[47] Symbols are expressive of more than mere words convey. The danger is to get stuck on the literal, even on historicity or in the old criticisms, important as they are, and not to read and hear the text and the message at a deeper level. So repeatedly the steps in the narrative move from the simple location of a plain event or story to its deep significance for faith. Metaphor is John's metier, and it becomes ours; it has to be ours. We move from the concrete to the intangible. We risk ourselves to "what opens in the space between our experiences of our self and our experiences of God."[48] And by trusting the space between each other as we read, we explore and ingest the uncertainties and certainties of the text, or rather this happens as the text reads us. Have courage!

12. Metaphor elides into symbol. The learning point for many (brought up on the literalist approach) is allowing for, and sensitizing oneself to, the flow built into imagery. So, simile—Jesus is *like* bread (not used in John)—to metaphor—Jesus *is* bread—to symbol—eating

---

47. Sanford, *Mystical Christianity*, 177.

48. Ulanov, *Finding Space*, 6; and see footnote 42 above.

Jesus/bread. In this sense of holding metaphor and symbol together, a symbol starts with what is familiar, part of experience in daily life. This is sometimes called the "vehicle," for instance, water, bread, light. In John images are gathered from the Old Testament. Because of background or cultural knowledge, and repetition, a symbol points to a meaning at another level, called the "tenor."

It has two parts, the mundane and that which mysteriously transcends it. The first is easy to know; the second teases us, puzzles us, expands us, leads us on. It challenges, changes, deepens us, changes our whole perspective, grants us meaning. It transforms us, joins us to a new vision of reality, unites us with those who perceive what we perceive, and provides endless stimulation and mystery. The reader is drawn into a new realm or sphere of thought and especially of experience. The symbol has a life of its own, without losing the connection to the original. The symbol is refined; "vine" and "bread," for instance, are identified, using one of John's key words, as "true bread" and "true vine." It points to a new reality, even a transcendent reality. Understanding is stretched. There is a living, changing quality or depth of life because simple words—water, bread, light, vine—are used symbolically. Symbols "often span the gap between knowledge, or sensible reality, and mystery."[49] They exist between knowing and not knowing and lead to deeper knowledge.[50]

13. This is how we are made! The process mirrors the mental development we all make from the concrete to the intangible in our mental processes and in the development of faith (Piaget, Goldman, Fowler). This process Jesus trusted and John used. We are still mulling over it, talking it, and writing it! We shall need to understand that in John "knowing" means not only the cerebral acquisition of knowledge, but the deepest changes in our psyche when we come to "know" Jesus and perceive that Jesus "knows" us.

49. Culpepper, *Anatomy*, 183.

50. See Dodd, *Interpretation*, 133–43; Culpepper, *Anatomy*, 180–202; Lee, *Symbolic Narratives*, throughout; Koester, *Symbolism in the Fourth Gospel*, 4–31 and throughout; Jones, *Symbol of Water*, 1–35 and throughout.

5. The Workshop Style: In Particular, the Nature of Sharing in Small Groups

The foundations of such groups living in such a style are: (a) historical, (b) theological, (c) psychodynamic.

5a. History

Historically, the belief in the supreme value of self-disclosure, much to the surprise of some, goes back a long way! For instance, the practice of the desert fathers was to share, not just in confession, but what was in the mind, "offering the secrets of one's heart to another person for discernment." The scenario was complete, with full awareness of the issues of self-deception, of finding the right person to share with, of waiting for a person to open his heart, of the stress on the value of the process itself (not just on the replies given).[51]

Perhaps the most notable example in the history of the church is in eighteenth-century Methodism. In the early Band and Class meetings there would be prayer and singing, but the core activity and discipline was personal sharing. "Speak your experience," said John Wesley. It meant more than "tell your story," it meant telling the group what your current experience was at the moment, and it was more than telling your "religious" experience, though that was the context; it was somehow conveying the essence of what was your being in the moment. The groups were foundational in and throughout the revival of "heart religion" in Germany, Scotland, Wales, England, and America in the eighteenth century.

John Wesley's *Preface to a Collection of Psalms and Hymns* (1739) contains the bon mot, "Solitary religion is not to be found here [in the gospel of Jesus Christ] . . . The gospel of Christ knows of no religion, but social; no holiness but social holiness." By the word "social" he meant, in this context, what we would call "fellowship," not a concern for social action (about which he was, of course, also completely passionate). "Faith working by love," Wesley's phrase, is the length and breadth and depth and height of Christian perfection. Both Wesleys were deeply attached to Milton. John Wesley included a selection of *Paradise Lost* in his *Christian Library*.

---

51. Stewart, "Radical Honesty about the Self: The Practice" and "Radical Honesty about the Self: The Tradition."

He to his own a Comforter will send,
The promise of the Father, who shall dwell
His Spirit within them; and the law of faith,
Working through love, upon their hearts shall write,
To guide them in all truth.[52]

We draw our minds away from the single interpretation of "holiness" as being ethical. Holiness *is* the journey of discipleship. "And we really misunderstand the whole thing if we think that holiness means being defended from our own humanity or other people's humanity: quite the opposite."[53] A fundamental point in early Methodism is that "discipline" meant the honest style of relating in small groups, and *not* just a matter of ethically behaving properly. Discipline was exercised over matters of behavior, but "the hedge of discipline"[54] was the interior discipline contained in the style of life operating within the Band and Class meeting. *The Rules of the Band Societies* (December 25, 1738) indicated the necessity for a willingness to be entirely open, to speak and be spoken to freely and plainly, and to be "cut to the quick" and "have one's heart searched to the bottom." It is, of course, essential to keep a balance in all personal group work, the safeguard being that the group process ensures that we do not try to "heal our own wounds slightly"! As John Wesley said, "in the multitude of counsellors there is safety."[55]

Joseph Sutcliffe in *The Mutual Communion of Saints: Showing the Necessity and Advantages of the Weekly Meetings for a Communication of Experience* (1797) writes:

> Tell your experience; and tell your conflicts; and tell your comforts. As iron sharpeneth iron, as rubbing of the hands make both warm, and as live coals make the rest to burn; so let the fruit of society be mutually sharpening, warming and influencing. Christians should also bewail their failings, infirmities, deadness, coldness, narrowness, and unprofitableness, one to another; to see whether others have been in the same case; what course they took; and what remedy they procured.

Many a rich tapestry is woven of sensitive group interaction, handling distress and despair, fear and shame, inconsistency, as well as

---

52. See Milton, *Paradise Lost*, book 12.

53. Williams, *Being Disciples*, 49.

54. Wood, *Directions*.

55. 1748, cited by Oden, *Intensive Group Experience*, 70.

greater security in faith. "Souls may perish through too much modesty and reserve." "When we hear people speak their own experience, there is something in their voice and manner which affects us with a degree of sympathy, tenderness and conviction of their sincerity, as cannot be communicated to the mere reader."[56]

> Love is their sole bond and soul of union . . . we love God in proportion as we know him: so also with regard to our brethren . . . We may know [them] . . . by being members of the same church . . . yet are we incapable of knowing, and consequently of loving them as we do those who disclose their experience in mutual confidence. Where a communication of experience is neglected, we can be acquainted only with the exterior Christian; but where it is improved, we see the interior: and discover at once the happy correspondence between their outward walk, and their inward piety. And, having long been accustomed to lay open our hearts, and to sympathise in all our temptations and distresses, to edify and comfort one another in the Lord, our love must have grown in proportion to our faith, and likewise in proportion to the persuasion we have of each other's piety: we must have formed an intimacy of the most sacred kind, and such an union of spirit as none can know, but those who now know it by happy experience.[57]

James Wood, in *Directions and Cautions Addressed to the Class Leaders* (1803), says of leaders, "they ought to be well acquainted with the human heart . . ." *The Methodist Class Leader, or, The Duties, Qualifications, Difficulties, and Encouragements of a Class Leader Considered with an Account of Class Meetings* (1818) by John Blackwell is a more extensive study, over 140 pages, and the core of the matter is clear. He points up the difference between "popular social discourse" like preaching, which deals with general principles, and the Class Meeting, wherein "they are particularly applied. The one relates to topics, the other to cases." It is intended "to advance experimental religion in the hearts of individuals." "In a class meeting, we learn what we are, and what we want." "The duties of a Class Leader should be performed in a feeling manner." "A leader should be a man of peace and energy." John Wesley says in *Plain Account of the People Called Methodists*, "I have often found the advantage of such

---

56. Sutcliffe, *Mutual Communion of Saints*.
57. Sutcliffe, *Mutual Communion of Saints*.

a free conversation . . . Every one here has an equal liberty of speaking, there being none greater or less than another."[58]

What is amazing is that the early eighteenth-century Methodist groups practiced a style of group life that has so very many similarities to the practice of modern group therapy or sharing groups. The analogies between then and now are compelling. I have identified thirty-two points of similarity between them; there is no space here to describe them.

We should note incidentally that there is much humor. I was in a Care and Share Group once at a conference and we had so much fun! "It is important to remind ourselves often that the cultivation of a right sense of humour can be one of the forms of piety."[59] It is also a creative part of group activity. The mere fact that people bare themselves and share their deepest hurts means there is a true seriousness. But true seriousness is not antithetical to true humor. It is more than "seeing the funny side of things," which can be an avoidance of hurt. Even then it may be permissible and useful, as our defenses *are* useful to protect us and give us a breathing space and a new platform from which to dive deeper. It is more that in sharing the deepest hurts we are sustained by the contexts of biblical narrative and a caring group. The richness of the latter experience will often mean the possibility of a lighter touch, a shared wisdom, a gutsy determination to get through, accompanied by a healthy joy and togetherness that will often sparkle with humour. In this context, "Cultivate a sense of humour in yourself about other people, and in other people about yourself: learn to laugh, rather than to be vexed by other people's foibles, but learn the ability also to let other people laugh at your own."[60] Well, not so much of the "laughing at," which in the wrong way can be cruel and distancing, but more of the "laughing with," which is engaged and empathetic.

An extraordinarily tense and obsessive theologian, namely, Martin Luther, respected and was aided at a critical time by the encouragement of one Dr. Staupitz. "It should not be forgotten also that Staupitz, in his role as Martin's superior, could afford to make Martin laugh; and laughter marks the moment when our ego regains some territory from oppressive conscience."[61] Nor should we forget the words once on a poster outside

58. Wesley, "Plain Account."
59. Vann, *Divine Pity*, cited by Handley et al., *English Spirit*, 220.
60. Vann, *Divine Pity*, cited by Handley et al., *English Spirit*, 220.
61. Erikson, *Young Man Luther*, 163.

Park Avenue Methodist Church, New York City: "Laughter Is the Closest Thing to the Grace of God" (Karl Barth!).

5b. Theology

Theologically, the nature of sharing is exemplified in the trust between Jesus and the characters in the New Testament Gospels, and within the fellowship advocated in the New Testament writings. *Koinonia* is the word for partnership, for "fellowship." It is of the essence of the church down the ages and interpreted specifically as the love that members have for each other in Christ. As H. A. Williams, former dean of Trinity College, Cambridge, and then a monk of the Community of the Resurrection, writes, "The confidence which leads us to abandon the shelter of our disguises and to open up the doors of our personality so that others may enter there, and both we and they be richer for the contact—that confidence is God."[62]

Van Deusen Hunsinger speaks of "Practising Koinonia" as depending on appropriate personal interchange. "Others cannot know us unless we consent to making ourselves known. Others may be able to surmise something about us, but if we want to be fully human, we need to reveal ourselves."[63] She quotes Karl Barth's "theological anthropology": "This two-sided openness is the first element of humanity. Where it lacks, and to the extent that it lacks, humanity does not occur. To the extent that we withhold and conceal ourselves, and therefore do not have to move to know others and to let ourselves be known by them, our existence is inhuman."[64]

I had a most moving conversation with a pastor whose wife and children were trapped in Rwanda at the height of the murderous civil war there. He did not know if they were even alive. I asked if he was able to talk to anybody, to share his acute distress, and he replied, "Oh yes! I talk with all my friends. They need to know what is happening to me." *They need to know!* That is a powerful theology of the church.

Analysing what it means for the church to be a Reformed church, Rowan Williams, the former archbishop of Canterbury, says, "And the . . . thing I want to underline about the Reformed Christian identity is that it

---

62. *True Wilderness*, cited by Handley et al., *English Spirit*, 227.
63. Van Deusen Hunsinger, *Bearing the Unbearable*, 111.
64. Barth, *Church Dogmatics* III/2, 251.

is <u>conversational</u>." He reminds us that "Calvin . . . speaks at length about how the church must come to stand under the judgment of God, and says that for this really to work, people have to learn how to talk to each other about God." "It is the mark of the Reformed 'style' of Christianity that it is interested in how ordinary people talk with each other about God and the things of God. Because, if the critical edge is about sharing attention to what God is saying to us, we need to learn common discernment, . . . finding words beyond our own—and that's why Reformed Christianity is anything but individualistic."[65]

The genius of the Wesleyan emphasis will add that such conversation, for it to be rich and applied, has to refer to the self. It is speaking of *the self, in that context*, that provides the breakthrough into fellowship and faith/trust. Speaking truth to our neighbor is enjoined upon us (Eph 4:25), but that must mean truth about ourselves first.

"But where was I when I was seeking You? You were there in front of me, but I had wandered away from myself. And if I could not find my own self, how much less could I find You?"[66] "Unless we know what it is to care for and value our selves, we shall never learn what caring and valuing are."[67]

5c. The Psychodynamic Approach

So what are the psychodynamic guidelines for, and the principles of, the activity of sharing, whether in a group of two or more?

For the first session, the leader welcomes and reassures. The aim is to have an experience together whereby we gain insight into others and ourselves so as to care more effectively, and to do this in a Christian context. This is not only a learning group, but also a fellowship. Activities are not "exercises" but a real exploration and encounter. Please try and let happen to you what is happening to you. And if the initial feeling is that "this is not for me," please try and be patient and hang in there. There is no compulsion on anyone to speak if they choose not to. The hope is that everyone will be able to listen, though there may even be times of great stress when even listening is too much. We are different and from different backgrounds as regards personality, faith experience, and

---

65. Williams, "Reformed Characters," underlining original.

66. Augustine, *Confessions*, 5.2. See Williams, *Wound of Knowledge*, 68.

67. Williams, *Wound of Knowledge*, 110.

churchmanship. We are seeking to be human together to share a *common faith and ministry*. So listen as much as you can. Listen to each other. *Do not cheat and chat. Open-ended* questions and grunts are allowed. Empathize. Listen to the feelings. Be aware of censoring. Reflect on how was it talking, listening? How has your relationship with the partner you are talking to changed?

The one golden rule is CONFIDENTIALITY. There are two aspects to this. "Do not speak outside the room what you have heard within it" was John Wesley's command. Speaking in Band meant that *nothing* that we hear of another's life will be repeated. It is dreadfully easy when tired, excited, voyeuristic, or needy of attention for ourselves to pass on what we have heard. Guard against it. And secondly, do not report even in the room the content of what your partner said to you without permission.

Paradoxically, we are free to censor what we say about ourselves (we do it anyway!); we do not have to say what we do not wish to, and that sets both speaker and listener free, the former because we are in charge, and the latter because if we ask a question, or get our response wrong, the speaker need not respond.

6. A Closer Look at the Guidelines for Sharing

I commend small group work and pastoral care based on a psychodynamic approach and integral with Christian faith. *It is NOT discussion, but sharing.* Communication is sought rather than socializing. It creates honesty and dialogue, and properly avoids the tendency to suppress negative feeling. It enables the showing of, use of, release of, enjoyment of proper emotion. It enables the avoidance of judgmentalism and the giving of advice. It teaches self-reflection. It uncovers both damaging and creative unconscious material. Its currency is *affect*, feeling, which is both joyful and painful. It analyzes patterns of personality, interaction, and group life. It explores transference. It creates a sense of the presence of goodness, of Christ, of the Holy Spirit, and puts into practice the doctrines of atonement, justification, and sanctification. It brings people together in love and in trust.

- Start with a primer, e.g., "What has happened to you this week?" "What has happened to you since last we met?" Move quickly from storytelling to "So what did that mean to you?" "How did that feel?"

- Not discussion, not argument, not establishment of points, not exploring truth "out there," not settling "facts." The method is *sharing*. For most of us, this requires a transitional shift from talking to listening, from a logocentric style to the active passivity of listening. "If we were apprentices of listening rather than masters of discourse we might perhaps promote a different sort of coexistence among humans . . ." "A listening atmosphere is not improvised. It is, on the contrary, the product of a strenuous process of conception, growth and devoted attention."[68] The only points to be asserted are about the *process of the group*.

- The facilitator may explain the process, steps, aims, rule of confidentiality, and guidelines, and use this to refresh, calm down, explicate. The process or method is transparent, open to all. The agenda is contained within the group. The method contains the message, namely, that each one is accepted, respected. The *work* is that the group is caring for each other and for the group-as-a-whole. Responsibility is accepted for the group life. There is a commitment to focus, when needed, on the group process. Focus on the present and permit owning of the past. *Describing* is the discipline, without judging. Personal sharing is preferred over diagnostic probing. Attacks are discouraged, observations welcomed. The leader is involved. Change is encouraged but not required.

- The purpose may be explained within the Christian context, the comfort and challenge of a common commitment and affection focusing on a shared faith and Person, a metanarrative within which all other stories are told. The goal is growth, sanctification (the work of the Holy Spirit). Caring and training, interests and skills, and spirituality interweave. These include recognizing the tendency to suppress negative feelings and the tendency to be judgmental. Leadership is mutual. Care will often be shown later outside the group.

- Trust should be built. Steer away from discussion to an expression of feelings. The theme and material of the group is not thoughts, but *affect*. People change because they share affect. Whenever one shares something of oneself with another, there is always an inner event.

- The Gestalt rules are useful: not why but how; here and now; I and Thou. In other words, share how one feels, without enquiring about

68. Fiumara, *Other Side of Language*, 57, 60.

reasons; permit owning of the past but stay with the present feelings, not anecdotes about the past; be in direct communication with a partner. Personal sharing is preferred over diagnostic probing.

- Listen. Give people a chance to talk. We all need to talk. We all need to talk about ourselves. Talking, even about ourselves, is not necessarily sinful. It is not necessarily pathological; not if it is related to growth, of the person and the group. Everyone is equal. All can learn to listen. "The Christian who cannot find time to listen to a sister or brother will soon no longer be listening to God either."[69]

- Let questions be open, not closed. Questions are meant to elucidate feelings, not ideas, and rarely facts, if the narrator can cope.

- Listen and make no value judgment. Hear and give no advice and *do not insert your own agenda*—so you need to know yourself pretty well! If need be, be vulnerable. Vulnerability will release others' narrative. But do not manipulate.

- Empathy means showing an equivalence of form and feeling.

- Especially allow for the *unconscious*, and for unconscious communication.

- Be aware of the transference of affect between members, and between members and leader. Be aware especially of the mechanism of projection, whereby we put *our own* feelings onto another person.

- Note that the facilitator and the group act as a "container," "holding" each other's experience, good or bad. She or he will know each member as a whole person, and also, when the group works as a whole, will be aware of all the movements, non-verbal and verbal, of all the other group members. These guide the leader to the inner world of each and of the whole.

- Allow for humor and lightness.

- Give affirmation of work done.

- Practice the ethos of mutuality rather than competitiveness.

- Allow for winding down at the end.

- Always allow time for feedback and debriefing. It is absolutely essential after *every* time of sharing, of personal disclosure, that those who wish to acknowledge openly what they were in touch

69. Bonhoeffer, *Letters.*

with have an opportunity to say what has happened to them. Not everyone will need or want to talk, but it is vital that the opportunity is available. This also has the effect of bringing the theme of the session and of the sharing to the fore, so that the group-as-a-whole can own the material that is current. It also means the leader can in any case offer a person who has been distressed a window to talk about it afterwards.

- The goal is growth. Sanctification is the work of the Spirit of God. Augustine's plea was "Let me know you, O Lord, who knows me: let me know you as I am known."[70] "Let me know you for you are the God who knows me: let me recognise you as you have recognised me" is the translation of R. S. Pine-Coffin.[71] "[K]nowledge of God in Christian faith is correlative with knowledge of self. The two are dialectically related. All true self-knowledge requires knowledge of God, but knowledge of God is sterile and 'academic' unless it discloses true knowledge of the self."[72] Only in personal sharing in a Christian context can our identity narratives be infused with the difference that belonging to Christ makes. "[T[he disclosiveness of Christian narrative is not only its revelation of the identity of God but also its revelation of the true identity of the individual, insofar as that person's history has been reinterpreted in the context of the community's life and history with God."[73] Prompted by John, we learn together who we are and manage to grow. We share with Augustine, "To know myself is to know you."

Awakening with a fresh sense of God's love and presence is always coexistent with a new relationship with others. There are a multitude of biographical examples of the corporate experience alongside the individual experience when finding the reality of God afresh. For instance, in Albin[74] and Hindmarsh amongst others, or in the *Arminian Magazine*, eighteenth-century biographies and autobiographies always point to the group experience as being integral with the personal. As just one example, Margaret Austin, married to a cruel husband who left her with

70. Augustine, *Confessions*, 10.1 (p. 207)

71. Augustine, *Confessions*, 10.1 (p. 207). Also quoted in Stroup, *Promise*, 176. See 1 Cor 13:12.

72. Stroup, *Promise*, 19.

73. Stroup, *Promise*, 247.

74. Albin, Empirical Study, 275–88.

two small children in 1739, heard the key preachers, and longed to join a Band, a small sharing group of committed Christians, and found comfort and support "hearing the others tell the state of their souls." She was emboldened "to speak of the state of mine." She at last experienced joy, as another prayed and sang hymns with her.[75] Hindmarsh's summary is, "if we look closely at the stories told by the evangelicals, we find a surprisingly strong countervailing emphasis upon the community of faith as well, a community that was as much discovered as it was constructed by human agency . . . When Thomas Oliver and Margaret Austin expressed such strong yearnings to join the Methodist band meetings, they acknowledged not only that they needed new hearts, but also that they needed a new community."[76] When people have shared as deeply as is suggested in these workshops, they will have a stronger sense of love for each other and a surer sense of belonging.

Given these guidelines, when a person shares in the group it will make manifest their presence, their joy, their confidence, their satisfaction, and often their sorrow or suffering. People initially are fearful of too much introspection; that is always a criticism of sharing groups, but indulgence will be monitored by the group-as-a-whole, by the facilitator, and by the person's own superego, the censoring part of the psyche. Soon the sense of tremendous privilege reassures us as we hear a person's story. We need to share our "psychopathology," in the literal meaning of the word: a *logos* of the *pathos*, suffering, of the psyche—all Johannine key words! It is a case of living on the boundary between, and also of deep calling to deep. It will be creative of *koinonia*, a close and trusting fellowship. Feedback by members or the facilitator will be non-judgmental and supportive. Our joy and our sorrow become gifts to the group.[77]

To tell one's story means two things. "Stories are transformative, and people need to learn to become the authors as well as the subjects of their own stories."[78] Yes, and it is also essential for us to know ourselves in the story, to become the subjects as well as the authors of our own story—to see ourselves.

We also have to be alert to the group process. *The value is in the process.* The value is in the event, the exchange, the happening, not just

75. Hindmarsh, *Evangelical Conversion Narrative*, 147.

76. Hindmarsh, *Evangelical Conversion Narrative*, 344.

77. A moving guide to the experience in such a workshop exists in Levine, *Poiesis*, 43–61.

78. Knights, *Listening Reader*, 71.

in what is said or heard. The message is in the medium. All we can say here is that there are many descriptions of what happens in groups, and sadly this is not the place for them. We need the best models, insight, and understanding we can get if we are to risk venturing into ministry with people in small groups. It is completely worthwhile to try to gain such skill, by belonging to a training group or reading about groups. To have an awareness of the phenomena occurring within groups is essential. The same elements are present whether the group is for psychotherapy or is just an "ordinary" group.[79]

Building on the wisdom in the three elements—the historical, the theological, and the psychodynamic—we perceive that sharing, focused on personally earthed story, is narrative defined as autobiography. Sharing means talking about oneself. It is autobiography, more than a memoir or reminiscence or factual narrative, because it permits significance, facilitates meaning, and constellates identity. In Augustine's *Confessions*, maybe the first Christian autobiography, in books 10 and 11 he dealt with memory at length, and time and change and who he was. "He wondered what the relationship was between himself in the present and himself in the past as a child and a young man and an adult."[80] He wrote, "O Lord, I am working hard in this field, and the field of my labours is my own self."[81] Rowan Williams's observation is, "Identity is ultimately in the hand of God; but this does not mean that it is a non-temporal thing. It is to be found, and in some sense *made*, by the infinitely painstaking attention to the contingent strangeness of remembered experience in conscious reference to God which makes up most of this extraordinary work."[82]

To tell my story involves: Who am I? What did and does my life signify? What do I say, and what does what I say mean? The listener will be holding in the scales of the listening process both trust and suspicion. He or she will expect both naivety and sophistication, blindness and sight, pretense and reality, and will be conjoined in the search for meaning. The presence of an-other is integral to the sharing of oneself. So nearly all of the questions in the boxes in each chapter/workshop invite a narrative of the inner world. Growth comes through reowning, in a caring context,

79. The bibliography contains a few of the many books on group work.

80. Hindmarsh, *Evangelical Conversion Narrative*, 4.

81. Augustine, *Confessions*, 10.16. Amongst much writing on Augustine, of interest are Anderson, "Historians of the Self"; Williams, *Wound of Knowledge*, 68–89; Taylor, *Sources of the Self*, 127–43.

82. Williams, *Wound of Knowledge*, 68, italics original.

the actualities of who I am. In the present moment of disclosure, the past is healed and the future assured. I know more precisely and more clearly who I am. Making autobiography enhances and sets a seal on identity. Self-interpretation is formed in the group. The sense of the good comes to us through the group, from John's Gospel. Our narrative is held in his. Hope and being is found, not in the resources of the self alone, nor in the group alone, but in Christ and "resting" in him, as John says.

Charles Taylor, in a chapter on "The Self in Moral Space," writes:

> I have been arguing that in order to make minimal sense of our lives, in order to have an identity we need an orientation to the good, which means some sense of qualitative discrimination, of the incomparably higher. Now we see that this sense of the good has to be woven into my understanding of my life as an unfolding story. But this is to state another basic condition of making sense of ourselves, that we grasp our lives in a *narrative* . . . that making sense of one's life as a story is also, like orientation to the good, not an optional extra; that our lives exist also in this space of questions which only a coherent narrative can answer. In order to have a sense of who we are, we have to have a notion of how we have become, and of where we are going.[83]

The "space" for questions is within us, between us, and between us and the text, and the "good" is offered in the Gospel. We risk ourselves so as to *feel* the answers.

7. The Need for a Model or Models

7a. The Dynamic Cycle

Sharing in groups and by self-narrative deals in the particular, not in the general. As we listen our reactions will put us in touch with the scandal of hard listening to the text and to each other, the particular and not the general, and we will be remembering especially the *skandalon* of the cross and the foolishness of Christ's sharing the human terror. Sharing groups deal with the concrete; that is why folk fight shy of them, and fight shy of the "scandal" of what happens inside people and between people. The scandal, of course, is the cause of much blessing! Our reading of John will point to and lead us across the threshold of the particular. So on a particular day, the morrow, he sees Jesus coming to him and says,

---

83. Taylor, *Sources of the Self*, 47, italics original.

"See . . ." (*horao*, 1:29), and at the end he says to Thomas, "Bring your finger here and see [*horao*] . . . and be trusting" (20:27). And sight and insight are close. With blinded, not-seeing Gloucester we shall say, "I see it feelingly."[84] In our reading of the text and in our reading of each other we shall see feelingly.[85]

In the core of many disciplines there is a notion of what is "normal." For the English lawyers, it was the "reasonable" man: for the purpose of deciding what behavior was "reasonable," it was what "the man on the Clapham omnibus would have done"! In medicine and psychiatry, it has seemed to be a negative: a person without . . . is "normal," health being an *absence* of sickness; hence a pathological model. Frank Lake responded with the quite distinctive notion that Christ is the "norm." It was by studying the life of Jesus that the model called the "Dynamic Cycle" gained life. He spent a day with the Swiss theologian Emil Brunner, who was visiting the Christian Medical College at Vellore, and pressed him "to show me where psychiatry could find a model of man's understanding of himself which could be acceptable to a Christian theology, he directed me to a long and repeated study of the dynamics of our Blessed Lord, as they occur in St. John's Gospel."[86]

John's *bios*, "biography," of Jesus shows him as having a supreme sense of his own identity, sharing life with God the Father, the source of his being, the one who has sent him. *There are four elements to that portrait: Christ's acceptance, sustenance, status, and achievement.* And here are a few examples.

1. *Acceptance*: Jesus knows (a Johannine word) he is the beloved Son, only begotten, with access to the Father at any time and all the time. Indeed, he abides in him and is one with him (17:5; 11:42; 16:28; 14:10; 17:21). John's commentary makes it clear that this is how he is seen (1:18, 3.17). This sense of *acceptance* is the foundation of his life.

2. *Sustenance*: Throughout he is sustained by the presence of the Father. He is always in a continuous state of prayerfulness with the Father. He is not alone (3:35; 11:42; 14:10; 16:32; 8:16). His well-being

---

84. Shakespeare, *King Lear* 4.6, 149.

85 For a discourse on the essential nature of "feeling" in a caring relationship as part of the way we communicate, see Pembroke, *Art of Listening*, 79–83.

86. Lake, *Clinical Theology*, 134–37.

is preserved because he abides in the Father and the Father in him. His *sustenance* is never arrested or interrupted.

3. *Status*: However much he gives of himself, even exhaustively, his *status* remains full of grace and truth, as the Son. His motivation is to love to the end because he is loved (5:26; 7:18, 28–29; 8:23). The strength of his sense of his worth is expressed most forcibly in the seven "I am" sayings, and in sayings where "I am" is used without a predicate (4:26; 8:58). They are used by Jesus in both his public ministry and in the private discourses.[87]

4. *Achievement*: There is a constant theme of the work that Jesus is to do, is doing, and has done. This flows from who he is and how he is energized, namely, by the Holy Spirit. He fulfills his destiny, even when he feels forsaken (5:19; 8:26, 36; 14:10; 17:4–10). The "words" his Father gives him and the "works" that he does (5:36) constitute his work in this sense. The "heavenly blueprint of his plan for the world" is communicated in substance both orally and through his "works."[88]

This life is the norm for *our* lives. Christ's dynamic cycle is paralleled in our dynamic cycle. This is how we may live. Here is a window into how we work. The Dynamic Cycle charts the process by which an infant acquires a sense of being, from the love and nourishment provided within the immediate family, then how he/she is sustained and nurtured to a point of well-being, and so gains a sense of worth, identity, and status, enabling him or her to achieve, to have a work outflow from the self. The cycle, of course, is continuous, not staged, and all the phases coalesce, and repeat themselves as life goes on. The model takes the form of a quadrilateral with a circular movement through the four phases.

1. The baby is looked at by mother lovingly and "sees feelingly" with all his or her senses. He or she gains a sense of "I-myself." A trusting dependence is normal, and security comes through being deeply accepting of the *acceptance* offered. "Simply accept the fact that you are accepted."[89]

---

87. See Brown, *Gospel*, 1:553–58; D. M. Smith, *Theology*, 111–13. The source is Exod 3:13–14.

88. Ashton, *Understanding*, 405.

89. Tillich, *Courage to Be*, 163.

2. Well-being comes through regular and reliable attention. The baby is, and feels, *sustained* consistently, both by food and a presence full of love.

3. Slowly becoming aware of a safe separation into a secure but closely relating self, the baby has and feels real worth, *status* (a good word), and value, and is satisfied in him- or herself to be a deeply loved and honored person; thus the baby has love and value in abundance to offer back and to others.

4. Thus the baby is able to *achieve*, to work, to contribute, and to respond freely with energy and to be only naturally fatigued in the process. Work, service and loving, learning and playing, are not falsely tiring. And the process starts again, i.e., is continuous. So this is how a human being lives.

6b. The Interruption of the Dynamic Cycle

However, being who we are as parents, maybe even through no fault of our own, the cycle is often blocked, fractured, impeded, interrupted, or breaks down. Especially when this happens in the first two phases, damage mild or overwhelming occurs. Failures at various points in the cycle may affect the developing psyche. Lake crystalized a range of defenses and positions by using the descriptive language of the psychodynamic world, sometimes adapting it with his own nuances. *These terms are simply useful* (not to categorize people, but) to illuminate how we are as human beings when the sources of our life waver. They will be used periodically as helping to illuminate John and ourselves. We need the resources to *witness* to the presence of Christ at the depths of mental pain, where acceptance and nourishment have been impoverished, and status and achievement thus compromised. We are describing features in every life, even if we have had "good-enough mothering" (Winnicott).

- Denial of or delay in the presence of mother and her nourishment provokes mild to severe *anxiety*, the *anxiety of separation*. Her presence holds at bay ontological anxiety, the threat to our being, the anxieties we feel just by existing in the world. Her absence prompts a decline in being and well-being.

- But our reaction to learned anxiety through deprivation is anger and aggression, *expressed* outwardly onto (m)others or *suppressed* inwardly. In simple terms, the anger is at the heart of one sort of depression and is either exploded or imploded, commonly both. Another reaction to the impending loss of the source person is the libidinous fantasy of possession of the source person or of her parts. To gain what we need, we seek to achieve in order to earn our own acceptance, nourishment, or worth, thus *reversing the Dynamic Cycle*. Acceptance is seen as a *reward* for work, and which we have to work for; it is not a gift freely given. We have to earn our acceptance!

- If mother still does not come or repeatedly fails to come, the child's sense of being is progressively reduced and he or she moves to a sense of "non-being" and knows that that is a "*dread*-full" place to be. Mounting separation anxiety is an experience of being rejected, shut out from life, the total opposite of "abundant life."

- The lonely child faces the prospect of being forsaken, and experiences the stress that cannot be borne, *transmarginal stress*. This prospect of the worst pain, of annihilation, is terrifying and a living organism fights against it tooth and nail: with anger and destructive rage against the source person who has "betrayed," and by clinging with the fingertips to a sort of hope. This is manifested in the *hysteric* (not "hysterical") defense and position whereby the child struggles to be close, to seek intimacy, to manipulate a response on order to repress the feeling that "I am nothing, no good," and struggles to prove by many words and posturings how acceptable "I am." This in turn only puts people off with demands that feel phony. And how can you trust a response that you yourself have manipulated? But people remain too distant and separation is a constant threat. So paradoxically there is always an *untrusting* move *towards* people, to cling, or to manipulate a response.

- On the other hand, when we go beyond the margin of stress to the far side, people are too close. If by neglect the child is pushed to the extremes of inattention, it is as if an *abyss* of non-being is opened up, which, by summoning all the powers of defense, the sufferer manages to cross away from the source person; but will choose determinedly never to recross. Never again! How can anyone be trusted ever again? This is the *schizoid* defense and position. The anxiety is *commitment anxiety*. All sorts of defenses protect the person from feeling such intolerable let-down ever again. The movement is *away from* people. The avoidance of heartache is by keeping your distance.

- If the absence of accepting and sustaining figures begins to feel persecutory (and maybe it *is* persecutory), the reaction is *paranoia*, and the inner conviction, mild or absolute, that the pain is inflicted by the (m)other on purpose. The locus of the suffering is sincerely and even passionately believed to be outside the self, which in a way it is, except that perspectives become warped and (to mix metaphors) flood into wider areas of judgment. There is a spread of blame; the finger is pointed. Accepting one's own inner truth is inordinately difficult.

- An early defense is to turn inwards to the self. The outside environment, including persons, becomes a mirror of the self. Like Narcissus, we get comfort and value by gazing at our own reflection. It is safer than risking relating to the world as it actually is. We naturally opt for safety. In *narcissism* the world is related to us.

- Another safety ploy is to seek to control everything. This is the *obsessional* defense and position. Ritual, organization, and routine protects, is safer than the terrifying chaos of a descent into the abyss, even though that is where Christ is!

These elements exist in us in different quantities and commonly mingle one with the other. The development we go through as we make this journey through our psychic pain and defend against it is sporadic; it is not in straightforward steps. And when we retrace our steps painfully through what we have become, the progress is not necessarily regular. Maturation, personal growth, individuation, working through our reaction patterns learnt over many years, is often a start-stop activity. The fact that old patterns and new insights weave in and out of us in our personal growth to a greater wholeness or maturity is actually reflected in the text we are studying, the Fourth Gospel.

It would be nice to have a step-by-step sequence in personality development and to have it matched in the text of John. But life and text are not nice like that. There is no routine schema for the human soul. Positives and negatives weave in and out the whole time, as they do in the Gospel. That is the nature of the relationship between Jesus and those around him, and the text reflects wonderful moments of clarity and desperate moments of disappointment. The energy in the story carries us along. So the words we have used in the model suggested weave in and out of our analysis of the characters and of ourselves. Regularity or sureness of response is not our experience. The descriptive labels will be invoked where they fit. Motifs will surface and resurface where appropriate.

We need to note three patterns that frequently occur in us.

- Anything that is painful in us, which we feel to be "not me," we *repress* into the unconscious and *split off* and deny the existence of. But the heartache remains at the heart of us, and is relieved only by catharsis and reowning through a process of disclosure that is managed in a bearable way. Update the eighteenth-century language, and Charles Wesley, in the brilliant hymn "Open, Lord, My Inward Ear," is appropriate: "Show me, *as my soul can bear,* / The depth of inbred sin."[90] We need to allow the depth of distress to surface, as much of the distress that we can bear at the time, and then we shall be free. This will happen naturally in the groups. (We are not interpreting the word "sin" in a narrow moral sense, but as alienation from self, (m)others, and God. Being "inbred" simply means it is part of our shared human condition.)

- A key defense against self-knowledge and an awareness of the pain within is *projection*. We put feelings, "good" and "bad," which are really our own, onto others in an attempt not to own them for ourselves. Projection involves "A mental image visualised and regarded as an objective reality"—not a new idea; it has been current since 1836. When we make a judgment on others, for instance, if the hysteric bit in us is speaking of another and we say, "He or she is always seeking attention," we get a clue to an element in our own personality. We may be right about the other, but the fact that that is what we have noticed indicates something about ourselves.

- *Transference*: In any relationship, and especially in a caring relationship, it is normal to use the mechanism of projection to color the relationship. Its field of operation is also *every group we are ever in*. It refers to a specific "illusion" that develops in regard to the other person, one which, unbeknownst to the subject, represents in some of its features a repetition of a relationship towards an important figure in our past. It is *felt* as strictly appropriate to the present, but

90. Hymns and Psalms, 540, italics added.

it is not; it is "a false connection."[91] The engine of transference is the defense of projection. This is the "as if" factor. The other is treated "as if" they were someone from our past; it skews the current relationship. Positive transference is where there is attraction to or idealization of the other; negative is when there is dislike or rejection of the other. Countertransference, positive or negative, is when the *helper* has such an attitude to the person being helped. The feelings may be extremely mild or dangerously strong. The aim is to use an understanding of transference to create a "working alliance," rather than to "act out" the phony relationship. What is needed is firm, holding warmth.

We have described in summary form a particular outworking of the psychodynamic style. "The psychodynamic model has assumptions implicit to it about how our minds work, how we develop psychologically, how we function emotionally . . ."[92] Understanding the relationship between helper and the person being helped is vital to the process. It safely owns the disclosure of unconscious material, of our inner world, hid from sight and feeling for so long. This happens between two people and also in a group. Given patience and trust, these experiences will occur in the workshops as people talk and share. The new awareness and knowledge that we gain swims through the whole of life, through every relationship, and permeates our faith response. The pervasive Johannine imagery of dark and light often expresses the experience. Awakening to one's own consciousness is like opening the window on to a sunlit morning after the dark night of non-being.

It is exciting and confirming that we may now be sure that this approach is consonant with the recent developments in neuroscience.

> In the last 20 years there has been an explosion in our understanding of how our brain develops and functions, which has brought neuroscience and developmental theory together . . .
> In particular there is an increasing understanding of the role of early experience in how the brain is sculpted, so that we can no longer think about nature (what we are born with) and nurture (the influence of our experience) as rivals . . . For example it has

91. Freud and Breuer, *Studies on Hysteria*, 390.

92. Howard, *Psychodynamic Counselling*, 3.

been discovered that the structure of our brains is formed by the experience we have as very young babies.[93]

This happens "because, although we are born with all the brain cells we will ever have, the connections between those brain cells happen as the result of the relationship between the baby and his [or her] carers . . ."[94] Cells that don't become connected die off, while those that do make richer connections, and this affects how the baby experiences the world. Caring nurturing, or as Winnicott would say, "good enough mothering," is essential and difficulties arise when it is not there.

> The brain is at its most plastic (that is, can generate new con-
> nections between cells) during childhood, but new learning,
> including emotional learning, can take place in adulthood so
> long as the right conditions apply. This explains why people can
> change in adulthood and also why some kinds of early experi-
> ence are difficult to repair but instead need to be managed . . . [95]

This is the world Jesus lived in. If we wish to be "in" him and he "in" us (John 17), then we must attend to our *inner* world.

We are not offering these models and insights to the text of John or to ourselves or to each other as watertight categories or solutions, but as windows or metaphors that give clues for a deeper understanding of text and person. How do we understand that Jesus can reach the parts others can't reach? This psychodynamic reading of text and person will help. There are many models in the psychodynamic field that are immensely helpful, and we have chosen Frank Lake's cyclical one as a key. As we go through the Gospel, these models and this language will be used, and will lie behind and inform the insights into the text. In particular, they will be of essential value in monitoring and understanding the sharing responses made trustingly to the questions in the groups in each workshop.

> The process of living in God's creative life comprises our spiri-
> tual journey. Christian doctrine calls this the process of sanctifi-
> cation. In the spaces among the persons of the Trinity, all life is
> found and created. Christ brings this life to us, which we are to
> live and have abundantly if we can take it and not turn away. We

93. Howard, *Psychodynamic Counselling*, 53–54,

94. Howard, *Psychodynamic Counselling*, 54–56. We now also need to note that a view is also strongly held that "neurogenesis" occurs, the creation of new neurons in the brain. See Lehrer, *Proust*, 38–43.

95. Howard, *Psychodynamic Counselling*, 54

are summoned, wooed, challenged, invited to participate *in the circulating life* of the divine.[96]

Edwina Gateley was so moved by the experience of sharing in pairs and in the group on a pastoral training course that she wrote the following poem, and very kindly sent it to me. I am deeply indebted to her.

We told our stories—
That's all.
We sat and listened to
Each other
And heard the journeys
Of each soul.
We sat in silence
Entering each one's pain and
Sharing each one's joy
We heard love's longing
And the lonely reachings out
For love and affirmation.
We heard of dreams
Shattered
And visions fled,
Of hopes and laughter
Turned stale and dark.
We felt the pain of
Isolation and
The bitterness
Of death.

But in each brave and
lonely story
God's gentle life
Broke through
And we heard music in the darkness
And smelt flowers in
The Void.

We felt the budding
of creation
In the searchings of
Each soul
And discerned the beauty
Of God's hand in
Each muddy, twisted path.

96. Ulanov, *Finding Space*, 136, italics added.

And his voice sang
In each story
His life sprang from
Each death.
Our sharing became
One story
Of a simple lovely search
For life and hope and
Oneness
In a world which sobs
For love.
And we knew that in
Our sharing
God's voice with
Mighty breath
Was saying
Love each other and
Take each other's hand.

For you are one
Though many
And in each of you
I live.
So listen to my story
And share my pain
And death.
Oh, listen to my story
And rise and live
With me.

John 1

When Two Worlds Meet

Touch my world with yours and let me follow, I pray.

THE GOSPEL BEGINS WITH a Prologue. The Word was in the beginning. The Word was God. The Word was made flesh. Then what?

Come close with John and feel the pulse of love.[1]

1. The Story Begins

The writer moves from this high philosophical background, from an attempt to use fresh language and thinking, perhaps reconciling Greek and Jewish wisdom, wisdom that came to dwell with men, with Christian thought, as he begins to paint a picture of Christ. Painting has an abundance of the philosophy of art behind it, but it depends on the slightest brushstroke as well. So the Gospel becomes localized, itemized, precise, particular. This is where the story begins. From the arena of philosophic debate and intellectual synthesis, it moves to the stones of the desert, the mud of the Jordan, and a fig tree in Galilee. To a person who acts, who does things; he preaches and baptizes. But with a question hanging over him, a question of identity, of meaning. Who are you?

1:19–23. I am not, this John says. I am not the Christ. I am not Elijah, not a prophet. We begin the "biography" of Christ with what a person is

---

1. Guite, "John," in *Sounding the Seasons.* Used by permission.

not. A negative definition. *Ouk eimi* ("I am not"—see chapter 9 for one person with a strong enough identity to be able to say "I am"). Certainly, *ego ouk eimi Christos*. This is in response to priests and Levites sent (*apostello*) from Jerusalem to ask him. Would even the use of this word "sent" spark a response in the first readers, who knew already that Jesus was the one who was sent? "Who are you? Let us have an answer for those who sent us." Even though these are lesser "sent" (*pempo*) people, is this a subtle echo of the whole theme of the Gospel. How do we respond to him who was sent? "[H]uman 'coming' corresponding to divine 'sending.'"[2] The more important and certainly more persistent query will be, not of John the Baptist, but of Jesus, "Who are you?"

This John answers, "I am a voice . . ." (*ego phone*). The Maori myth of creation starts, "In the beginning was the voice . . ." This word *phone* will be often used at critical moments throughout the Gospel. We shall have particular words repeated time and time again. We shall get used to listening for all sorts of hints in the words used and the nuances of their use. John is a very "wordy" gospel, and we are just remembering it started with the Word! So, strangely, as we get into a new habit of checking out each word and spotting whether it is significant, we are already aligning ourselves to something quite basic to what is spoken of in the large-scale narrative of the coming of Christ. Word, and words made flesh, and dwelling in us is what the Gospel is about. What we experience as we work our way through John is that "The Word that had been Word only in my head, became flesh."[3]

We shall find words repeated, so as to hang like beads on a thread, or better, beautiful shining pieces of glass, or gems at which we may look longingly and lovingly. We may even peer through them at some mysterious reflections within. They will dazzle us by their brilliance, amaze us by their arrangement, fracturing the light around us so that we shall gasp both with surprise and recognition. We will trust the flickering of words and phrases. So what if we make an odd mistake or so; we shall have seen some gems worth seeing. And we ourselves will have changed. We shall have avoided the old bland ignorance and exchanged it for hints, puns, metaphors, ironies, and connections, made rich by the jewelery of the words scattered through this Gospel.

2. Schnackenburg, *Gospel According to John*, 1:251.

3. Woodman, *Pregnant Virgin*, 185.

The life of this one, who calls to us first, has been so stripped down that he is simply conscious of being a voice. Imagine being a voice crying in a wilderness. Not many hear much in a desert!

Choose a partner and share with a partner your response to any of the following:

Can you remember an experience similar to that? You had important information to share but no one wanted to know. Who were you trying to tell, where were you, what were you trying to say, how was it when they did not listen? What did you feel toward the one or two who did attend? How did it affect you?

Have you experienced the sense of isolation we may feel in a desert place? This may be actual physical isolation or a personal isolation experienced in some other way. Share as bravely as you can.

Are you conscious of having had a question put to you at some point? How did you respond? What did you answer? Was what you said "satisfactory," was it "adequate"?

At a deeper level, are you aware of any sense of the way life questions you, of the questioning of life? What is the answer you are trying to give? Do people hear, see you as you see yourself?

Are you ever conscious of a voice crying out of the wilderness of your own heart? What does it cry? What do you cry?

2. John Bears Witness

This is the witness of John (*marturia*, from which we get the word "martyr"). We have joined the story at its first scene. The message was one of preparation for the appearance of Jesus. Make straight the way of the Lord—into the world, into people's hearts? The rationale for John's movement was not just his own faith response to Old Testament texts and to his unique vocation, but to point to the advent of Christ. As the very start of the other three gospels, the Synoptics, it is shepherds and wise men and the pious who do the pointing; here it is John the Baptist (though John never calls him that).

1:24–28. He baptizes with water, but paradoxically the setting for his "pointing" was the presence of one standing (a special word in John) "whom you do not know." We begin the "biography," the *bios*, of Christ with an unknown one. The first appearance is full of mystery. The reader asks, "Who is he? Where is he? What does he look like? How do we see him?" Yet he has a thong on a sandal, so incarnate is he, that "I am not worthy to untie."

We note here that two important ideas have been introduced, which we shall reflect on later. "Witnessing," the noun and verb, is used thirty three times in the Gospel and six in 1 John, compared with thirty-two in the rest of the New Testament. The second is "knowing," which is a vital theme in the Gospel, and is linked to "seeing."

This event took place in Bethany across the Jordan. Place and time defined are very important in John (the writer). It is one of the ways he moves from the general to the particular. He is very conscious of time, especially nearness of time. It is one of the ways he emphasizes immediacy, immanence, and a pressing *incarnate-ness* in his story. We assume this introducing of the idea of the Baptist and the unknown one—who by definition is not seen, even though he is standing there—is on the first day, because we are then told, on the next day, on the morrow, he saw (*blepo*) Jesus coming towards him (1:29). Time links give energy to the story, and bring us into it.

We have turned into the first room of the art gallery, and in each room he who is not known is going to be made clear to us. There will be a series of great murals and of tiny cameos, of portraits and scenarios. The pictures will amaze and stir us and leave us questioning, and with answers, till the end of our lives. With a simple phrase repeated three times we are led on and on: "the next day," "the next day," "the next day." You can't get much more mundane than that.

The next day he sees Jesus (*1:29–34*). "Behold [see, *hoaro*] the Lamb of God, who takes away the sin of the world." The next day, "Behold, the Lamb of God." Two disciples and Simon (35–42), "a scene full of mysterious silences."[4] The next day, Philip and Nathanael (43–51). On the "third day," a marriage at Cana in Galilee (2:1). The Passover of the Jews was at hand, (nearness of time again) (2:13). "On each day there is

---

4. Van Tilborg, *Imaginative Love in John*, 87.

a gradual deepening of insight, and a profounder realisation of who it is that the disciples are following."[5]

It is possible[6] or probable[7] that there is an intended time structure here, though there is discussion as to what it is if there is one. "The difficulty of basing a convincing chronology of events upon this datum is notorious. But 'the third day' was in Christian tradition from earliest times the day when Christ manifested His glory in resurrection from the dead."[8] Brown and others do list the events as pertaining to each day. Could it be that the whole start of the ministry of Jesus is set so? It is suggested that there is a span of seven days here, up to 2:11, and that the public ministry began at 2:12 with an interlude at Capernaum, where they stayed (meno).

What would the first readers have been thinking? They could have thought in terms of the days of creation in Genesis—"In the beginning," a reminder of which they have noted already in reading the Prologue. This is the start of a new creation.[9] Or they may also, knowing the story well, have sensed in advance a hint of the days referred to at 12:1, "six days before the Passover," the end of the ministry, the period just before the dreadful climax of the last week of Christ's life. Passover being referred to in verse 13 is a chill echo of what is to come, a point of interpretation this early of what the life of Jesus means. What a cost is involved in taking away the sin of the world (cosmos)! The mind of early Christians would leap from "on the third day" to the resurrection. A new beginning at Cana there certainly is, of "signs" of the old order being superseded.

What happens inside you when you meet a very distinguished person?

Share how time impinges on your life. What is it to have "free" time? How do you find places to rest when you are busy? Are you conscious of your feelings about changing times?

---

5. Brown, Gospel, 1:77.
6. Brown, Gospel, 1:105–6; Gospels and Epistles, 24–28.
7. Barrett, Gospel, 158.
8. Dodd, Interpretation, 297–300.
9. Phillips, "Third Fifth Day?," 328–31.

3. Seeing and Seeking

The declaration John makes identifies Jesus at his Baptism as the one who will baptise with spirit (*pneuma*) because he is blessed by spirit descending (*katabaino*) and remaining (*meno*) on him (three special words), and that he has "seen" him and "witnesses" that he is Son of God.

1:35–42. Again John is standing, and fixes his gaze (*emplepo*) on Jesus, and points to him, but this time he is with two of his disciples who heard him speaking (*laleo*) and then followed Jesus. Jesus turned and saw (*theaomai*) them following. So now two follow Jesus and he contemplates them, "looks at" them with wonder. Brown would give the word no special meaning here; it would mean mere physical sight. Yet it is elsewhere used at 1:14, "we beheld his glory"; at 1:32, John saw the spirit descend as a dove and remain on Jesus; 4:35 Jesus says the fields are white unto harvest; 6:5, Jesus "seeing that a multitude was coming to him"; and 11:45, the Jews had seen what he did at the raising of Lazarus and believed. These were all experiences full of significance and emotional charge. This is how he first sees the two following (*akoloutheo*) him. Surely, Jesus had more feeling for his first two disciples than simple ocular vision?

How does Jesus feel when he sees you following him?

The whole of the subsequent narrative and dialogues describing what it is like to become a disciple reinforces that it was no formal moment when he met them and they met him. The first two "follow" before he sees them. "What do you seek?" he says (*lego*). Or "What do you want?" It is Jesus who asks the first question of them. He is not so elusive after all! The word he uses is *zeteo*, "seeking." These are the first words Jesus speaks in the Gospel, the start of a dialogue that will continue with each one he meets—to this day. If the word "follow" "has more than a locomotive sense,"[10] witness the meaning with which it is charged when applied to Peter in the final chapter (21:19); how much more is it the case that "seeking" speaks of a quest. Seeking Jesus will be a constant in

---

10. Marsh, *Saint John*, 134.

discipleship. The verb is used thirty-four times in John; that is a quarter of the uses in the whole New Testament.[11]

Then, how is it that John records the strange response to "What do you seek?," namely, "Where are you staying?," and the response to that is "Come and see"; and their response to that was that "They came and saw where he was staying and stayed with him that day"? Surely it is so that he can introduce and emphasize the important word *meno*, "stay," "abide," "remain," rest."

The first-time reader will be puzzled by the mystery involved in the phrase "lamb of God," and by the introduction of "staying," and by a disciple who is not named. Those familiar with the text in later years would know their significance. It is of the essence of how Jesus gives himself to us that he stays with us and we stay in him. They stayed for the rest of the lives. "The Gospel teaches us that the bottom line in thinking about discipleship has something to do with this *staying* . . ."[12]

Andrew and Philip here do actually find him (*heureka* from *heurisko*, used nineteen times in John). "Eureka!" Archimedes cried out in the bath. And the crowd crossing the sea actually do (6:25), but it is also a rare experience to find him! We will be put in touch with uncertainties here, and even with the concealment of Jesus, both in respect of his actions and his word. It may be that this *not finding Jesus* syndrome is not just not unlucky; it may be that the way the life of Jesus and our lives coalesce is through a sense of him not being found, of being not available, of being absent even. Nevertheless, and therefore, these first words of Jesus "are a question whose meaning can be extended to existential depths." We are seeing that the character of Jesus is being introduced "elaborately but somewhat indirectly."[13] Yet we are so soon already sure both that his feet are on the ground and also that he represents a teasing, elusive dimension of reality. Charles Wesley, taking the story of wrestling Jacob to himself and describing our quests as well, wrote, "Come, O thou Traveller unknown / Whom still I hold, but cannot see! . . . With thee all night I mean to stay, / And wrestle till the break of day." And "Through faith I

---

11. Stibbe, *John's Gospel*, 16.

12. Williams, *Being Disciples*, 1.

13. Culpepper, *Anatomy*, 108, 107.

see thee face to face, / I see thee face to face and live!"[14] Jacob "wrestling for a benediction . . ."[15]

Share with a partner an early memory which you can associate with an impression of Jesus.

Share how and when did you "find" Jesus. What did he mean to you then?

Share how it is that you "stay" with Jesus and that he "stays" with you.

Share how you feel in the dark night when it seems that Jesus can't be found.

---

4. Seeing, Finding, and Staying

We are confirmed in this experience as we watch the calling of the disciples more closely. We have already come across four Greek words for "seeing" (*theaomai, horao, blepo, emblepo*). In the first chapter alone they are used twenty times. That is no accident. Every word in John matters. This is the optical Gospel, the ophthalmic Gospel. The Greek words, some think, carry a consistent shade of meaning, whilst others sense a graduated intensity of meaning, which can make sense of their use in the resurrection story, and which are partly hinted at in the English translations here. For now we focus on the impact of the whole use. The reader of the Gospel has been given a huge clue in 1:18. "No one has ever seen God; the only Son who is in the bosom of the Father has made him known." Yes, but what does it mean? "Rabbi [originally "Sir," later "Teacher"], where are you staying [*meno*]?" A strange question which we return to later. Come and you will see (*horao*). They came and saw and stayed! One was Andrew, who first found (we are familiar with *eureka*) his brother Simon and said, "We have found"—in the perfect tense, therefore, "so as to keep"—the Messiah, the Christ. He brought him to Jesus. Again, the initiative is with Christ. Jesus looked at him (*emplepo*) and gave him a new name! "The same understanding gaze as John had directed upon

14. *H&P* 434; *STF* 461.

15. Erikson, *Young Man Luther*, 99, describing Luther as a young man.

Jesus."[16] "So you are . . . you shall be . . ." What a greeting! Jesus is going to attend to the *identity* of people. When he meets Simon, he looks carefully at him, as John had looked at him (*emblepo*, v. 42). "Seeing" is a fundamental step in discipleship.

Who did you see, or who saw you, on your journey into faith? Share your memory of them, your appreciation for the part they played in your life.

We can only truly live if we are acknowledged by another, an Other. "Almost everyone is desperate to be recognised, confirmed, approved. Just as it can annihilate with a cold stare, so can the Other through a loving glance infuse the flagging spirit with life-giving warmth." And this is our learning point. "But our neediness prevents us from being Other for others."[17] The way to live with our own need and the need of others is to be centered in love. Love is seen by very many, Jung included, to be the healing force in the therapeutic experience. Resistance against the idea is great! At a lecture in London at the Institute of Group Analysis, a speaker was trying to identify what it is in group work that exactly produces healing change in group members. All the (important) standard words were used like empathy and so on, when one brave soul stood up and said, "Why can't we just call it love?" There was a shocked silence! The discussion moved on!

The small caring groups that will develop through the personal sharing in the workshops will create love and the experience of love. Allow it to happen! Love one another! For John Wesley, the beating heart of heart religion was the small group, the Band or Class meeting, both part of the wider society group in each place—and the beating heart of these was love. There were many guidelines for the groups, for instance, *The Rules of the United Societies* (1743). "Such a society is no other than a company of men [there were very many women as members and leaders!] having the form of godliness, united in order to pray together, to receive the word of exhortation, and to watch over one another in love, that they may

---

16. Barrett, *Gospel*, 152.
17. Smail, *Illusion and Reality*, 140–41.

help each other to work out their salvation."[18] "In his letter to Edward Perronet, Wesley indicated that once classes were meeting weekly, fellowship was the vital ingredient that gave them purpose. This was enhanced by class member's "'intimate acquaintance' which gave them 'more endeared affection for each other.'"[19] Believe me, "more endeared affection" will grow as sharing takes place in the workshop groups!

1:43–51. The next day . . . Jesus decides to go to The Galilee. What a risk to go home; what will happen, will any more follow? But he was desiring to go. And he "found" Philip. "Follow" me! Phillip "found" Nathanael, who is dubious. "Come and see!" says Philip. Jesus saw and said, "Behold," see, an Israelite who is pretty honest. "How do you know me [ginosko]?" The most profound question anyone asks of Jesus. And the answer: "I saw you." He first sees us. This is the genesis of discipleship, of following. It is because he first sees us. It is also the continuance of discipleship after failure. See Charles Wesley: "Depth of mercy! can there be / Mercy still reserved for me?" "I have long withstood his grace, / Long provoked him to his face," "Whence to me this waste of love? . . . / See the cause in Jesus' face."

> Pity from thine eye let fall;
> By a look my soul recall;
> Now the stone to flesh convert,
> Cast a look, and break my heart.[20]

In sight of Jesus it is the renewal of the right balance in the relationship with God. Michel Quoist creates a meditation as a dialogue: "Help me to say 'Yes.'" "Say 'yes' son . . . For it is my look that penetrates, and not yours."[21]

When did you say "Yes" to Jesus? What were your circumstances of spirit? Share.

Are you being called to say "yes" to a person, a happening, a situation, or to a deeper trust in some part of life? Share.

---

18. Found in many places, e.g., Goodhead, *Crown and a Cross*, 318–22.

19. Goodhead, *Crown and a Cross*, 166.

20. *MHB* 358.

21. Quoist, *Prayers of Life*, 95.

Understanding Nathanael's swift change of orientation in the encounter with Jesus is helped when we realize the subtext of the exchange. The "enigmatic interchange" reflects the weaving in of OT allusions. There is the Jacob story, who is noted for guile (Gen 27:35–36), but who observes the commerce between heaven and earth (Gen 28:12, as the disciples will see, John 1:51), and who becomes Israel, the first to bear the name Israel (Gen 32:28). Then there is Zechariah 3:6–10, when in a single day the guilt of the land is removed and every one invites their neighbor under their vine and their fig tree (in the LXX "under" is *hupokato* as in John 1:50); there is also sensitivity to the advent of a messianic Branch or Shoot. It is also the place for studying the scriptures. So Nathanael's response is to use titles fitting for a Davidic ruler, acclaiming Jesus as the "son of God" and "king of Israel."

Readers had sensed in the Prologue "a second level of meaning" so that "Son of God" became "more than a royal title"; Jesus was God's "only begotten Son" whose power is from above. "The encounter between Jesus and Nathanael unfolds through a subtle interweaving of OT allusions." "[W]hat appears to be an obscure interchange is a subtle and engaging conversation."[22]

I remember being invited to the evening meal at his home by the Palestinian headmaster of a school in Hebron. We sat, we men, in his "garden," really a small vineyard, in the cool, still, and scented evening "under" his vine, a royal moment of peace and Palestinian hospitality with delicate and deep conversation and the meeting of minds. It lingers in the memory as a golden moment. So Nathanael was transformed, he was *seen* and called to be neighbor of all because the words of the promises are made flesh. This disciple who thought no good could come out of Nazareth learns that the Lord will come and dwell in the midst of his people.[23]

Originally, it may have been intended for it to appear that Nathanael's faith was evoked by "a comparatively trivial exhibition of supernatural power."[24] (Is such possible?) But, no, we must be in the realm here of the mystery of how Jesus is connected to us, knows us. "Where did you come to know me?" "I saw you under the fig tree before Phillip called

22. Koester, "Messianic Exegesis," 23–34.

23. The absence of fruit on the fig tree is a symbol of affliction, but the image of the fig tree is used to signify peace and safety, of walking in God's way; see 1 Kgs 4:25; 2 Kgs 18:31; Zech 2:6–12. The symbol of inviting the neighbor in is of a time of hospitality and openness.

24. Barrett, *Gospel*, 154.

you" (1:48). Phillip "called" (*phoneo*) but Jesus "saw" (*horao*)! He does not pick his disciples only on the basis of character (one of them is evil); he chooses those God had given (17:6).[25] His perception, his engagement with, his penetration of another human being will be continually exemplified during his ministry, and point to that mystery of his knowledge of us, of his abiding presence in us.

This is soon made clear (2:23–25). He was in Jerusalem for the Passover, full of suggestiveness of the tragedy of his end, but he did not trust (*pisteuo*) himself, his own being and identity, even to those who trusted (*pisteuo*) him, not even his own! It is an extraordinarily strong statement. He keeps his own boundaries, a model for those who care for others! And the reason is "because he knew [*ginosko*] all men" and needed not that anyone should "witness" concerning anyone, "for he knew what was in man" (2:25; see 1:48; 5:42; 6:15; 21:17 where Peter knows he knows!).

We anticipate. The hint we have had, however, is the use in this passage of the word *meno*, "remain" or "stay." The spirit "remained" on Jesus, John was convinced, at his baptism (1:32–33). The first request made by any of the disciples is to "stay" with him (1:38–39). They stayed with him the rest of the day from four in the afternoon, or even, if it was a Friday evening, through the Sabbath the next day. What impression did he make on them in that short time? Maybe we are meant to read more than a superficial meaning into it. Certainly, there is a theological slant in these pictures of call to discipleship, staying with, and attending a wedding, and certainly this theological slant is intended.

Nathanael's response, "You are Son of God, King of Israel," shows a response apparently out of all proportion to what has occurred. Even Jesus remarks, "Because I said I saw you sitting under a fig tree, do you now trust?" The answer is "Yes." Yes, we do trust because he sees us first. The Word, the Lamb of God, notices me! Yes, because, or when, Jesus sees you, even if you started by following him, you will trust. The first prompting to follow is by what John Wesley called "prevenient grace," the grace that comes before. It does not all depend on you! And you will see greater things than these, heaven opened, and the relationship between your opening heart and the world—which, Jacob like, you open up to—will become clear. You will see a direct connectedness between heaven and the Son of man (*anthropos*). You will be part of this vision. This vision will be part of you.

---

25. Grayson, *Gospel of John*, 25.

We can't see God. People of his time could see Jesus, but John makes it clear that there is seeing with the eye and seeing with the eye of the spirit. So seeing Jesus in the fullest sense is not just seeing him with physical sight. It is seeing him for who he is, with the change that takes place in the person as part of that seeing. It arises out of a surprising mutuality, a flow of interest, a knowledge between Jesus and his disciples, in which he does the same actions, of looking and finding, as they do. This pattern of mutuality will be a mark of the encounters between Jesus and the characters in the Gospel. It will signify an approachableness, an availability of the God made man, which will both display what God in Jesus can do and what humanity can be. The inner world, and therefore the outer behavior, of the human being can be abundantly full of life.

How does it *feel* to be conscious of Jesus looking at you? Your discipleship does not simply depend on you.

What do you want? Be precise. Never mind how extreme or unobtainable, spell out what it is you want. Hear the sound of your own voice saying it. Allow your partner to hear it. See if it connects with another question, What are you searching for?

How does he know you? He knows me as . . .

You hear "follow me"—how is it that you respond? In what way can you sense that "faith," or "Jesus," brings some answer to your search?

Familiarity should not blind us to the astonishment we should feel that Jesus took these people on as disciples. He accepted them. This is the core experience of religion. They were accepted. And that acceptance continued to the very end, and even at the end was still creative. Even the transformation desire was an expression of total acceptance. We see this quite lucidly in the accommodation offered to Peter in the washing of the disciples' feet (13:6–12) and in his restoration after the resurrection (21:15–22). This changed their psyche. "No self-acceptance is possible if one is not accepted in a person-to-person relation. But even if one is personally accepted, it needs a self-transcending courage to accept this acceptance, it needs the courage of confidence."[26] We rejoice in the gift of their "courage to be."

Share what you feel when you feel deeply accepted.
Share some of the courage it takes for you to be a Christian.

Whenever we come to a point of growth, transition, or breakthrough, it is because there is a personal dilemma, a moment of opportunity to synthesize part of our personality with something new. Our personal history, our current existential condition, and our yearning to make sense of our inner world in relation to the outer move us forward. With the new awareness will come some disequilibrium; what has been not known is now experienced. This will happen in the groups outlined and experienced in these workshops. That is, so long as the questions are honestly faced, and group and leader are caring. For our mentors in the text we have Nicodemus, the well woman, the thirty-eight-year weak man, the man born blind, and especially Peter. They all moved through a personal dilemma through the presence of Jesus and a group of followers studying how to care—a true therapeutic group!

> Let there be life, said God,
> Let there be God, say I
> Let life be God[27]

> Everything in me and around me is in a state of becoming.[28]

5. The Prologue: 1:1–18

"The Prologue is necessary to the Gospel, as the Gospel is necessary to the Prologue; the history explicates the theological, and the theological

---

26. Tillich, *Courage to Be*, 161.

27. Siegfried Sassoon, "Power and the Glory." Copyright Siegfried Sassoon, used by kind permission of the Estate of George Sassoon.

28. Gustave Mahler, whilst creating his first symphony, "I can't help it, I just have to compose." Cited by Lebrecht, *Why Mahler*, 51.

interprets the history."[29] The Prologue "is a fair barometer of the atmosphere of the Gospel generally."[30]

The "normal" pattern of commentary is, of course, to start with the Prologue, the "beginning," at the beginning! But it is also true that, historically, the "story," the events, came first. It seems sensible also from a literary creative point of view to presume that the profound reflection we call the Prologue was penned when the "story" was well known, and was already embedded in Christian consciousness. Out of that consciousness came the "theology." So *we* began on our journey in Palestine, with our feet on the ground!

Now, having met him and his downright earthiness and his heavenliness, we can see how the Prologue is the introductory text in the anteroom of the art gallery. It operates at more than one level. This passage starts with the God dimension, Christ's place within it and his coming from it and the daring connection between the pre-existent Word and the earthly Jesus. "In the beginning [*arche*] was the word [*logos*] . . . and the *logos* was God." He was/is intrinsic in the process of creation, in the process of becoming (*ginomai*). Life (*zoe*) itself is in him. John will speak of his descent from above. It is as if light (*phos*) shines in the world, in the cosmos, and that "life" of his was the "light" of men (*anthropos*). The "life" was the "light" of human beings. It shines in the darkness (*scotia*) and is not overcome [*katalambein*] by it; the darkness is as light to God (Ps 139:11–12). Brown identifies four interpretations of *katalambein*, which the darkness has not achieved:

- to overcome, to grasp, to comprehend;
- to welcome, receive, accept, appreciate;
- to overtake, overcome in a hostile sense, c.f. 12:35 "walk while your have light lest darkness overtake you";
- to master or even to absorb.[31]

The Prologue is like the overture, introducing the themes of the symphony. (For Mark, 1:1, the "beginning" [*arche*] is the beginning of the gospel, the good news, the evangelion, and also the "first principle" of the gospel; both meanings reflect the Greek.)

29. Barrett, *New Testament Essays*, 48.

30. D. M. Smith, *Theology*, 11.

31. Brown, *Gospel*, 1:8.

However, there was one *anthropos* sent (*apostello*) from God. This earthing was necessary because this man, John, is a "witness" who is meant to witness so that all might "believe" through Jesus, the true (*alethinos*) light. We focus on the importance of witnessing later.

There is a shadow side, however. The light which enlightens every *anthropos* "was in the *cosmos*, and the *cosmos* was made through him, but the *cosmos* did not know him," and knowing signifies not just "intellectual apprehension . . . but personal response."[32] He came to what, after all, is his own, but his own did not receive him. He suffered "extensive rejection."[33] The negation will enable him to identify with every negative in our own lives. In John the *cosmos* is the world as the dwelling place of people, which God loves, and then it also takes on the meaning of the world of humanity as it is. But—and this is the theme—"to all who did receive him, he gave power/right to become children"—yes, of God! They, we, become children through the work of his will in us, obviously not through biological process, nor through body meeting body as such, and certainly not through our own willpower.

1:12–13. This happens because of two steps which we make: we *receive* him, as they "received" him into the boat in unstable circumstances (6:21), and we *trust* him. We are born of God. It is an image of God's family, to which we come to belong, of which we are part (13:8). Natural birth is both painful and joyful (16:21). Being "born of God" is also painful, letting go a privileged part of our self, and also joyful. It is different, however; being born, not of "bloods" (the word being plural, in accordance with the current physiology that it was the mixing of male and female blood that caused conception), not by the wish or intention of the flesh (*sarx*), which precedes the mixing of blood, and which is preceded by the will and desire of a man, who was seen as taking the leading part.[34] We need not assume that "flesh" is "a wicked principle opposed to God,"[35] nor that "desire" is lust. The carnal and spiritual are complementary, not opposites, and give way to another dimension. Becoming children of God means being "born of God."[36]

---

32. Lindars, *Gospel*, 90.

33. Carter, "Prologue," 39.

34. Bultmann, *Gospel*, 60 n. 2.

35. Brown, *Gospel*, 1:12.

36. Van Tilborg, *Imaginative Love*, 33–47.

It is a vivid comparison; we need not denigrate the God-given human activity of creation; it indicates difference. Being "born of God" is a metaphor pointing to another way of being. Just as we use the word "conceived" as a metaphor for, say, the thought process of invention, so "born" points to a realm of human change and being, gestation and growth in person, which is quite distinct from, but suggested by comparison with, the physical procreational process. The whole Gospel is about a new way of being (20:30–31).

Becoming children of God happens because the *logos* became (*ginomai*) flesh (*sarx*), pitched his tent (the root of the Greek word is n. *skene*,v. *skenoo*) with us, took up residence with us, full of grace (*charis*) and truth (*aletheia*); and we have looked with wonder upon his glory (*doxa*), the sort of quality an only-born son of the Father would have. This was remarkable in itself, but just as remarkable is that that fullness has been transferred to us; we have received it. New and decisive qualities came through Jesus Christ, namely, grace and truth, and were shared with us.

Yes, but how does he get himself into us? No one has "seen" (*horao*) God; this only Son who was totally accepted and shares intimate nourishing life with the Father (Lake's model), has revealed the secret, and is embodied in the narrative we now read and the narrative of our lives (v. 18). The invisible God is visible in Christ, in such a way as to transform humanity. It is more than simply having a look at what God is like; it is through participating in him in a new way that we can live with ourselves. We see what we could not see before. "The invisible appears on earth, / The Son of man, the God of heaven."[37] "God the invisible appears."[38]

> Faith lends its realizing light,
> The clouds disperse, the shadows fly;
> The Invisible appears in sight'
> And God is seen by mortal eye.[39]

So John's great theme is conveyed to us with his intense series of great words, which will become like identifying tints and colors, and brush marks. We shall be able to tell his style, but also we shall see and know the style of him who is his chief character.

---

37. Charles Wesley, "To us a child of royal birth," *MHB* 141.

38. Charles Wesley, "Glory be to God on high," *H&P* 101; *STF* 199.

39. Charles Wesley, "Author of faith, eternal Word," *H&P* 662; *STF* 457.

Pick on one word from the Prologue, get under the surface of what it means to you, and share what it means with your partner.

6. Comments, Gloss, and Application. Anxiety.

6a. Living Without and Living With

My contention is that St. John's Gospel stage by stage speaks to our deepest being, the core of our existence, and that therefore we can parallel each chapter with a stage of psychic development, or at least with a mechanism consciously or unconsciously used within our development. This is never going to be a watertight scenario. For one thing, John had no access to a modern understanding of personal development, or of the personality, or of dynamic psychotherapeutic approaches. On the other hand, we never stop short of applying the Gospel to our modern condition, nor should we. That would be to defeat the whole purpose of a scripture which is living and is constantly being reinterpreted for the age. So let us try!

We start with the *elusiveness of Jesus*. I was blessed with being brought up in a loving Christian home and there never was a time when Jesus and the church were not honored. I have often had a sense of his presence, and sometimes that has involved high points of great certainty, a certainty of the experience I was having, not just the thought I was thinking. In those moments of disclosure, even of a mystical nature, I had a sure sense of Christ being in me and I in him. But a lot of the time throughout life it has naturally not been like that. In these other times I have not been particularly aware of him. He has been elusive; he has been missing. Correction: He has not been missing; he has always been present and I have known that, but I have not known him present, not felt him present. So I am speaking about me and not about him. To speak of the elusive Christ is, since the ascension, inaccurate. And yet what I often feel is that I don't know him. My superego, coupled with depressing, ethical preachers, tells me I should and ought, and if only I prayed more or . . . I would know him!

Maybe I have to learn—no, drop the ethical compulsion—maybe I *can* learn that I don't know him and start in that place—at the bottom, in ignoring, in ignorance, in not knowing, where the Gospel started—and that I need not beat myself with mea culpas. That he is not known or not easily known is a good starting place for me! As we read John, our learning curve is to uncover how he gives himself to us.

Jesus is my hero! The paradox is that although in post-ascension history I know he is available all the time, it does not feel like it. Many things get in the way, my anxieties, for instance. So paradoxically I go through just what the people around Jesus went through. People did not necessarily find him. Stibbe, echoing Gerd Theissen's *The Shadow of the Galilean*, describes Jesus as "a shadowy figure, a man whose radicalism meant that he was constantly on the move."[40] He was certainly mobile geographically, but, to our great comfort, he was constantly on the move within the psyche of those he met. John expresses totally that he has his role *within* people. Yet there is also a mystery.

Stibbe stresses the elusiveness of Christ in his character as hero. He is not apprehended and comprehended, not understood and grasped (*katalambano*) by the dark forces of the cosmos. So the fundamental theme of the Gospel is: How is he to be "grasped"? He is an enigmatic figure, not pinned down till his hour has come. He is a Scarlet Pimpernel. The further paradox is that searching and being on a pilgrimage with a Christ who is, step by step, slowly to be revealed to us in a coalescence of his life and ours, will only have the possibility of its consummation just at the moment we do not have him. "Receiving him" and "seeing his glory" is a process and not a one-off! As R. S. Thomas in his poem "Via Negativa" says, "Why no! I never thought other than / that God is that great absence / In our lives, the empty silence / Within, the place where we go / Seeking, not in hope to / Arrive or find . . ." Or in "The Absence," on the one hand, "It is this great absence / that is like a presence . . . ," and then on the other hand, "What resource have I / other than the emptiness without him of my whole being, a vacuum he may not abhor?"[41]

Can I live with such anxiety, the anxiety of not having him when I need him, and then the anxiety of surrendering my anxiety when (it powerfully seems) he is not around?

40. Stibbe, *John's Gospel*, ch. 1.
41. Thomas, *Later Poems*, 23, 123.

> What makes you anxious?
>
> Can you live with your anxiety? How? Can you surrender your anxiety?
>
> Share what you feel when you do not have a sense of the presence of God.

6b. The Theme of Anxiety

If I am looking for a "human" theme subsumed in chapter 1, or a theme to set over against it as a counterfoil which it illumines, it is the theme of anxiety. Our primal anxiety is of not having a presence, initially of the absence of mother. Separation anxiety is learned very, very early, even in the experience of parturition. If mother is not available, is withdrawn or withdraws herself, the flow of supplies of essential nourishment of body and spirit is interrupted. Such early learned anxiety is reinforced by subsequent anxiety-producing separations. Woven in with this, reinforced by it and reinforcing it, is the ontological anxiety which we encounter just because we are human and living in the cosmos, and which we encounter because our environment of places and people will frequently cause us alarm, lesser or overwhelming, transient or chronic.

> Can you try to discern and share the difference in yourself between the anxiety that is intrinsic to our living in the world, and the anxiety you have *learnt* through early experience?

We may presume both John the Baptist and Jesus had a loving home and childhood. Mary spent the first trimester of her pregnancy resting at Elizabeth's, who was in her third trimester and needing support, at least sharing chores and chat. There was a unified extended family. Of the actual matrix of nurture, encouragement, and instruction, or of the bonding then between mothers and fathers and sons, we know little, though we assume, with the pointers we have, that it was good. Mary was a good mother. Whether she was a perfect mother rather than an "ordinary de-voted mother," or perhaps an extraordinarily devoted mother, or only, like the rest of us, offered "good enough mothering" (Winnicott) is a truly fas-cinating question! It bears more than closely upon the question of whether Jesus could cope with ontological anxiety, assuming he had no morbid learned anxiety, or, like the rest of us, he had experienced not only onto-logical, but also learned anxiety, and had grown (like us, but far better than us) some way of processing it so as to synthesize it into his maturity. It is a quite central question. How does the divine-human figure handle what we have to handle?[42] John Donne raises it, almost, in "Annunciation."

> That all, which always is all everywhere
> . . . yields himself to lie
> In prison, in thy womb; and though he there
> Can take no sin, nor thou give, yet he will wear
> Taken from thence, flesh, which death's force may try.

It affects not only how we see Jesus (his foundational human re-sponse aimed for in this Gospel), but also how we define our terms in an attempt to understand human personality in the light of Jesus. People instinctively sense this dilemma. In group after group, when reflecting like this on the impact of his early childhood on Jesus, I have asked, "Was Jesus ever anxious?" Virtually 100 percent will say "Yes." When I ask if he was ever depressed, nowhere near so many are sure about that, perhaps varying from 10 percent to 25 percent. We will need to use psy-chodynamic language and allow what it describes to tally with how Jesus enters us. Ontological anxiety is part of being human; being depressed is not, apparently! Learned anxiety is half and half? So in our thinking, the words "anxious" and "depressed" do not have equivalence. And we shall need to explore how the mind of Jesus, the psyche of Jesus, abides in us and how ours abides in him!

6c. Living with Anxiety

It is a truism of *incarnational thinking* to say that *the characters in the plot were children of their time.* The disciples were born into second-generation immigrant families from the south who had settled an area on the west side of the Sea of Galilee, looking across at the Greek area, the Decapolis or "Ten Cities." The area later spawned the second strongest resistance

---

42. These are christological questions with hints at answers!

movement against the Romans, which held out at Gamla as others notably held out in the south at Masada. Christ's early days were spent on the
road or in exile, and then four miles from Sephoris, the focus of Roman
rule and pseudo-Jewish culture of the Galilee. They all lived in a pluralist
society which was multireligious, multiracial, and multi-political. They
were settled but not settled. The country was occupied; there was frequent inflation, famine, and illness.[43] It was an age of anxiety. They were
children of their time.

When they "got religion" there must have been a heightening of anxiety. John the Baptist left home and led a pioneering life in the wilderness.
Possibly the disciples left home, with no time to first go and do what had
to be done! On the other hand, from 1:35 to 2:11, "On each day there
is a gradual deepening of insight and a profounder realisation of who it
is that the disciples are following."[44] However, Brown notes that there is
no suggestion that they returned for a time to their normal livelihood.
Their response apparently was immediate and not delayed. Did they have
inklings of what was to come? Jesus certainly did; the Baptist could not
have been blind to the possibilities; the disciples had to make the journey
into the full horror of what lay ahead. But they shy away from it quite early
on. It is not inaccurate to say that Jesus actually calls them into anxiety.

Like the Baptist, the disciples, and the Word, we also are born in
time. We are children of our age. Some of our anxiety derives from our
own period of history, especially at the time of our upbringing. Our own
local or national history is the crucible in which our personality is fired. I
can remember when a soldier was missing at Dunkirk. I can vividly recall
for few days picking up (exactly) the worry of my parents, and the next-
door neighbor who was related to him, and the house down the road
where his sister lived, and the surge of relief when it came through that he
had been on a ship and was safe. I was four. To this day I still have dreams
of crawling through hedges and fields to escape from German soldiers!
Interviewees in East Anglia recorded, with the prospect of invasion, how
terrified they were of meeting Germans coming down the road. "We were
not allowed to say. We couldn't tell anybody." Ontological angst, learned
angst, and a learned response to it.

The task of a helper, and of a text, of a counselor or of faith, or of a
hero who comes and goes, is not to take anxiety away, but to strengthen

43. Jeremias, *Jerusalem*, 120–44.

44. Brown, *Gospel*, 1:77.

us to live with it. It is to help us to see through the learned patterns which are now out of proportion to the current threat so that we will not to be anxious when we need not be. Learned or morbid anxiety, part of our "self-care system,"[45] can reduce, and ontological anxiety can be borne, faced, contained, understood, and courageously contemplated as a living and dying experience. Our memories, individual and corporate, are met by the counter-memories of Jesus; we can "appropriate the memories of the destiny of Jesus"; we internalize the story of his life, death, and resurrection; we live "by the incorporation into our deepest psychic processes of the story of Jesus Christ."[46]

It has helped to get in touch with the earthing of the Jesus story, not only to remember the stress of that time, but also the stress of our own time, the time of our lives. We do it by remembering our own beginnings (*arche*), which are of the anxiety patterns we learned in our own bonding with mother and father or guardians. This is intensely personal and many have memories of such. Even in good, loving, or Christian homes, we experienced separation, real or constructive, from the source person. We also always need to note that we also are children of our time.

Search for and share an event of influence in which you were a child of your time. Uncover how it influenced your personality.

Or, can you remember what you were doing and what you felt the day Kennedy was assassinated, or on September 11, or at some other significant event?

People have said:

"I was born in 1945—I still can't celebrate things" because of living through the austerity of the postwar world.

"I remember, aged four, something—my first day at school, my mother letting go of my hand and disappearing."

"The war. I was very aware of pushing down feelings—sadness."

We have been studying the call of the disciples, to be disciples.

---

45. Northridge, *Disorders*; 36–48; Kalsched, *Inner World*, throughout.

46. Elliott, *Memory*, 218, 130.

> Reflect on it. How do you see Jesus working? What do you hear John (the writer) saying? What do you see the disciples learning?
>
> What did Nathanael not like about Jesus?
>
> We see Jesus how we want to see him! How do you want to see him?

What about the moments of calling, of conversion or breakthrough, in a religious search? They are often charged with emotion, a large part of which may be the build-up of tension and its release. Going through a change of mind can often be fraught with anxiety.

> How did you hear "Come and see"? What were your feelings as you responded?
>
> Or, share a memory of a person who was there when faith came to mean something to you.
>
> What part did they actually play? What did you feel towards them?

These activities are designed to enable you to feel that it is safe to talk about your anxiety, and about your faith experience personally.

When asked how they felt talking about such material, different people said:

I felt I was organising it. I was almost a witness. You can share any confusion about where you are at or come from. You can express it and put it in place. It felt in the here and now. I felt confirmed. Something has clarified for me. I feel calm and serene. Whenever I tell someone, I feel better about it.

> Share any moment when your meeting with Jesus has been obscure, ambiguous, subtle, engaging, embodied!

None of the analysis above belittles the reality of a sense of God's presence, of "simple" faith, of assurance of faith, of trusting in dark times, of living in Christian hope!

7. Comment

After much reflection, an introduction was written. It is *after* an experience that we reflect on it.

1:1–18. With regard to the Prologue, Carter asks, "Why was such a *poetic* unit employed as the beginning of the Gospel narrative?"[47] There are similarities of content with the rest of chapter 1, and of vocabulary (seeing, life, light, darkness, world, sent of God, witness, believe, glory, know), and it is written for an audience of "knowing" readers. There is a similar focus, as in the rest of the Gospel, especially in regard to the way Jesus is presented, as being with God from the beginning, in personal and intimate relationship with the Father, as revealing who the Father is. The debate over his origins is pervasive throughout the whole, in the mind of friend and foe alike (see chapter 3, Nicodemus; and chapters 6–9). The dual response to Jesus, of acceptance or rejection, runs through the whole Gospel. The world did not "know" him, which meant a lack of thinking appreciation and an absence of personal response, with "extensive rejection"[48] by "his own" and the world.

However, the positive reaction is of those who "receive" and "believe," become "children," and "see" his glory. Both responses are vividly portrayed in the rest of the Gospel. His descent from heaven, from "above," and his remaining at one with the Father is the authority for his grace and truth; indeed, they are mediated through him to those who are "in him" and in whom he is. So why two different styles, the poetic and the narrative, which starts at verse 19? Because of the power of symbols, because the Prologue launches us on a sea of symbolic language that persists in the succeeding story, interwoven (intertextually—the root meaning of the word "text" is "woven") with the narrative form. The Prologue is integral to the Gospel.

The Prologue especially, in summary form, attests (witnesses) to the community's special nature and role. Its members have this clarity of revelation and experience (see chapter 14); this is the group to belong to;

---

47. Carter, "Prologue," 39, italics original.
48. Carter, "Prologue," 39.

here is life and truth—because of Jesus. There are similarities to the sense that prevailed about the role of Wisdom. In previous Jewish thinking, *Sophia*, "Wisdom," though John does not use the word, is intimate with God, and is the agent of creation, and the primordial light, and enlightens all wise people; she comes to her people, finds a resting place in Jerusalem, teaching, guiding, showing what pleases God, and was embodied in the law of Moses (Ecclesiasticus 24). Her role, by John, is transferred to the Word, that is, to Jesus, who is preeminent.

Religious groups love wordiness in definitions, in daily life and in dallying with the truth, but their essence is shaped, guarded, affirmed, and communicated in symbol. Witness the universal symbol of the cross, or crescent. As humans we form our symbolizations in the "space between" ourselves and others, or in the "space" within ourselves. Symbols both express and create meaning. Symbols affirm for groups, identity, understanding, purpose, function, reality, ethos, worldview, and boundaries and distinctiveness. The Johannine community need not have been negative about itself, but it was distinct from society and synagogue, felt under threat, and needed the deeply felt reiteration about itself we find in the Gospel. Positively, it cherished its own role and its own truth.

The idea of *space* as the place where, from infancy on, we create the value of our symbols is vital. There is space between the authors and the readers, the community and the synagogue, the Christians and the world, and the time of Christ and now (for the readers and ourselves), so the space will be filled with symbols of who Christ is and who we are. The space between is "transitional space" (Winnicott), where we, from our earliest days, form our symbolizations of the world so as to make meaning of it, and it is thus the place where communication happens through symbol as well as through telling the story. Writing about seeking the meaning of symbols in texts, Northrop Frye comments, "It is not often realized that all commentary is allegorical interpretation, an attaching of ideas to the structure of poetic imagery."[49] "Thus as a symbol, the Prologue expresses the essential understanding and experience of the community—rejected by the surrounding society, yet unique and special in perceiving the divine act. Of course the narrative (1:19 onwards) will express the same understanding and experience but will do so in a different literary form and with a host of different expressions and metaphors."[50]

---

49. Frye, *Anatomy of Criticism*, 89.

50. Carter, "Prologue," 50.

The Prologue forms the climax of many a carol service. When our sensing is satisfied with the procession—the lights, the color, the candles, the choir, the music, and the narratives, with expectation in the air—then our perception can take in the profound symbolic of the first part of this Gospel with all its hiddenness and mystery, and we are satisfied. It sinks into our conscious and unconscious memory till next year! The Word made flesh! Words brought to life, the light of life.

Share a moving moment in a carol service when the Prologue was read. Recall it and respond afresh.

Pick one word from verses 1–18 and cherish it, let it live in you, and share it with another. Listen to their memory and their word.

So the Gospel starts with the fact of Jesus as the centering of faith, "but at the same time introduces new ways of describing him and thinking about the character and implications of this faith."[51]

We are trying to suggest frameworks for shaping the answers to the question, "How does God give and share himself with us?" You have to describe Christ! Here God is known, seen, and heard (metaphors all). The life of God is shared with us through Christ. All things came to be through him, including the fact of getting him to us, sharing him with us—that's creative! If he is in the bosom of God, how can we be so intimate? We need an image of closeness, like, say, a union of a man and woman in marriage (chapter 2). "Jesu, lover of my soul, / let me to the bosom fly,"[52] The one who has seen God can make him known—but how? That is the theme that is now developed step by step through the narrative of the Gospel, through the rooms of the gallery. How does he get into us?

8. Key Thoughts

1:5. When we look at this verse, we notice that it has a present-tense "shines" and a past-tense "grasped." The evangelist holds together the

---

51. Moody Smith, *Theology*, 2,
52. Charles Wesley, *H&P* 528.

shining of the light and the refusal of people to let the still-shining light into their lives (3:19), and who thus prompts us to look at ourselves. "'Darkness' in John means primarily the world estranged from God, the place of man's existence not yet (or no longer . . .) illuminated by divine light. Then it comes to mean men themselves, as they yield to this darkness and are oppressed and blinded by it. It is of this blinded world of men ensnared by evil that the *scotia* (darkness) of 1.5 is to be understood."[53] (This is the first occasion of the contrast between light and dark. See also 3:19; 8:12; 12:35, 40, 46; cf. 9:4, 39; 11:9–10; 1 John 1:6; 2:8–11.)

It is an interesting concept—blinded by darkness! It is made very real when we walk on a dark night on a road we do not know—many urban dwellers never have that experience. How can we use modern concepts of the human personality to relate to this theme of John's? It feels like a dark road sometimes when we walk into our own personalities!

We are prompted further by the preference for the light shining in the darkness, but the darkness did not "grasp" it, the alternative being did not "master" it. The metaphor of putting a light on in a dark room and the dark disappearing does not work, since we retain in ourselves a mixture of light and darkness, and indeed, according to Jung's useful and powerful idea, we have a "shadow."

The notion of process helps in that we struggle for the light to "overcome" the darkness, which is the process of sanctification, theologically, or maturation and individuation, psychodynamically, and is the work of the Spirit of Jesus in us. A model using the idea of synthesis helps. It gets away from a dualism between good and evil as a black-and-white concept, if I may use the phrase, even though we are all capable of a willful refusal to accept the revelation bought by the Word.[54] We are a mixture, and even when the light shines for us there are still pools of darkness in us, and in society. Somehow the work of the Spirit is to transmute the dark in us, the negative, into a positive. Then we can sometimes see that the negative had potential. We move away from identifying our shadow side, for instance, our depressiveness, as alien, not part of who we are, and move to reintegrating it. We shall think more like this later.

53. Schnackenburg, *Gospel*, 245.

54. Moloney, *Belief*, 40.

> Share a moment when you were suddenly conscious of a darkness within you, when you could not see, or had chosen not to see.

1:14. The mystery of the incarnation! This is the climax of the hymn to the *Logos*, a synthesis of all that has been said on the incarnation so far.[55] It is a departure from all previous thinking. True, God has been active in the world with all his attributes, and often accepted and often rejected, but now he comes in the flesh, pitches his tent amongst us (literally "in us"), and is a man. "Was" has occurred four times; now the word is "became" (*ginomai*) flesh, but because of the context, namely the whole verse and its key nature, the word feels stronger than the *ginomai* in verses 3 and 10b, "made," the coming to be of creation, and even than in verse 12, "becoming" the sons of God, and John "appearing" in verse 6. Light has always been available—in human reason (Rom 1:19–23), in the Prophets, in the Law—but now it is available in all its fullness in flesh, in the human situation.[56]

Allusiveness gives way to what is specific in verse 14. A huge step, a huge event in human history, and as Jerome wrote, "The Word became flesh . . . and did not cease to be what he was before."[57] "Flesh" indicates the earthiness of man, the perishable and transient, the whole human condition. "[T]he Logos has become one with the whole human condition in Jesus." "[T]he Logos's involvement in creation culminates in a specific relation with the human condition in Jesus." "The incarnation in Jesus is not the sudden arrival of an otherwise absent Logos, but rather the completion of a process already begun in God's act of creation."[58] Here is the genesis of Christology, the Son of Man descending and ascending, the "above" and 'below' of John's image of the journey of Jesus, who will enter humanity and lead us back to the Father. It is *now* the case that the marks of *human living* are grace, truth, and glory (1:16–17). When we look at ourselves now, the view is distinctive and different. There must be hope for us!

55. Moloney, *Belief,* 40.
56. Moloney, *Belief,* 41.
57. Schnackenburg, *Gospel,* 267.
58. Need, "Re-Reading the Prologue," 403.

What sounds simple is profound. The idea of God pitching his tent with us is an easy metaphor. We need to see the depth of the thought (in John's mind) behind it. It is a strong Jewish idea. In the Old Testament, "tenting" is found in Exodus 25:8–9, where Israel is told to make a tent so that God will dwell with his people, "the site of God's localized presence on earth," the tabernacle. God "dwells" in Zion (Joel 3:17). After returning from Babylon, rejoicing is possible because God "dwells" in the midst of his people (Ezek 43:7).

Have you had any experiences of being camping, under a night sky perhaps, and being conscious of the prssence of God?

Jesus is where God is. He replaces tabernacle and temple. The wisdom literature has wisdom making her dwelling amongst people. There is also a comparison with the Hebrew *shekinah*, the sign of God's presence. Jesus is now the wisdom of God, and the *shekinah* of God. And we have seen his glory![59]

How does it feel to be sharing in the life of Jesus, if you like, part of the stream of creation, part of the wisdom of God, part of the *Logos* of God, sharing in the indwelling of God?

1:16. From his fullness we all have received "grace upon grace." Charles Wesley:

> Closer and closer let us cleave
> To his beloved embrace;
> Expect his fullness to receive,
> And grace to answer grace.[60]

---

59. Brown, *Gospel*, 1:32–34; Barrett, *Gospel*, 138; Moloney, *Belief in the Word*, 42.
60. *H&P* 752.

Share in *discussion* what you understand 'grace' to mean, and then share the inner feeling of grace that you have. It is the active life, or energy of God in you.

1:18. No one has seen (*horao*) God; this is stressed elsewhere (5:37; 6:46; 1 John 4:12, 20) as part of the wonder of "seeing" Jesus. Uniquely, the "only begotten" can bring direct knowledge of the Father, and the verb used (*exegeomai*) for bringing tidings, making him known, is the word from which we derive "exegesis," the term for the explication of texts. The "exegesis" of God and the testimony of the Son are the same! He alone has this knowledge because he rests in his Father's bosom, like one reclining at a meal and resting on the person next to him, as did the Beloved Disciple at the Last Supper (13:23). In the Old Testament, the image is used of married life, of the infant with mother, and of God's care for Israel. Charles Wesley personalizes this image and sees it as expressive of our relationship to Jesus: "Jesu lover of my soul, / Let me to thy bosom fly . . ."[61]

Can you try to share the beauty and consolation when such an intimate moment has been experienced with another human being?

Can you share something of your longing for it? Can you enter into sharing something of the lack of it?

Can you in any way carry the experience over into your relationship with God or Jesus?

This chapter has been well extended and can be taken in workshops in many stages. John's first chapter gives birth to all the key words and the key motifs and themes of the Gospel. The poetry of the Prologue is followed by a telling narrative as we plunge into the ministry of Jesus. The message is universal. The Word, to the first readers, meant not just the God Word that brought everything into being, and not just the message of prophets, but the reason and mind, the wisdom behind all things, and it now shines for everyone; all truth is embodied in the Word made flesh and is pictured now "in this book" (20:30–31).

61. *H&P* 528.

John 2

Jesus Gives a Sign

I am nervous of your presence; be kind to me, I pray.

CAPERNAUM IS AT 690 feet below sea level, Cana at, say, 900 feet above, and Jerusalem 2,500 feet above. We begin in the middle, but we remember that one of John's main motifs for Jesus is that of descent and ascent. Here his physical journeying (similarly to the way that the journey up to Jerusalem in Mark and Luke becomes an image of discipleship) may also speak of his elevation and depression, his rising and descending within himself, for himself and alongside us.[1]

2:1–11	The wedding at Cana
2:12	A few days interlude down at Capernaum with mother, family, and disciples.
2:13–22	The public ministry, the "cleansing" of the temple in Jerusalem.
2:23–25	A final reflection.

1. Wedding Nerves

After the Word, the *Logos* with us—John the Baptist pointing, the disciples being seen and seeing, being found and finding—the last thing we now expect is a wedding! The village celebrated from before the seventeenth

1. 2:12, 13, 19–21.

century is traditionally the one four to five miles on the road northeast, down from Nazareth to Galilee, a lovely little Galilean village with two churches, one Roman Catholic and one Orthodox to remind us of the difficult relationships between Christ's followers! The latest archaeology suggests that the site is the ruins of Khirbet Qana, nine miles or so north of Nazareth and five miles northeast of Sephoris. In Roman times it was a vibrant Jewish village near a junction of Roman roads from Magdala on Galilee to Akko on the Mediterranean, with a synagogue and ritual baths. Archaeology has uncovered stone vessels, which incidentally were not subject to Jewish purity laws, a cave complex with layers of plaster, Greek graffiti, one "*Kyrie Iesou*," and crosses from the fifth to sixth centuries, a sarcophagus lid used as an altar, two more stone vessels, and space for four more. So it was regarded as a Christian site from very early on with a major underground worship and veneration complex, as is found under the Church of the Holy Nativity in Bethlehem. Six early guidebooks for pilgrims point to this site.[2] We readers journey to Cana feeling "spirit's Cana-spark."[3]

2:1–11. "On the third day," perhaps after the call of Philip and Nathanael, with a day for traveling in between, and perhaps therefore it was the seventh day from the first recognition of Jesus, with the two disciples overstaying the Sabbath with him. It would be thus the Wednesday, the day in the Talmud for the marriage of a virgin. On that day a marriage took place ("came into being," *ginomai*) at Cana, Nathanael's village.[4] Though for us there is a chapter break, this story is really part of what has gone before. How can Jesus, in the writer's mind, begin to convey the message of his engagement with humankind? How does he give himself to us? The answer is at another genesis, where flesh and spirit meet, where families gather, greetings are exchanged, old relationships are shifted into a new historical setting; where folks are touched and get touchy, impatient and passionate, critical and forgiving, for all human life is here. But there also is anticipation of the mingling of bodily fluids in hope of the creation of new life, not just of a child who may be born,

---

2. McCollough, "Seeking for Cana."

3. Clemo, *Selected Poems*, "Wedding Eve," 78 (also quoted in Hurst). He lived with poverty, deafness, and blindness, and with loneliness until fulfilled in a late marriage. He was a poet of rigorous and developing faith, seeking integrity in the world as it is, who "strongly asserts the transforming nature of redeemed sex in Christian marriage." "It is a life beyond tragedy, of lived faith." Hurst, "Awkward Blessing," 268–71.

4. Brown, *Gospel*, 106; Barrett, *Gospel*, 158.

"become," into an environment of nurture, but of a new unity between husband and wife. As the new disciples and familiar family cluster round Jesus, an ordinary marriage becomes the symbol of his theophany, his manifestation, of what John calls a "sign."

When we ask why this story is introduced here in the Gospel, part of the answer is surely that it is an everyday human event. It is an ordinary Jewish marriage. That is, it is far from perfect. *And this is where Jesus is known and where we see who he is!* In all human gatherings, however mixed, this is where he is. We resist the idea, and dress our churches in architectural beauty and our functionaries in glittering vestments. It all has meaning, but it also avoids meaning. John radically starts Jesus' ministry in a binary situation where there is both joy and pain.

Gustav Mahler's Jewish father ran a tavern; the little white coffins of his dead children were carried out the back door while the raucous jollity of the inn continued at the front. At the first performance of his First Symphony, there was critical (in both senses) and vitriolic resistance to the third movement, where the nursery rhyme played as a funeral march is joined by a joyful klezmer tune, a jig. Audiences need to know whether to laugh or cry! We don't like ambivalence. The message is "a very Jewish recognition that no act is ever totally tragic or entirely happy." (After my father's funeral, we all with the grandchildren played impromptu cricket on the lawn. We celebrated his life; he would have approved!) "The conjunction of gravity and gaiety is a facet of Jewish psychology and a driving motive of Mahler's First Symphony."[5] How did John dare so prominently to tell the gravity and gaiety of a Jewish wedding and dare to identify Jesus with both, and to tell it as a way of introducing the ministry of Word made flesh? How did he dare to call it a "sign"?

"Was the mother of Jesus there." Stephen Verney translates the Greek literally just to refresh our reading![6] This was a term of respect. John never calls her Mary. She is Jesus' biological mother. She gave him *bios*, life. Here we find her an enigmatic presence at the *first* picture or image or cameo, which is chosen to say something profoundly significant about Jesus' new relationship to those around him. She represents the creative past, the old humility, a family member; in legend, the aunt of the bride; part of social life, part of the earthy order of things. She was there and Jesus and the disciples were "called," a word of the same root

5. Norman Lebrecht, *Why Mahler?*, 58–60.

6. Verney, *Water into Wine*, 30–31.

as *ecclesia*, the embryonic church. They are getting settled with him. John always describes them as "disciples," never "apostles." He is historically accurate. "The general presupposition of the story is that Jesus was a person likely to contribute to the success of a convivial occasion."[7]

> Share a memory of a moment at a wedding, perhaps of the gaiety in the occasion.
> Your affect, emotion, feelings?

> I was a boy at the wedding
> With the fishermen and Joshua and the good woman,
> When the steward whispered to the bridegroom at midnight
> 'The cask is empty.'[8]

On a Galilee hillside with its village resourcefulness, at an occasion planned in advance somewhat, the wine runs out! Life has its limitations! Presumably they did not know that it would! This moment has a contemporaneity in which the Christ effect is felt straightaway, and from which flows a long view of who he is.

> Share with a partner a memory of such a moment. You are entertaining and run short of an essential item. What happens to you, within yourself?

It is of course Mother who realizes. Why does she tell Jesus? Was it a request, a demand, a conversational aside? Was it her anxiety or her embarrassment speaking? We do not know. "Wine they have not." "What [is it] to me and to you, woman?" (2:4, and see Mark 1:24; 5:7; Matt 8:29). To us it sounds abrupt, even extremely rude. But again we do not know the intonation, or inflection of voice. "What would you have me do then, madam?" "[I]t is not easy to interpret." "It is impossible to deny that Jesus

---

7. Dodd, *Interpretation*, 226.

8. "Corpus Christi," in Brown, *Collected Poems*, 314.

holds himself aloof from his mother (and her request) to some extent."[9] The Greek phrase is widely used,[10] and sometimes paraphrased as, "What concern is that of yours and mine?" (Schnackenburg). Depending on the tone of voice, it could be "Leave me in peace" or "What would you have me do?" And the aloofness is also connoted by addressing his mother as "woman" (*gunai*). "The word 'woman' is certainly not a disrespectful form of address, but when used towards one's mother, at least among the Semitic peoples, it is unusual and astonishing." It is used also in 19:26 at the cross, where there is "no trace of disparagement,"[11] although it is not proved to be a mark of honor.

On the other hand, some commentators see this as a routine Semitic expression, and the address "woman" as respectable and proper. Jesus refers to her again in the same way on the cross, a moment of supreme altruism. Others are conscious that he distances himself from her, is not grasped by whatever is happening in her—her desire to help, her shock, her embarrassment, her panic, her need. Was she stepping out of line? An imperfect Mary. Does she have some sense of something important about to occur, or is she (just) an ordinary mother now stepping back and being tactful? Jesus had (only) "good enough mothering"?[12]

If you have been pregnant, can you share something of what it meant to have new life "cloistered" within you?

If you have been involved closely and watched someone carrying a child, can you share what it meant to you?

You may feel you want to start by sharing negative feelings and move to positive feelings. You may start by sharing positive feelings and move to negative feelings. We shape our narrative in our own way. Share how it was that you started where you did. What was your (non-biological) relationship to the new human being?

Pastorally, we often start at a different point from where others start. There are reasons for that.

---

9. Schnackenburg, *Gospel*, 327.

10. For example, by the demons to Jesus, in Mark 1:24; 5:7.

11. Quotations from Schnackenburg, *Gospel*, 328.

12. See Luke 2:44–50.

There also has to be a relation to the saying about his "hour" having not come yet (2:4b). In 7:30 and 8:20 it refers to his death, which John thinks of as his "glorification." Was Jesus already thinking like that?—though it was far too painful for him to admit it, to himself, or to his mother on such a happy occasion as a wedding; he was human after all. "Immensity cloistered in thy dear womb."[13] Or is John wanting to alert his readers (who know the outcome anyway) to that? We can say that Jesus has a strong sense of timing, of completing his work and the Father's, and John certainly has. For us, Jesus has to live out his life in the timing pattern of his Father and the timing structure of the evangelist. "The evangelist uses double meaning terms and symbolic language . . ." He often uses calendar time,[14] but he invests time with symbolic meaning; "day" and "hour" frequently have significance beyond counting the clock.[15] Jesus knows about his "hour" and all that it means; his mother does not. John presents a depth below the surface of things. There are many occasions when Jesus' words only become powerfully clear later after the resurrection (2:22). Yet we realize that the "sign" presents his "glory" now, and also is lodged in the disciples' memory for the future.

We need to ask whether we project our own feelings onto Mary, our feelings of embarrassment or shame or tension, as though we were in a situation of running out of liquid refreshment at our own daughter's wedding. *But* so long as we do not then seek to define the text in some objective way as carrying in itself (in the old way) this meaning, we are still reading it legitimately. Or rather it is reading us! It is making us become conscious not only of how we respond to it, what it does to us, but also of what is inside us, our reactions, our personality patterns. In that sense, we are completing the text. It teaches me who I am and where I am meant to grow, or change, and as we shall see, step by step, it teaches how Jesus aligns himself with this "me" who is me.

If we can let the text make us aware of what strong material we are dealing with in ourselves here, then it is doing its job! One person spoke with remembered and current distress of how one family Christmas, much longed for, was totally ruined till the shops opened again, and was then irretrievable, because she had forgotten to buy the cranberry sauce for the turkey. And her mother would not let it rest! Her chagrin, shame,

13. John Donne.

14. E.g., 12:1; 18:28; 20:1, 19; 21:4, 11, 17.

15. Neyrey, *Gospel*, 62–63; Brown, *Gospel*, 1:517–18; Culpepper, *Anatomy*, 53–70; Davies, *Rhetoric and Reference*, 44–66; Ashton, *Understanding*, 269–70.

self-blame, and anger colored, clouded, and obscured the celebration. No one could lighten it.

Have you been at a wedding where there was shortage of love, patience, understanding, or insight into what someone was going through? Did anyone resolve it? How? Or was it unresolved? Your feelings?

Another enigmatic saying is prompted: "Whatever he says, do it," an encouragement to obedient listening to what he says. If only we knew the intonations and inflexions of voices. We are strictly in a position of not knowing. So much of Scripture is veiled by this not knowing, and it frustrates us when searching for the "facts," as though they would help us! Interest us, yes, but it may be that this open text through which we may construct all sorts of insights, relative and not absolute, yet absolute when they touch us, is better for us. Is it too strong to say John forces us to speculate, "What on earth is going on here?"

There seems to be a resistance on Jesus' part to do something, a distancing of himself, a disengagement. He is not involved. "My hour has not yet come" (v. 4). Could it be that he himself is anxious? Two anxious people make for tension. If he is human, his adrenaline would flow. Here he is immediately conscious that this is the start of his public ministry, and he is put on the spot. He knows his hour will come; the start of that journey is an anxious time and the need to postpone the journey overwhelming. Then he comes round to it, and Mary backs off, sensing or causing a change in him. "Do what he says"—she is surrendering her influence. He will always be anxious when he faces a crisis in pursuing his destiny, in the fracas in the temple, in the conflicts with the "Jews," when facing knowledge of his death, and, according to the Synoptics, in Gethsemane, for instance.[16] He stays human till the end!

Slowly we sense that Jesus is reflecting another timescale, another order of things. John's sense of a timeline, of the appropriate moment for Jesus to act, follows him throughout the Gospel and is part of the plot. The time will come when he pours out his life, but not yet. Two worlds

---

16. See, for instance, Dolto and Séverin in Rollins and Kille, *Psychological Insight*, 177–80.

meet in him. John's metaphor is of the higher and the lower, that from above and that from below (*ano* and *kato*).

Can you share the feeling you had on an occasion when another person seemed to be working to a different timescale from you, and you had a different sense of timing within yourself?

Can you share an occasion when your anxiety coalesced with someone else's and you resisted it?

Then John seems to have Jesus changing his mind. "There were six stone water pots there." Was it an imperfect number (i.e., not seven; life is limited), or would the disciples say, "Yes, of course we have been with him six days," or are they aware these sources of ritual washing symbolize the old order? Or is this how they become conscious that he represents something new? (Even we wear something old, something new at a wedding!) The jars, used for "purification," were empty. Each held from seventeen to twenty-six gallons, though estimates vary considerably. But how do you get pure? How do you get a drink at a wedding? Is there a need to find between 102 and 156 gallons of water in the middle of the celebrations? How long would it take to fill them, where from, and by whom? However hard you work, you cannot purify yourself. It is a gift. The disciples and others are on the threshold of new discovery.

Draw the shape of six water jars and fill them with a sentence each that speaks for something you want to get rid of or purify.

Draw the shape of six water jars and fill them with a sentence each that speaks for or of the fullness of life, e.g.: "I like to keep something old, namely . . ."; "A memory of a celebration"; "I'm looking forward to . . ."; "The core of my faith is . . ."; "I enjoy eating and drinking"; "The relationship which fills me up is . . ."; "What does Jesus mean to me?"

One preacher enthused about the fact that Jesus had created the equivalent of so many bottles of "best plonk"! That would be anything between 960 and 1090 bottles! Some wedding! John Julius Norwich, the writer of books on the Byzantine Empire, said, "I only discovered the other day that St. John's Gospel lets you know how much water is converted into wine at the wedding at Cana. You can work it out from biblical measures that it was 1112 bottles and that was after they had run out for the first time. And Cana was a very small village!"[17] Another has equated the amount with 6,000 glasses of good wine. A superstar's wedding!

It is only rarely in these suggestions in this material that you will be invited to discuss! Sharing is a different activity altogether and is aimed at the building of trust and of maturity in faith. If you have time, however, discuss how you believe in this story. In a nutshell, do you believe literally or symbolically?—though that classification fails to do complete justice to the issues. But make sure you focus in your thinking on the nature of Jesus, and of his way of showing what God is like. You could remember, for instance, that he has recently refused to create bread to feed himself—he could have fed the hungry! The text gives you permission to feel free to believe literally or not to believe literally! And still to find meaning. You all belong to the same fellowship and seek to follow the same person—remember that, if you disagree strongly with others.

The drink that was there was taken to the "ruler of the room with three couches" (a literal translation of the Greek word), the friendly MC, the Master of Ceremonies. It was water that was put in the jars, and "filled to the top," up to the heaven (v.7 *ano*). When the steward took the water, now become (*ginomai*) wine, he said to the bridegroom, in whose house they were and where his friends had brought his bride, "Every *anthropos* sets forth [*tithemi*] the good wine first, but you kept it till now." He did not know "whence" (*pothen*) the wine had come from, any more than the mystery running through the Gospel, of whence Jesus had come, the

---

17. *Daily Telegraph* May 30, 1998.

continual pressing enquiry.[18] Schnackenburg summarizes, "the narrative is of masterly brevity and nonetheless vivid."[19]

This, whatever it was, was a "sign" (*semeion*), was "the beginning of the signs," earthed in time and place (2:11). It was invested with meaning. It manifested (*phaneroo*) his glory (*doxa*). John the Baptist did not know him, but came baptizing in water so that Jesus might be "manifested" to Israel. This was the first sign. There is a new vision of meaning and purpose rising above shortages and personal need. There is no long discourse here; the narrative has to speak for itself, as after other signs. Event, words, and meaning have to come together.[20]

His disciples' response was that they trusted, believed (*pisteuo*, v.11). This is not the first time (1:49–50), because trust is a continuous process. It even ebbs and flows because it is the content not just of an attitude but of a living relationship. There are key steps throughout the Gospel, thresholds of faith, where John records the response of faith, of trust, and also of distrust. "True faith matures without discarding . . . I have grown and explored / In my faith's undivided world."[21] As faith grows, it synthesizes and remolds former elements. It is not just that as our faith grows, new depths of truth become apparent in this Gospel; the Gospel itself has some incremental change built into it. But is also rich for the simplest as well as the most complicated minds! And for all stages of faith.

In a group, role-play a wedding reception, members of the group taking on the role of typical characters at a wedding, members of the families and friends, all with their distinctive characters and personalities.

But make sure you have a warm, skilled facilitator who can offer or highlight points of insight, *and* pick up the pieces afterwards! Debriefing of each person with all listening empathetically, and consequent reflection, is vital, with a recognition that role-plays are revelatory, not judgmental, and that they touch the depths and are

---

18. 7:27–29; 8:14; 9:29–33; 19:9, Pilate: "Where are you from?"

19. Schnackenburg, *Gospel*, 334.

20. "Here our problem is not a poverty of detail but an embarrassment of riches. As we shall often discover in the Johannine use of symbols, the evangelist shows many different facets of his theology through one narrative." Brown, *Gospel*, 1:103.

21. Jack Clemo, "Broad Autumn," quoted in *Expository Times*, June 1992, 269.

powerful in the releasing of affect. It may be hilarious, or deeply sad, very moving and quite real.

Mary was a real person, and is also a source of inspiration to all Christians, whatever our view of the traditional views of her. She has been an inspiration to more people than any other woman in history, "Model of models."[22] However one wrestles with the theological issues, she is blessed among women!

Share in your tradition how you have sensed the worth of Mary, talking not just about her, but about your sense of her in your own life.

Then find or remember a "Mary figure" in your own life and share what she means to you. Carefully identify your idealization of the woman you see in this way! Get in touch with your own need for an ideal mother figure and what that means. Then withdraw your projections, if need be, and honor the real person you have identified and your real relationship with her.

Return to Mary and honor her. What kind of a woman was she?

Now acknowledge the worth of your own mother. See her positively and leave any negativity associated with her for another time.

2. Reflections

2a.

This Cana episode is certainly not the beginning of the end, but it is the end of the beginning. What does it signify? John uses "sign" as a point of revelation as to the person of Jesus. He is the primary focus. This "miracle" is distinctive to John. So it maybe that we have only snatches of dialogue so that we concentrate on the person and role of Jesus.

Names and numbers had significance in early Christianity. Jews and Christians understood them as gifts from God, which express an

22. Thomas, *Later Poems*, 170.

extralinguistic reality beyond what other words are capable of transmitting. The name Jesus means "helper" or "savior" and is a powerful and natural representation of an unseen reality and was essential in their need to preserve memories of him, to read the scriptures of Israel, and to actualize the message in life. Numbers were signs of a divine and providential order. This may be seen in the tradition behind John, and his stress on "days" and sequences.

2b.

Here is a suggestion. Mary felt that surging need for a solution at the point of chaos, of embarrassment, or at least at a point of practical inconvenience of which she was aware. Whatever it was, John saw it somehow as a way in which, this early on in the narrative, a profound insight into Christ and his relationship to needy people is shown, "manifested." Mary has a need which she brings to Christ. Maybe she reflects others' concerns and so acts as a conveyor or purveyor of need. She is the symbol of having to have need met. This need does not conflict with the piety attributed to her. One may be pious and anxious. (That statement obviously begs the debate about states of mind and "sin.") The hysteric element in us[23] finds the time lag between wanting and getting or having very trying.

Get in touch with and bravely share how you satisfy your want. What do you *imagine* will satisfy? Too much to drink, too much chocolate, showing irritation to another, distrusting the response you do get? How do you manage to go on when you feel needy?

Need arises ontologically; a baby needs to drink, else it dies, as do we all. Unmet needs can be survived, endured within limits, to different degrees of intensity, and endurance produces personality and character.[24] Unmet need, real or imagined, becomes a "want." Painful wants are suppressed—for a range of reasons.

---

23. The avoidance of separation anxiety by wanting closeness. See above in "Introduction 2" under heading 6b, "The Interruption of the Dynamic Cycle."

24. Rom 5:5

We use all sorts of defenses to protect ourselves. It is safe not to face and feel the neat pain, so we use all sorts of strategies to avoid feeling it. We even construct strategies which to others look infinitely worse than the original, but are safer for us. We strive to have the need, legitimate and learned, natural and morbid, met in illicit ways, by shortcuts, by taking in more than we need, by yearning for attention or to be accepted, to have contact with a rescuing hero/heroine figure who will take the need away. Source persons are expected to give more than they can, to fill our empty reservoirs. The principle is the same whether it is low-key as here, a bit of fuss in a social occasion, or whether it is fairly substantial like, say, working one's way through half a dozen husbands![25] Maturity is not identified just by denying our wants, but by synthesizing them back into genuine need. We can tolerate wanting when we do not get or have, positively not negatively. We *can* live without, without what we believe to be the wine of life. It is by knowing that there is another who pours out his life for us, the core of the Christian faith!

My guess is that Jesus did not overreact, and that the supposed distancing response was a neutral, "on the level" response where he was stating something clear about their relationship at that moment. He kept his boundary, was not sucked into Mary's panic, and somehow contained the situation. He could not rescue her just then and he was not going to. In his presence she recovered herself!

Share any memory you have of a tussle with your mother. Looking back, can you recognize the energy employed by both sides? Could you call it a "power struggle"? How did the dust settle afterwards and how did your relationship change? Share the feelings you had/have when your mother has to step back, and allow you your space and *your* power.

---

25. As in John 4!

2c.

Then he did intervene! But how? Some will believe water was chemically turned into wine. Some will not, and will find the miracle, the "sign," located more intimately within the matrix of happenings between Jesus and the people. A reader-response reading gives clues without us having to come down on one side or the other of that debate. I hope a narrative or reader-response reading unites those who read here a miracle of chemical creation and those who read a miracle of a different sort, the transforming perspective that comes to our neediness in the joyful or humorous presence of Christ. The panic falls away in his presence, our want is transmuted. We can *wait* for fulfillment. And we can accept profoundly that ultimately our fullness will come from his emptiness, as he pours himself out for us.

How easy is it for you to wait? Can you link your capacity to wait or not with your personality? You are not alone in the waiting.

What in life are you waiting for at the moment? Share as much as you can.

There is a new order, a new world, and the emptiness of lives will be filled. Water tastes as good as wine in the presence of Christ. They were all touched by him; the mood of the gathering changed, not just through a crudity. A seismic shift of meaning, of focus takes place as when a desert traveler has been stranded for forty-eight hours and one glass of water is needfully and joyously drunk. It is water that is John's theme. They don't understand, but their needs were met because their wants were held in a firm relationship with Christ. He kept his boundaries and yet was a reality for them. We shall see this happening again in the next two chapters.

We may see that chapters 2–5 deal with the psychodynamic effects of the lack of acceptance and sustenance, and the wounds that flow from this.[26] Our response to deprivation, and the hurt that ensues, is to create a variety of personality patterns. Our anger at the separation results in depressiveness, passive or active (possibly chapter 3). We compensate

---

26. For a summary of symbolism often associated with John's vision, see, for instance, John, *Meaning*, 46–83.

with attention-seeking lifestyles so that the experience of separation anxiety develops into the hysteric position (certainly chapter 4). When it is too painful to move back into relationships, commitment anxiety leads us to avoid relationships, the schizoid position (possibly chapter 5).[27]

These are the areas his disciples will be led through *both in themselves and in training for ministry to others.* The modeling of responses to these needs and patterns of response is what we readers of the text will observe. We shall sense how they can be transmuted into new personality. Anxiety was recent for the disciples, in chapter 1; as they leave home and follow him, life is totally open-ended. Now we are shown that in his presence we can live in anxiety without a phoney attempt to assuage it. We notice that he does not rush to the rescue, but he does promise resources in the future, and he sets in perspective and proportion the clamant want arising out of a *genuine* need. We learn to wait again knowing that need will be satisfied and want will be able to be reowned and our reaction patterns will mature.

Jesus keeps his place of integrity within his boundary, not swamped, not sucked dry, but modeling what it is to be a resource person and demonstrating the fact that his presence leads us through.

Will you try to share what is stagnant in your life?

Get in touch with how it feels when you ask for something from someone and they avoid you—or can't give you part of what you need. Focus on your need, not on what you want.

Get in touch with how it feels when someone asks for something from you and you feel it to be a demand.

What are the resources in yourself that you draw on? What help do you seek from another?

It is possible to imagine a social and even a religious occasion where a hiatus occurs, as at the wedding, because there is an absence or unwanted interval. Superegos and parental elements or child elements in us will classify this experience as an embarrassment, as shame, spoiling, demeaning, and detracting from the "enjoyment" of the occasion. Then a

---

27. The avoidance of commitment anxiety by avoiding closeness. See above in "Introduction 2" under heading 6b, "The Interruption of the Dynamic Cycle."

leader-type voice and personality will "save" the situation by inducing a change of mood with a joke, a game, a social fiction, a distraction, or an empathetic attitude. The mood changes and everyone can see how *relative* the issue was. Proportionality takes over. Really, what does it matter if the cranberry sauce is missing on Christmas day, or even if the oven was not turned on!? We can live on another part of the Christmas dinner, on sausages and bacon! There are far more important things in life, like choosing the right moment to announce important decisions or to offer to make a sacrifice. It is the family love that matters, not just the drink. We can live on water in fact. And this Gospel has plenty of that; in at least fourteen chapters water is part of the theme!

2d.

So do we ask, "What really happened?" If we do, we need to focus, to stay focused, on what seems to be John's summary. What happened was a sign; it revealed God's glory (*doxa*). Sometimes John *is* explicit. A "sign" is a happening where who Jesus is and how he deals with us is revealed; it is a pointer to truth. John the Baptist has pointed to him; now Jesus points to himself, and author John points to Jesus.

Truth is deep and is seen in symbols. The old is coalesced with the new; it is not scrapped. It was for purification according to Jewish practice and Old Testament provision, but now the new has come. An abundance of wine was "One of the consistent Old Testament figures for the joy of the final days . . ."[28] The "new" was kept to the last and is the best, Jesus. We who read are purified in him.

The disciples trusted him. What is old inside them will be synthesized with what is new inside them. They shall all (except for one) be changed; ordinary old water becomes like new rich wine. Anyone who can do that with human personality is glorious and reflects a glory not his own only, but that of the Father whence he came. We often do glimpse that in a wedding—the light of the eyes, the playfulness of children, the sad and satisfied wisdom of the older generation, the purpose of living, the good lives that have been lived, and the hope of the new.

Jesus' life has a timing, a momentum, and an effect, which is the Father's purpose for him and thus for us.

---

28. Brown, *Gospel*, 1:105.

This passage was traditionally read on Epiphany, January 6. That was the date of the festival of Dionysus, the god who was credited with turning water into wine. So the early church declared that what early religion and clamant, bucolic, oral[29] human need sought, is fulfilled in Jesus. The oral society we live in, with its craving for satisfactions, for alcohol as the answer, for thousands of items on the supermarket shelves, and for endless foodie programs is not satisfied by the promise of more, but by hearing this story and knowing that unmet need can be met, contained, and transmuted. The hysteric quest finds, through humor and the pointedness of this story, a capacity to trust, even in absence. This is a miracle, whether it is wine in the old jars or not! If only the consumer society would consume the life of Christ poured out for many! And the fact that his name is so frequently used as a swear word is a minute residual memory that Christ is a resource who can be invoked!

The "sign" is of a profundity to life, which is more than eating and drinking—though those themes are vital—and which is attached to the person of Jesus. The disciples see that gradually. This interpretation is speculation, but it satisfies me more than the speculation that these guests could only find love, life, and truth through the prospect of all that wine. It is the wine of Christ's life that is the theme. That is good news.

Look at some of the old things in life—a photo, a hymn, a memory, a person, a family gathering, a film—that sustain you and share precisely how this helps.

Share what happens to you when the old thing, a person or a memory, does not sustain you, and fails to satisfy you. When the person or thing does not satisfy and heartbreak looms, what do you do with your want?

Share how a sense of Jesus sustains you when you have a great need.

The power of the imagery lives on. Literary references abound. The metaphor is extended; it carries weight and expands our understanding and insight, for instance, in the way psychodynamically one person's life is

29. Relating so the psychodynamic insight into the mouth being a main source of pleasure, of seeking satisfaction of need.

ingested by another. R. S. Thomas inserts it as a commentary on the death of that lover of Scotland, the Marquis of Montrose, lover of a Scotland free from royal imposition of bishops and prayer book, yet lover and defender of royalty, loyal soldier, and brilliant strategist, who was betrayed at Ardvreck castle on Loch Assynt, was tied to a nag and led to Edinburgh, where he had been condemned in his absence. He was twice by hostesses offered the chance to escape and declined. So R. S. Thomas writes:

> It is said that he went gaily to that scaffold,
> dressed magnificently as a bridegroom,
>
> His red blood was the water of life,
> changed to wine at the wedding banquet;
> the bride Scotland, the spirit dependent on
> such for the consummation of her marriage.[30]

Or there is Brian A. Wren:

> . . . drink the joy he offers you
> That makes the simple moment shine
> And changes water into wine.[31]

There is Charles Wesley's number 81 of his 166 hymns on the Lord's Supper:

> His presence makes the feast;
> And now our spirits feel
> The glory not to be expressed,
> The joy unspeakable[32]

Again:

> There is a moving passage in D. H. Lawrence's novel, *The Rainbow*, in which the young wife Anna is sceptical about the story in St John's Gospel of the water being turned into wine at Cana. Her young husband, Will Brangwen, loves the Church and its dark mysteries. He agrees that the miracle at Cana seems impossible: "Very well, it was not true, the water had not turned into wine. But for all that he would live in his soul as if the water *had* turned into wine. For truth of fact it had not. But for his soul it had."[33]

30. Thomas, *Later Poems*, 80.

31. Brian Wren, "As man and woman we were made," *H&P* 364.

32. *H&P* 61.

33. Wakefield, *Methodist Recorder*, 24.

> For once feel free to *discuss*: How do you believe in this sign (miracle)? Please allow others to have a very different opinion and listen to them! And monitor yourself as you do so.

2e.

One question, not easily resolved, is whether the use of "woman" is respectful or otherwise. Commentators are evenly divided. It may be part of a larger pattern in the Gospel. It is pointed out that "The shepherd who knows his sheep by name rarely uses their names prior to his death."[34] But after the resurrection he does! True, he mentions Simon (1:42), though less effusively than in Matthew's account, but Nathanael is greeted in the third person (1:47); he addresses others as "you" or uses imperatives (4:7). He also shows affection: "little children" (13:33); love each other "as I have loved you" (13:34); "will not leave you orphaned" (14:18); lays down his *psyche* for his friends (15:13). In the resurrection, we have "Mary," "Simon" three times, "children," and blessings of peace. So there may be some contrast in the pre- and post-resurrection narratives, but we need to note also the substantive situation. He knows people very well—Nicodemus, the woman at the well, the man by the pool, the blind man, even if John did not know or tell us their names—and there is the definitive phrase, "for he knew what was in people."[35] We do not doubt his attitude.

John's portrayal is of a person full of love, and it even answers the question, "Can the disciples still love him when he has gone? Can the next generation love him, without having had a personal relationship to him?" Bultmann observes that in chapter 14 the word "believe," "trust" (*pisteuo*) gives way to "love" (*agapao*). "This love in fact can be nothing other than faith."[36] For Brown the change of focus happens in the transition from chapter 12 to chapter 13. His image is of a pendulum, foreshadowed in chapter 1, swinging from high to low to high. And the lowest point is

---

34. Brant, *Elements*, 176–77.

35. 2:25. See 1:48; 5:42; 6:15; and lastly 21:17, where Peter knows he knows!

36. Bultmann, *Gospel*, 612–13.

where "The Book of Signs" (they refused to trust him, 12:37) gives way to "The Book of Glory" at chapter 13.[37]

That still leaves us with the dilemma of "woman": and we noted that Jesus addresses his mother in the same way from the cross (19:26). We can only admit that commentators are completely divided as to whether complete respect or gross disrespect and all shades in between is shown.

When your name is used to address you, how do you feel?

When your name is called, say, in a public place, how do you feel? Does it affect your sense of identity? How do you find using another's name affects the relationship? Remember, "I have called you by name, you are mine" (Isa 43:1).

---

3. An Interlude

2:12. "After this he went down [*katabaino*] to Capernaum," on the side of Galilee, and stayed (*meno*) for a few days. Up till now the days had been counted, but now the pressure is off. However, John's sense of time process still frames the action. This is repeated in verse 13: "The Passover of the Jews was at hand."[38] We are even now, so soon, given a sense that the Passover and all that it means is pressing. At 12:1 a period of six days is clearly defined. He now went up (*anabaino*), a definite act, to Jerusalem.

Jesus is now itinerant. He goes down to Capernaum, a village on the edge of a fertile plain on the edge of Galilee. His mother, brothers, and disciples form a group and travel with him. The first-time reader will be shocked later (7:5) when his brothers do not trust him. They stay (*meno*), reside, abide there, as the Greek says, "not many days." This retirement, followed by a very public ministry, represents what is much clearer in the early Galilean ministry in Mark 1:21—6:6, namely, a coming and going, dealing with the crowds and then finding the privacy of a home or the solitude of the hills. Jesus exemplifies the balance in himself between coping with intimacy and the need for space. There is a sacred oscillation

---

37. Brown, *Gospel*, 1:541–42.

38. *Engus.* For *engus* signifying nearness of time, see 6:4; 7:2; 11:55.

which fuels his energy. It is between isolation or withdrawal, and engagement with needy people. He holds the tension between both the exhilaration and fatigue of closeness and also both the exhilaration and fatigue
of separation. That symbolizes, or signifies, or represents the holding of
the tension between the hysteric and schizoid polarities in himself. He
models for the disciples, and for the first readers engaged in pastoral and
preaching work themselves in the community to which they belong, an
integrity which comes through a proper sense of self with clear boundaries and a proper contact with the world (my word, not John's).

How do you find an "interlude"? Where do you go? Share with a
partner the place, time, need, feeling, and the restoration that is then
and there. What effect does it have on you?

Share a memory of a withdrawal with family or friends prior to
a new venture, journey, or engagement. What emotions are present,
what affect is in you?

---

4. The Cleansing of the Temple: 2:13–25

4a.

We note that this whole community to which the Gospel is addressed has
grown into, or been forced into, its own sense of separateness. "The Jews"
are often referred to by John as a people set over against the recipients of
the Fourth Gospel.

Jesus now "ascends" perhaps through Samaria, and through the hill
country of Judaea, but *anabaino* is also a term describing pilgrimage *up*
to Jerusalem.

This section is the first part of a longer section, 2:13—4:54, in which
Barrett[39] sees the theme as the fulfillment that Jesus signifies in various
aspects: what the temple represents (2:13–22), Pharisaic Judaism (3:1–
21), Jesus and the Baptist (3:22–36), heretical Judaism (4:1–42), and the
Gentile world (4:43–54). There is still the steady march of time.

---

39. Barrett, *Gospel*, 2:164.

John's plot has three Passovers. John has an act of cleansing as the opening of Jesus' more public ministry. The original Passover meant survival and escape from the threat of violence. His disciples remembered that honoring the temple and thus being single-mindedly devoted to God was an expression of zeal (2:17). "If zeal is the affirmation of the sovereignty of God, then it is a mark of his zeal that the Temple is the primary location where Jesus claims the absolute authority to speak for and represent God who sent him."[40] Here he finds vendors, and the driving out is very physical. There is probably a reference to the last verse of Zechariah, 14:21, where after a lot of nasty threats, "And there shall no longer be a trafficker in the house of the Lord . . ." The injunction is to cease making the house of God a house of trade. Worshippers were supposed to offer only pure, clean animals, hence the trade, and to use only a particular coinage, without a human head on it, not Roman or Greek, hence the money changers.

The temple treasury was extremely rich. The gold market throughout Syria slumped by 50 percent after the sack of the temple in AD 70. The first readers saw the irony: it had all gone anyway! Their minds were focussed on the inner importance of temple space. The disciples contribute to the narrative a shared memory of a text, verse 17, an example of intertextuality.[41] "The Jews" contribute a question, "What sign [*semeion*] do you show [*deiknumi*] us?" Is this John's irony? Every other usage of *deiknumi* is about Jesus showing the Father and his works, and the marks of his suffering.[42] If this shrine is destroyed, Jesus says, he will raise[43] it in three days, "shrine" meaning his body. Does "the third day" of 12:1 prepare us for this, though it is not mentioned in chapter 19? The readers probably assumed that it did. Jesus meant himself. There is a progression of terms: *hieros*, temple, being used by the people, *oikos*, house of God, *naos*, shrine of his body. The "shrine" signified the presence of God. We need to remember that the readers would possibly know of the image of the church as the body of Christ and the temple of God.

40. Lieu, "Blindness," 68.

41. Using one text to illuminate another, or an event.

42. 5:20; 10:32; 14:8–9; 20:20.

43. *Egeiro* is used of the resurrection.

Share, if you can, and so long as the group you are in can adequately hold you, the experience you have had of violence and its effect on you. Or try to share at least some of it, holding back some of the worst; or at least make a *statement* that you have experienced "physicalness" against yourself, or witnessed it against another. Any indicative statement helps because a listener witnesses our story and by their presence affirms our reality, but you are also free to make no reference to it all.

Share, as bravely as you feel able, a time when you yourself resorted to physical violence, and your feeling about it then and now. Trust that your listeners can hear what you say and be non-judgmental. You will be censoring what you say anyway, but if you are not sure, say as much as you feel you can.

4b.

At one level, one could argue that the sign was that the true meaning of the temple would be realized when that which sabotaged its proper use was removed. That would be a real sign to the people. Early on, Origen wrote, "I believe he wrought a deeper sign, so that we understand that these things are a symbol that the service of that temple is no longer to be carried on by way of material sacrifice."[44] John's all-knowing comment is that "he spoke of the shrine of his body [*soma*]," which, of course, will in fact in due course know the extremity of violence. When he was raised (*egeiro*) from the dead, the disciples, in the second act of memory in the text (2:17, 22), remembered he had said this; Jesus the Word had become the text for them and all subsequent readers. And they trusted the scripture and the *Logos* Jesus had spoken. Here is another step of faith, another threshold of trusting, and many believed. They trusted, "and of the inspired corporate recollection of the Church John is itself the most

44. Dodd, *Interpretation*, 301.

striking monument."[45] So we live in the church, founded on memory and experience. So how can we be sure about our inner world? Chapter 3!

Reflect on how much of your current faith is built on your memory of a previous moment when you sensed the reality of Christ, and/or on a memory of the exposition of a text.

The artist Stanley Spencer imagines the scene. He has a great figure, clothed in a great white sheet, shirt, or smock, his arms upstretched, and a huge red table with sturdy square legs, upended and about to go! "Overturned" is *anatrepo*, the only use in the New Testament, except for a metaphorical use for two men upsetting the faith of some (2 Tim 2:18), and for deceivers upsetting whole families (Titus 1:11), a picture of the church, with the inner world upset! We too live by the force of our inner experience and have to work it out. As Carl Jung wrote, "We live not only inwardly, but also outwardly."[46] We might use the Latin derivation, "subvert"; Jesus was subversive, countercultural.

Is the quality of life in your church sabotaged in any way? Share *your* feelings.

(Do not tell anecdotes or criticize others, however much you think they deserve it!)

There is often a choice. Charles Pearson, the visionary and founder of the London Underground, was instrumental in achieving the creation of the Metropolitan Railway. The directors wished to reward him but he declined the money offered, as his duty was to serve, and he asked them to put it towards the railway. He was a philanthropist in spirit and in practice. He "had a long line of social campaigns behind him." "His vision, therefore, was never simply about transport but had at its heart the

---

45. Barrett, *Gospel*, 168.
46. Jung, *Selected Letters*, 13.

aim of creating a better life for his fellow citizens."[47] He was concerned for the life of ordinary people, especially those who lived in the terrible slums of Victorian London. He fervently hoped that the railway would enable people to live in better housing conditions and fresher air further out of central London. The structural changes he had to insist on, uprooting many Londoners, was in the true service of the people, as was the action of Jesus. Pearson focused not on himself but on a higher cause, and gave up financial gain because of it. Jean Vanier reminds us, "we often seek life in the culture of money and forget that we too are the dwelling place of God." Each of us in the words of a victim of the holocaust, is called to be "the home of God."[48]

A question in Jean Vanier's chapter heading is, "Is the world only a market place?"

Reflect on any choices you have felt that you had to make for a truth and not for gain. How do you feel looking back on the decision? Or perhaps it is one you are having to make at the moment.

Share a moment or a time when you felt subversive of the established order of things, at whatever level? Your feelings?

Share feelings of being for or against an established order or routine or position, in the church or in the world.

2:23–25. Indeed, to return to history again, many trusted in that period during the Passover in Jerusalem. They trusted in his name beholding (*theoreo*) the signs that he did, though no signs have been described in Jerusalem! This word for "seeing" here suggests that they were watching with some attention and that this was leading to some faith but not a full comprehension. Maybe their attention was more given to the sign and whether they were persuaded by that.[49] As part of the same sentence, John writes, "but he did not trust [*pisteuo*] them"; he kept his boundary, his discernment and discretion, because he knew [*ginosko*] all men, all humankind. In Jewish thinking there was a strong conviction that only

---

47. Wolmar. *Subterranean Railway*, 16–18, 40.

48. Vanier, *Drawn into the Mystery*, 63, 69.

49. See also 4:19; 6:2.

God knows what is in man.[50] Jesus had no need for anyone to witness (*martureo*) of anyone because he knew (*ginosko*) what was in anyone. This is the "knowing" Gospel. He was wary, as we also sometimes are.

Jesus knows what is in a person. This is the key that will unlock the hearts of Gospel characters, and of ourselves.

Can you recall a moment when you knew what was in another person? How did it feel? Were you right or were you wrong? How did that feel when you realized it?

Share a moment and the feelings when you thought someone knew what was in you!

---

5. Reflection

5a.

Jesus clearly keeps himself to himself after an eruption of physical action and oral utterance (2:24). Some English versions translate, "he did not commit [*pisteuo*] himself." Barrett sees this sense as comparatively rare in the New Testament, "the specifically Christian sense having excluded it."[51] But does that not beg the question? He knows when not to give himself. It seems here that the people that he does not give himself to are those that trust (believe in) him. It seems another indication of his ability not to be a presence just when you think he would be. The most striking example is of his absence when the "man born blind" needs him in 9:12, 35, 39; his *absence* paradoxically is a factor in his *presence*. His elusiveness, and also the delays that are carefully noted, have a psychodynamic explanation and import. In our infancy and later, there were many moments when our need for dependence was baulked, and we learned to defend against the actual or perceived loss, but the pain remained. Dependence though runs with us all, especially when we are properly or supposedly needy. So, at those times, paradoxically, as Ulanov writes, "our emptiness remembers us as parts of community." We reluctantly discover

---

50. 1 Sam 16:7; 1 Kgs 8:39; Ps 94:11; 139:1–4; Jer 11:20; 17:10.

51. Barrett, *Gospel*, 168.

that "Religion ushers us into places of emptiness where we are emptied out in our efforts to reach God." "But the emptiness is also where the new happens."[52] Sometimes, like Mary, we have to hear, "Do not touch me" (20:17)! "We are afraid that no one will be there calling our name, that we alone will know what we are going through."[53] Like Jacob, in crisis we need to know with whom we are wrestling. He does know my name, but I need more!

> I need not tell thee who I am,
> My misery and sin declare;
> Thyself hast called me by my name,
> Look on thy hands, and read it there:
> But who, I ask thee, who art thou?
> Tell me thy name and tell me now.

And then the answer, out of not knowing, "Thy nature and thy name is Love."[54]

This can be a very moving and searching activity. As a group, mill around in the room and as you meet another person give your first name—just that, nothing else. Then the other person repeats it, addressing you. Then that person gives their name and you repeat it. Nothing else is said. When everyone has greeted each other, together reflect and share what it meant to you. What were and are your feelings?

5b.

Was Jesus angry? The traditional view is that he was motivated by righteous anger. He need not have been angry. Strenuous moral and physical action need not contain anger. One can speak and act with passion. For instance, Dr. Frank Lake, in the early days of Clinical Theology, was once arguing a case and getting very heated. It was for the application of faith in a particular situation. When someone, a little shaken, said, "There's no

52. Ulanov, *Finding Space*, 59–60.
53 Ulanov, *Finding Space*, 60.
54. Charles Wesley, "Come, O thou Traveller unknown," *H&P* 434; *STF* 461.

need to get angry about it." He replied, "That's not anger, that's passion!" Conviction produces word and deed. The passion of God for his created world produced *Logos* and the deed/descent of incarnation and crucifixion. Speech and act go together.

We do not have to read anger into the text. But we may do. At least the text forces this debate upon us, about his nature! However, if he was angry, then righteous anger is that anger which is not contaminated by our own history. We are then the vehicle through which flows a corrective energy in a situation which owes nothing to contaminants in our own material. There may have been antecedents of a similar nature, so that we have known before what it is like to be justly angry, but we have not carried any anger over from previous experience to the current situation. We may get energy for perception from it, but the decisions and attitudes we now bring are pure, are unique to this moment. We may have had brushes with this schoolboy, or this oppressive government, or this awkward client or church member before, but they do not affect our judgment on this occasion. Maybe Christ was capable of this single-mindedness. He could be trusted for justice de novo on each occasion. We find it vastly harder, if possible at all!

Such anger is righteous because no anger previously has been suppressed, repressed, and stored in him to mild or dangerous levels. With us, often it becomes a reservoir of anger. When trapped within us, it is at the root of psychodynamic depression. There is then often a pattern (triggered by new hurts to which anger is the response) of passivity or activity, of implosion or explosion. If we are saying Jesus had no trapped anger inside him, then we are suggesting that somehow if he felt incipient anger as a response he was able to metamorphose it and keep it synthesized with his true self. This is half to assume that he did feel angry when rocked about on two long primitive journeys to Egypt and back, as he recalled the experience of exile later on, when he worked hard long hours at the carpenter's bench, when he watched the Roman domination of Galilee and the oppression of its citizens, Herod's luxurious buildings sapping resources that could have helped the poor, and when he experienced the hardships afflicting his countrymen and women, or reacted to the misuse of his Jewish faith by Herod and the Hellenizers, or later to the senseless beheading of his cousin. It would be impossible to say on these and many other occasions he felt nothing. He would cease to be human! But what did he do with the feelings? We are assuming he could process them. He models to us ways of processing them. This is the work of the spirit of truth and the spirit of comfort. Jesus held together up and down, above and below, *ano* and *kato*,the earthly and the heavenly (3:12).

5c.

A director of a counseling service once said, "Our task is to take away people's anxiety." At best this is a very ambiguous statement. It is not possible to take away the existential anxiety that we experience just by living a short spell on a dangerous planet. We are often threatened. Such ontological angst is part of our being. We live with it. So maybe he meant the learned or morbid anxiety which remains in us long after its usefulness. Fight and flight become motifs of our reaction pattern. In both kinds of anxiety and the reactions to it, which notably include anger, we do need help to process it, to bear it, to live with it, to transmute it, and to synthesize it. To synthesize negativity, we need help.

This is the help of a loving father/Father or mother, a good friend, a Christian (or other) community, a skilled and caring pastor, a caring group, or a counselor or psychotherapist, for instance. The task is not to "get rid of" old fantasies, say of power, or outdated resistances, or subterranean anger, but to link them up with and integrate them into a new reality. Thus we grow and, for instance, old anger will not contaminate our current judgment.

Some situations fill us with anger; we hold onto it and then displace it onto undeserving targets within ourselves and onto others. The lifelong process of living with inescapable angst, and the usual way we shift it onto others, is helped by an accommodation we can best call "synthesizing." We can hold together negative and positive in a way which uses the negative creatively. It is the work of maturation, of individuation, of sanctification, and it is the work of the Spirit of comfort and of truth. Jesus could do this surely. That is assuming, of course, that he had feelings that we would identify as an angry reaction!

> Share something of your anger. Try not to talk about what other people "do" to you, or "make" you feel. Focus on owning something of how angry you sometimes feel. You will not be judged. Note that others may start to feel angry as you talk about your anger!

The style of management is to learn how to say, "Can I share with you that when you do/say that, I feel angry." The focus is then on *your* experience.

Vincent Van Gogh was an evangelist and sacrificially compassionate pastor from 1879 for a couple of years amongst the impoverished miners in the Borinage, the mining area of Belgium, and was horrified at their treatment: "anyone who wants to preach the Gospel must carry it in his own heart first," he wrote. His father, whom he loved dearly, came to rescue him, emaciated and starving. But by 1881 there was a deep and angry split between them when old reactions surfaced and he rejected the ordered church Christianity of father and uncle, both ministers: "ministers are the most ungodly people in society"; "The real reason was that I didn't go to church"; "I don't remember ever having been in such a rage in my life"; "Oh I am no friend of the present Christianity, though its *founder* was sublime." Thus Christ holds us. But perhaps his anger at his father and at the treatment of the miners was contaminated by his rejection by the "missionary" society he had been serving, by his failure to prepare for the ministry himself, and the rejection by his cousin Kee, who found him "disgusting," with whom he had been patiently in love.[55] So he drew and painted in a sublime light the men and women he had met, and the world around him. *Sublimation* is a defense, but a positive one in its affect,[56] and in its effects. Anger does give us energy for reform; it is good stuff, but we need to separate out the anger which we have learned in previous bitter experience.

The poet John Donne became secretary to Sir Thomas Egerton, the Lord Keeper of the Great Seal/the Lord Chancellor, and thus was embroiled in both law and politics. He lived in York House with the family, including a well-guarded young niece of the Egertons, Ann, who later became his wife, but he was still searching for his own meaning in life having moved into the Protestant camp, and was frustrated with the persecution of Catholics as with the victims of the slow legal apparatus of Chancery. "[T]he work began to eat at his patience. His anger was a complex disgust for a societal organism that he could not separate himself from, nor identify himself with. Only his writing provided a means

---

55. Wessels, *Kind of Bible*, 52–58, 112–13, italics original.
56. The feeling or emotional content of an experience.

of controlled release."[57] He writes, "now Injustice is sold dearer far."[58] Writing it out is a good form of sublimation.

Jesus is the only one who never brought to a situation a previous negative *dynamic* agenda. We do. Almost invariably. It provides good energy but can skew us dangerously. In far from objective ways, we can dish out to others disbursements of our own unresolved anger, anger previously felt and stored. Displaced anger is the common pattern for us. It was not so for Christ. His anger was pure, unpolluted by his inner world.

Van Gogh's sermons reflected his own need for love—of course! That is the only way we can work. It is not wrong to want to be loved, so long as we are aware and constantly monitor the expression of our need, and choose occasions of catharsis which harm no one. It is like disciplining a child. It is often contaminated by our own anger, or by displacement from an immediately prior situation. As I heard myself dealing with my children, I was shocked to hear my father's voice, mannerisms, and words in me. Jesus and the Father were one, and in him were his Father's words (14:9–11). Like his Father, his anger was subsumed into his love, his wrath into his mercy. We call it "grace."

Share, as honestly as you can, where you put your anger. Do you project it onto yourself and do you project it onto others? Implosion and explosion?

What means do you use to channel or sublimate your anger?

Do you get angry with the establishment? And so . . . ?

(Be aware that talking *about* anger will make some of the group, or your partner, feel angry. It is catching! It is easily internalized, ingested, and introjected.)

57. Stubbs, *Donne*, 104–5.
58. John Donne, *The Fifth Satire*.

John 3

Beginning Again

When we are aware of birthing, in body and spirit, pull us through, we pray.

FURTHER AND DEEPER LAYERS of activity are treated in this chapter. We are compelled to read this material on two levels by John's Jesus himself. The text reinforces "this purposeful ambivalence."[1]

> Nicodemus is a model of the subtlety the evangelist is capable of achieving in a severely limited characterisation. Nicodemus appears in only seventeen verses, three scenes, and speaks only sixty-three words, yet he is both individual and representative, a foil and a character with conflicting inclinations with which the reader can identify.[2]

There are many little touches:

- The last words at 1:51, "son of man" (*anthropos*); the last word at 2:25, ". . . he knew what was in a man" (*anthropos*); and the first words at 3:1, "Now there was a *anthropos* . . .";

- * 2:1, "A wedding there was . . ."; 3:1, "Now there was a man . . ."; 4:7, ". . . comes a woman . . ."—all speaking of new life;

- * 1:1, "In the beginning . . ." (*arche*); 2:11, "the first [*archen*] sign . . ."; 3:1, "a ruler . . ." (*archon*)—all from the same root.

---

1. Ashton, "John and the Johannine Literature," 261.
2. Culpepper, *Anatomy*, 134–35.

They are all part of larger pictures and of a larger scheme of things, stitches holding threads together.

John's pictures of Jesus are so stunning that it is easy to fragment the text, easy for us to feel fragmented, and to subtly resist the connections that live in the text, that live in us and the text! So people have focused on water into wine, or being born again, or that God so loved the world, or the Spirit blowing where it wills, or the judgment of the world, all in chapters 2 and 3. We can hold the pictures together, not so much like a series of portraits or landscapes, say, by Renoir, but more like Monet, whose series of paintings, substantially as well as formally, are facets of one theme—the River Thames, a series of poplars, or of Rouen Cathedral, or of the Valley of the Creuse. I shall never forget the exhilarating thrill of walking into a room of sixteen *Haystacks*.[3] It was plain that what held them together was an overriding theme, say, of the nature and power of light. I was not looking at one haystack after another, but at the carefully crafted expression of an overarching conviction. This is truly a Johannine theme!

The comments made on all the series can easily be applied to John's artistry. "Monet really set out to paint what he 'experienced' in front of those stacks, and not so much what he saw . . ." Monet was interested in the way that "immutable objects constantly took on new forms, [in] the unceasing flow of changing sensations in front of an invariable spectacle, one interwoven with the other, [and in] the possibility of summarising the poetry of the universe in the restricted space [of a canvas]."[4] He went along to the Impressionist's soirées "with their interest in the continuity of experience and its subjectivity as well as their attempts to meld imagination and reality, dream and consciousness to arrive at higher level of awareness."[5] The poet Mallarmé, a member of the group, "felt that one should never fully describe things in an empirical fashion but rely instead on the powers of suggestion." He said, "To evoke an object little by little in order to reveal a state of mind, or, inversely, to choose an object and to derive from it a state of mind by a series of decipherments—that is the perfect use of mystery."[6] Monet's interest was in expressing the intangible and the inexpressible. All this is so Johannine! As well as telling a story, John uses allusion and

3. Tucker, *Monet in the 90*.
4. Tucker, *Monet in the 90s*, 101–2.
5. Tucker, *Monet in the 90s*, 101–2.
6. Tucker, *Monet in the 90s*, 101–2.

metaphor to prompt depth of meaning. We now turn to a story that blends simplicity and mystery, the subjective and "reality," where what is said or written does not quite contain all the meaning!

Can you share an experience where looking at a painting or hearing some music or watching a film gave you an extended sense of meaning, a moment of insight which built on the intangible?

Chapter 2 had two sets of scenes: one in Cana, promising the new in place of the old ritual; and one in Jerusalem, of Jesus confronting theocracy and temple money/morality, and setting himself in a temple context with the threat of the future looming. Now there is a new scene, where the things about the earth (*epigeia*) and the heavenly are both mixed and distinguished.

3:1–21   Nicodemus. The first exchange (3:1–8): "Seeing God" happens with a newborn spirit. The one who achieves that is the Spirit.

The second exchange (3:9–15): That will be possible because a communication between the earthly and the heavenly is possible through the Son of Man.

Loving judgment (3:16–21): Eternal life, love, gift, light, and truth come through the Son of God.

3:22–30   The witness of John, a second time. The narrative continues. Arising out of John the Baptist's baptizing, the question is about being purified—in the process of having a new spirit—and it has to do with Christ.

3:31–36   Reflective summary.

1. Nicodemus: 3:1–15

If people who don't know—not-knowing people, like the "master of the three couches" at the wedding at Cana, or the crowd in Jerusalem—are impressed and trust Jesus, what is the prospect for those who know? If a not-knowing person (John the Baptist) is impressed, and is set (by John) in a scene where Jesus' glory is manifested and his disciples trust, and if people so not knowing that they ask for signs but are impressed enough to think that if they ask for and see signs they may be persuaded, how then does Jesus deal with a man who already knows?

John answers. We know a man, an *anthropos*, and we know his name, Nicodemus. He knows, and he says, "We know you are a teacher come from God." So often we do not see that the translation of the *same* Greek word is varied in English. See 2:24–25, where Jesus did not trust (*apisteuo*) himself to those who believed in him (*pisteuo*, "trusted"), because he knew all and had no need that anyone should bear witness to man (*anthropos*), for he knew what was in *anthropos*. "Now was there an *anthropos* of the Pharisees, Nicodemus his name" (3:1; cf. 1:6, "there was an *anthropos* sent from God, his name John").

What Nicodemus knows is that the signs cannot be done by one "unless" God is with him (3:2). So he is somewhat on the way. Is he a spokesman of those in Jerusalem who trusted (2:23)? It requires great courage to come, even by night. He has dignity, learning, and status. We need not take Nicodemus's words as containing a piece of politeness, or merely the opening gambit of a conversation, either respectful or sarcastic. We *can* take them at face value. He is an enquirer.

Have you ever had an enquirer about whom you felt irritated? Whom you felt was shallow? Or one with whom you felt pleased?

Have you ever made an enquiry and been fobbed off? Or felt accepted? Feelings?

Perhaps Nicodemus is a "crypto-Christian" continuing an attachment to the synagogue with inadequate understanding of Jesus. Coming at night, in the non-symbolic sense, may mean that he desires an uninterrupted meeting, and the "we know" (3:2) may just refer to his own small group of disciples. So he may or may not be part of the group who believed but did not dare confess (12:42); but he still acts publicly in burying Jesus (19:39–40); only Jesus' disciples see him as a king in death, and Nicodemus offers a king's burial. Jesus is rejected by all the rulers (19:15) except for Nicodemus and Joseph.

There is a high probability that Nicodemus belonged to the wealthy and powerful Ben Gurion family, though he may not be the person affectionately remembered in the rabbis' traditions. He was a "ruler" (*archon*) and one of the "authorities," speculated about by the crowd as to whether they knew Jesus as the Christ, with some even secretly believing;[7] but in any case they were "the effective Jewish government."[8] We may see Nicodemus as a real person who sought out Jesus. His failure to understand need not be recorded as "an act of unbelief."[9] We meet him again at 7:45–52 and 19:38–42, caring for the body! He may be a minor character, but he is "always in a significant role in relation to Jesus."[10]

Rensberger suggests that in addition to being a historical figure, Nicodemus has a symbolic role—but as what? Traditionally he has stood for the individual, inner change of "new birth," but Rensberger favors him as a communal figure, standing for the resistant, distrustful class of rulers that the Johannine community were up against: "he is clearly meant to portray one of these untrustworthy believers." But in Rensberger's account there is special pleading. The audience is indicated by the translation of the plural, "You people must be born again" (3:7). That could be taken at face value; there is no evidence that Jesus ironically calls him "teacher of Israel"; the protection of Jesus in 7:45–52 is denigrated as a "timid legal quibble," but every good lawyer would defend the fundamental right to be heard even in those days! It is putting a selective interpretation on the text by alleging that Jesus rebuked him for lack of faith, and asserting that he "appears as a man of inadequate faith and inadequate courage."[11] It is strange that we think of him as a symbolic figure but depend heavily on such supposed historical niceties! (When we come to chapter 4, we shall see how it is that we selectively interpret a text.) A contrary view, Brown's verdict is that "Nicodemus's role is not to illustrate or personify the attitudes of a contemporary group in the Johannine experience, but to show how some who were attracted to Jesus did not immediately understand him . . . but some like Nicodemus did."[12]

---

7. 7:26, 48; 12:42.

8. Bauckham, "Historiographical Characteristics," 162.

9. Rensberger, *Overcoming the World*, 40.

10. Rensberger, *Overcoming the World*, 37.

11. Rensberger, *Overcoming the World*, 38–40.

12. Brown, *Community*, 72 n. 128.

Have you ever been misunderstood as a representative of an opinion
or of a group that was not yours?

How did you feel, and how did you deal with the misjudgment
within yourself?

With Jesus' reply, 3:3, we are plunged with no warning into another
world of the human spirit and God's way of working in it. It requires a
birth. We have moved from a wedding to a baby! It is as if Jesus has been
living, thinking, concentrating at a much deeper level than any man since
2:23, and the character coming to him, who does not even get to state his
purpose, has to join him at depth. "In Johannine terms, symbols span the
chasm between what is 'from above' and what is 'from below' without col-
lapsing the distinction."[13] "Unless" anyone is born, again, from above (*anothen*), he is not able to see (*horao*) the kingdom of God![14] We have moved
from a new consciousness of what God will do, which is like an awareness
of water tasting like the richest wine, to a sense of God as the Spirit of God
who comes through water as a symbol, not through H2O itself.

Share how you came to know Jesus Christ, bearing in mind that there
is no prescribed route; "conversion" may by quick or slow.

Are you aware of a "moment of discontinuity"[15] between an old
life and a new?

And then are you aware, even when a Christian, of moments of
renewal when a new sense of God, a new language for your experience, has occurred?

Anothen is ambiguous, a "riddle," and telling thereby. Nicodemus
opts for the more literal line, "again," "anew," "afresh" (3:4), and so advances the argument. For every succeeding generation he has raised

13. Koester, *Symbolism*, 4.

14. Nicodemus used the first "unless" but Jesus sent it back; 3:2 and 3:3. Neyrey,
Gospel, 77.

15. Barrett, *Gospel*, 172.

the question of what it means to be born again. Incidentally, these are the only two references to the kingdom of God (3:3, 5) in John. It is a mainspring of Synoptic thought about the Rule of God and what disciples enter. Here the focus is on how. New life comes through encounter with who and what is from above. Chapter 4 makes it clear new life comes through encounter with Jesus, who is Christ.

In chapter 2 there was talk of his death and resurrection, his being a temple in himself (2:18–22), and in chapter 3 it is of his descent and ascent, the gift of his life and his being lifted up. The reader cannot escape being conscious of this dimension. The person who is now being taught is a teacher of Israel. What should Israel now learn from a teacher come from God? Every answer by Jesus takes this consciousness to a deeper or higher level.

At every point there is emphasized the connectedness between the two worlds, the heavenly and earthly, the above and the lower. The process of descent and ascent incorporates somehow the one who wants to believe, trust, and the one who does believe, trust. But how does this happen inwardly?

Anothen is capable of the two meanings, "and here it probably has both."[16] It may mean "from above" but it can also mean "again," "anew," "afresh." The birth which is here offered is a new birth, not a replication of the first one. An *anthropos* cannot be born when he is old. New birth is "spiritual" in the sense that it is not another fleshly birth, but is of the Spirit (*pneuma*), subtle, unseen, coming of its own will; its sound, its *phone*, is heard like the wind (*pneuma*), but what you are not knowing is whence (*pothen*) it comes and where it goes (3:8).

Nicodemus's anxiety is so great, apparently, that he comes in darkness, a profound image in John of the absence of God's light. Yet he is searching. He has believed, trusted the signs, maybe beginning to see who Jesus is, maybe acknowledging the sight of his glory in a most humanly typical situation, say, at a wedding or at prayer in the temple. He has poured over the Scriptures and knows God will do a new thing; a new consciousness of him will arise, but how? Can even the dregs of life be renewed? It will not be through an old search for old wine, through an old system of purification, an old cleansing, an old catharsis. The word "catharsis" nowadays means a releasing of affect and a point of growth through the letting go of old material in the psyche. It is derived from

---

16. Barrett, *Gospel*, 171.

katharismos, "purification" (2:6; 3:25); *katharizo*, "to cleanse," of disease
in the Synoptics and from "sin" and "unrighteousness" (1 John 1:7–9);
kathairo, "to prune" (John 15:2–3); and *katharos*, "clean" (John 13:10–11).
To let go of the old will mean a new joy through a new catharsis, the best
wine at last. It is his life that will be poured out, but what will happen to
mine? Can I be renewed when I am old? How will I be released "from the
pain of earlier living"?[17] How do I share the new? How does his life get
into mine? How can these things come to be?

> Share an experience of catharsis, either an awareness of a loss of
> an old position and adapting a new one, or of an emotional release
> through letting go of what was in you. How were you helped?

The theme of descent and ascent is prevalent (v. 13). The son of *an-thropos* has descended from heaven and is the only one who has ascended
there. The one coming from above (*anothen*) is above all (v. 31). It is like
a baptizing process, a going down into water. Such a going down it is
when you know also your own emptiness and need, the bankruptcy of
your own tradition, and you chose not to project it out onto another but
to query it within yourself. Such a going down it is as to Capernaum for
rest (2:12), with loved ones around; such a going up it is as to Jerusalem
for Passover (2:13); or as the collapse of a temple that took forty-six years
to build (2:19–20), and the raising of it up in a new religion, like the
dying and rising of this man, this object of quest, this guest, this family
man, this lamb, who next year (the readers know) will live six days before
Passover, who will stop the loop of descent and ascent in his own body,
and who will be lifted up. Like Moses lifted up the serpent in the wilderness, the serpent not always being a negative symbol even in the Old
Testament.[18] It may be the Passover of the Jews, but he was a Jew and it
will be his Passover. Afterwards, memory begat trust (2:22)!

17. Fred Kaan, "God! When human bonds are broken," *STF* 649.

18. John 3: 14; Num 21:8–9, Exod 4:1–5. The ambivalence continues in early
Christian writings, where the serpent can be seen as a source of healing, wisdom, and
"knowledge," attributes then associated with the forgiving and life-giving "Serpent-Christ" on the cross, the antidote to sin and evil. See Young, *Construing the Cross*,
82–95.

Share moments of your own brokenness, of being "down." You may receive a word of comfort but, if not, there is value in just telling and being heard.

This is how deep and high is the descent and ascent. It is like a man used to authority, very learned, very skilled, very religious, even strict, having to become like a trusting helpless child, getting in touch afresh with the flowing water of life that held him in the womb, water without which he cannot live for more than a couple of days, water made of hydrogen and oxygen, of the air he breathes, water and spirit, *pneuma* (v. 5). He will be so "low" he must envisage getting in touch with his own birth, his mother's birth canal, her pressure on or retention of his very life, the risk he runs between her legs, her juices, her life, and the threat of death and infection. "We experience ourselves as living mush, fearful of the journey down the birth canal."[19] He will be conscious of his own inner primal loves and hates, his perinatal psyche surviving into adult life. He must walk the line between flesh and spirit, must fight for survival, be thrust forth alone yet embraced, held, held with eye contact even in the darkness. He can do this. "The possibility of rebirth constellates with the breakdown of what has gone before."[20] This man has life. Here is a new picture for the great art gallery which John is. The question is asked in the dark. That is where we are when we ask our questions always, because we do not know the answer. But at least we are asking, we are searching! And here like Nicodemus we listen; "Darkling I listen . . ."[21]

What is your deepest question about yourself? And whom will you ask?

R. S. Thomas chides Paul with the wrong focus on the Damascus road when Paul asks, "Who are you, Lord?" "Wrong question, Paul. Who am I, Lord? is what you should have asked."[22]

---

19. Woodman, *Pregnant Virgin*, 7.
20. Woodman, *Pregnant Virgin*, 24.
21. John Keats, "Ode to a Nightingale."
22. Thomas, "Covenanters: Paul," in *Later Poems*, 172.

> When you listen in the dark, what do you hear?

If only we knew *how* Nicodemus said "Rabbi." Was it the kind of honor one would give to a Puritan preacher of the sixteenth century, or to a popular preacher of the twentieth, one whom one could readily approach with a question? Did they speak "on the level," as the modern jargon has it? Neither looked down on the other. There was no false superiority either way. We are meant to level with Jesus. It is only when we look lovingly to Jesus and let him look lovingly back that our search begins to make sense. Then we need to go along with the answer to the question. We can indeed relive the struggle, pain, and gifts of the moments of birth and nourishing. The change that Jesus brings to us is not a one-off. It is a continuous process; it is always happening; the dynamic cycle is always circulating within us. "If, without our choice or contrivance, feelings arise within us which cause distress, then Christ is there in the distress itself, not to save us from the pain of rebirth but to assure us that we are indeed being born again."[23]

Lila was brought up in a cruel, neglectful home, but was rescued and taken up by Doll, an eccentric, wandering but caring character, so that Lila became an uneducated but intelligent, wandering survivor. She drifted into Gilead and in the rain sheltered in the church. "The candles surprised her. It might all have seemed so beautiful because she had been missing a few meals. That can make things brighter somehow." The pastor, "a big, silvery old man," was tenderly baptizing two babies. One cried a little from the water on its brow, and he said, "Well, I bet you cried the first time you were born, too. It means you're alive." "And she had a thought that she had been born a second time, the night Doll took her up from the stoup [veranda] and put her shawl around her and carried her off through the rain."[24]

> Share a moment when you have felt "born again."

23. Williams, *True Wilderness*, 41.
24. Robinson. *Lila*, 11–12.

2. Key Themes

2a. Key Motifs

Let me suggest a model which may help understanding of the plural experience suggested in chapter 3. There are *four polarities* needed to hold together interpretations of the renewal described here. There must be a core experience of renewal, an actual change in the person, a "real change," as we say. The word for it is "conversion." But it is not simply a one-off but a continuous experience. That is the first polarity. The second is baptism, where we try to hold together the symbolic and the actual. The third is a modern suggestion, the gaining of self through psychotherapeutic work, and the fourth is through Primal Therapy.

Within each of these there are *four elements*. Loosely, it could be held that in each there is:

i. an experiential element, a change wrought in the heart, with considerable emphasis on the affect;

ii. an effect within the psyche whereby patterns of personality are reformed to some degree through integration with the person's past.

iii. the creation of a sense of belonging with an affirmation of such a sense; this is an institutional dimension;

iv. a "theological" dimension, in the sense that there is conscious faith reflection on the part of the person or those around. This is not to suggest that God is not a presence in the other elements, but an attempt to recognize the formal as well as the substantial, the outer as well as the inner reflection on what the meaning of the experience is.

Some may stress form rather than substance, the outward sign rather than the inward change, but the essence is a renewing of the psyche. *Outer* and *inner* are interrelated.

All four are present in St. John's Gospel as a whole. Briefly, for instance, many scenes highlight the response of trust people make in Jesus and the change this brings about within them. There is much evidence of the psychic shifts that occur within people wherein their personalities change.[25] The sense of belonging to a new community is emphasized, in chapters 1, 13, and 15, and shown in the persistent theme of "abiding." The "theological commentary" is everywhere; the descent and ascent

25. E.g., chapters 4, 5, 9, 13, 18, 21.

theme, the "Word" theme, and after virtually every narrative episode, the reflections by Jesus and/or the author.[26]

All *four elements* are important in all Christian traditions, but the emphasis varies substantially. The emphasis is different for each of the *four polarities*.

For *conversion* the order could be the experiential; and then the theological, in that a divine discourse, a theological framework, will often have been undergirding the process leading through the moments of conversion, which has an interiority to it not present, for instance, in infant baptism; then belonging; then the psychic, with awareness of a mental shift that brings for a time peace.

You might say the order of emphasis for *baptismal regeneration*, at least for infant baptism, is the theological; then the declaration of belonging, incorporation into the body of Christ; and then the experiential; and then the psychic.

The order for any *psychotherapeutic/growth process* that focuses on the early childhood experience, or Primal Therapy, will be concentration on the psyche; then on the experiential, especially on catharsis; then on a renewed sense of belonging, to the group where the sharing takes place, for instance; and then on the meaning of what has happened in a religious and theological context.

These categories are not watertight and not meant to be, but are meant to alert us to distinctive ways of thinking about the experience of new birth. If as readers we share the bewilderment of Nicodemus, we need to be able to hear the text afresh. We need to know whether Jesus is saying something distinctive about the way God works in us or we are really only dealing with a pretty metaphor or two!

Feel free to discuss the emphasis you would make in balancing the elements suggested, with an awareness of your own reactions to others' positions.

---

26. E.g., 3:16–21, 31–36.

2b. Primal Therapy

Primal Therapy is a style of counseling or therapy that allows the surfacing of very early "unconsciously remembered" experiences. It permits the pressing back beyond childhood memories into babyhood and even intrauterine experience. We now know that the emotions, especially those associated with adrenaline, are passed from mother to foetus. And for long it has been recognized that the traumatic events of parturition have an effect on the child. It is clear that the baby "remembers" the blissful and bitter experiences of infancy. In a supportive group with skill and awareness, a person may "regress" and get in touch with early perinatal experience. This is done by deep and steady breathing, which allows repressed and suppressed material to surface. This is often accompanied by physical movement, where instinctively the birth process is acted out. The person feels "born again"! Neither Jesus nor Nicodemus knew this! The pioneer of research, theory, and practice was Frank Lake. Chapter 2 in *Tight Corners in Pastoral Counselling* is fairly accessible.[27]

Primal Therapy is briefly mentioned here so as to make a link between the teaching and life of Jesus and the practice of a form of psychotherapy closely relevant to his words in chapter 3. It is added here for interest, if for nothing else, in that the chance of experiencing it is not easily accessed. Much more could be written about it which would be totally relevant to the ongoing experience of being "born again"; it would make Nicodemus's question less bizarre! We can understand his hesitation. "Penetrating into that tunnel of death and potential rebirth demands supreme effort, tenaciously holding on with no conscious orientation until a light shines in the darkness."[28] We are speaking of course of psychological death and rebirth, which is a common, widespread model in the psychodynamic literature, and of the experience of breaking through in personal growth.

Sanford focuses on verse 5, "unless a person is born from water and spirit," and points out that "from" is the preposition *ek*, which means "from," "out of," or "separate from," and thus easily refers to physical birth, so the one who is born again has come out from water and wind/spirit,

---

27. There is a PhD thesis on Lake's Primal Therapy by Stephen M. Maret from Drew University from 1992. A description of the theory and the practice is also to be found in the work of such writers as Arthur Yanov, Stanislav Grof, Verney and Kelly, Philippe Ploye, Ridgway and House, Geoffrey Whitfield, and John Rowan.

28. Woodman, *Pregnant Virgin*, 75.

has made a passage through the birth passage and through a psychic point of growth. Lake shows that many parts of our language can point to the intense heritage in memory that we each have of the stress of being born. (Vivid metaphors describing personal experience in common use may well have their original power from the birth experience: stuck, can't breathe, drowning, getting through, swallowing, strangled, helpless, no matter how hard I try, crushed, dead end, can't see a way out, in a tunnel.) Whether through the catharsis of physical or psychic/spiritual birth, we are assisted by a "doctor" of body or mind and spirit who draws us through the constriction of birth to a new life. Sandford quotes Jung:

> Our language is full of the most extraordinary things of which we are not aware, we use them without stopping to consider. For example, when you say, "I am under the treatment of Dr. So-and-so" you are using the Latin word *trahere*, "to pull." The doctor is pulling you through the hole of rebirth, and when he makes you whole and sound, you say, "the doctor pulled me through."[29]

Share what your mother told you about your birth. Can you identify any feeling you have now about it? Work hard at this!

If nothing was, or could be said, how do you feel about the absence of such knowledge?

2c. Intuition

Let us speculate a little! Nicodemus comes in a lowly, passive way. Was he passively depressed, hurt and anger turned in on himself, and hardly spoken of? What were his feelings towards his mother? Resistance to looking inside himself may suggest that there is unprocessed material from his early relationships. Jesus is not putting him down. Jesus does not "curtly reject" him. We can't go along with, "Jesus' responses to him appear to be nothing short of sharp, uncalled for rebuffs . . ." They are not sharp rebuffs.[30] "Are you a teacher and you don't know?" If we change

29. Sanford, *Mystical Christianity*, 87–88.

30. D. M. Smith, *Theology*, 26–28. Moody Smith then has to backtrack: "Jesus'

our intonation, Jesus is not criticizing (because he wouldn't, would he?), but he is aware of his rigidities, the suppression of a free spirit, and of his risklessness. Jesus can see into the heart of a man (2:25). His is the intuition that is "knowledge," in the Johannine sense, not guesswork of human nature, and he knows this one person standing in front of him. He is the shepherd of all shepherds, the pastor of pastors, teacher of teachers, psychotherapist of psychotherapists, counselor of counselors, man of all men and person of all persons. It is no good saying he was not a counselor or psychotherapist, for neither was he a shepherd, rabbi, or woman. He will facilitate a spirit of truth and comfort combined (chapters 14–16). He has a representative capacity to give himself for all (especially when his "hour" comes).

Some have more, some less, but intuition is a reality. All have to check out its accuracy and how much to trust it, at any one time. We recognize its "enormous delicacy" and "fluid sensitivity." And we note that for us uncertainty is part of "truthful" (1:14) relating.

> Indeed, it is almost impossible to say how one reaches the intuitions one does about other people—how for example, one knows the difference between a true and a fake smile, catches the flash of anxiety in somebody's eye, becomes aware of a current of sexual interest between two strangers who have only just met . . . It gives access to a world we all share . . . [to] the intricate and finely balanced subjective world in which we conduct our relations with each other, register and react to the impressions we give and receive, administer and respond to offers of love or threats of annihilation.

We do not often turn our sensibilities in this area into language, because we sense that it feels "far too crude to be allowed, as it were, to clothe our transactions in the coarse obviousness of words." "And yet we rely on this unexamined and mercurial faculty to tell us the truth about what is going on between us far more than on the verbal accounts we

---

sharp rebuff of Nicodemus should not be understood in normal relational categories applying to conversational and similar interchange between persons, so that Jesus could be described as arrogant or rude." If we wish to preserve the humanity of Jesus, it is easier to do so by withdrawing our negative projection and by changing the intonation we read into the narrative, replacing it with a positive one! It is quite possible to hear Jesus' words as calm, kind, and affiliative. But at least we are alerted to the role of reader as supplying his/her own material to the text, as will be seen especially in chapter 4.

give each other and ourselves as 'explanations' and excuses."[31] As helpers and as humans we rely intrinsically on the accuracy of our instinctive perceptions.

> And it is only because the therapist knows (trusts) that the patient *shares* the categories of understanding yielded by intuition that he or she is able to appeal to the patient's good faith (i.e. abandonment in the safety of the therapeutic relationship of the possibilities for deception offered by language) so that the truth may be acknowledged.

Substitute the word "Jesus" for the word "therapist" and read that passage again! We shall then also be sensitized to the way John's words and concepts creep into the modern caring relationship! "There is nothing special in these respects about psychotherapists and their patients. The immediate knowledge of interpersonal 'truth' afforded by intuitional sensitivity and the possibilities for obscuring it inherent in language are universal phenomena."[32]

These factors, intuition and obscuring by language, with the Johannine words of "truth" and "knowing," are encountered in succeeding chapters as Jesus meets the woman at the well, the poorly man, the crowd and disciples, the Pharisees, the man born blind and his parents, and so on.

> Do you have sometimes a sense of intuition? Can you trust it? How do you monitor it?

2d. Trust the Process of Inner Personal Change

It is the work of the Spirit, not merely self psychology (though that model is useful), nor pop psychology. The wind blows.[33] The movement within is not just about psychological development, but about the work of Jesus/ Spirit in our personality. Where else can he work? If you are not born (*gennao*) anew/from above, you cannot see (*horao*) the kingdom of God

---

31. Quotations from Smail, *Illusion and Reality*, 34.
32. Smail, *Illusion and Reality*, 35, italics and parentheses original.
33. *Pneuma pnei—pneuma* is both "wind" and "spirit" in Greek, v. 8.

(v. 3). So it is with everyone who is born (*gennao*) of the spirit (*pneuma*). What Nicodemus hears is "again," "a second time"; there is no need to call it a "misunderstanding," in a simple way. John's device, and that of Jesus, is to draw attention to the double meaning.

Nicodemus is just not in touch, as many since, with this revolutionary way of conceiving (to use a phrase) of growth in the inner spirit. If you don't understand how the personality works, this earthy knowledge, how will you understand that it is the heavenly contact that makes the difference? In every human being! It is the divine dimension (felt in Jesus) that transforms the earthly in us (vv. 10–12). He bears witness to what we know (*oida*) and have seen (*horao*). The point is not so much that Nicodemus is "well intentioned but theologically inadequate,"[34] but that it is the very way that ordinary people work, the ordinary workings of the human mind living out its common life on earth, that he doesn't understand. Like us, he is resistant. We all are blind to the way our psyche works till we allow the experience and gain the models that allow us to see inside ourselves. The spirit of Jesus is part of psychological change, of maturation, of growth. Paradoxically, when moments of breakthrough come and a new awareness of self is born, with a renewed sense of personal worth, we can often say of ourselves, "It is as if I have known this really all the time."

When being born is mentioned, Nicodemus immediately shies off the idea and yet constructs an imagination of entering the womb again. His mind pops up with a vivid image, about which he is ambivalent. There is much material in us about which we are deeply ambivalent. Some strong images shock us. Maybe he desired mother comfort and could not acknowledge it. That desire can last a lifetime! When we countenance what is in our minds, we are not then being judgmental, but describing the *process* of the way our minds work. It is normal.

Can you get in touch with any way in which you handle, your mind handles, material from a fairly early stage of your life? Share a deep memory of where you now see yourself as reacting to early experience.

---

34. Brown, *Gospel*, 1:138.

What we speak *does* reflect our thinking, conscious and especially unconscious. It is a window through which we see what is happening inside us. Maybe Nicodemus's preferred way of dealing in part with his sexuality, or his mother's sexuality, was to suppress some of the strong feelings associated with it, till such an odd, out-of-the-blue comment, "unless you are born again . . . ," releases a quick response. His defenses are down. They had to be partly dismantled to give himself permission to come to find Jesus. The constraint on his "knowing" is relaxed. Here he is apparently seeking a disclosure from Jesus, but yields a disclosure about himself. As well as a response to the simple literal question, it is a disclosure yielding up of something at the center of himself. We hear it if we write in an intonation of surprise or doubt or shock.[35] Murray Cox, writing of a clinical setting, but with a general application to all helping/healing relationships, describes disclosure.

> A disclosure is not an end in itself, but it is always an important step in the therapeutic process. The patient gains insight when material which had been repressed 'dawns' upon him. He may find that he is reliving early experiences and, within therapeutic space, a corrective emotional experience allows him to restructure the frightening, buried past. It can be an alarming experience to discover that, emotionally, 'a man can enter into his mother's womb', but he is only safe enough to do so with the reinforcing reality sense provided by the therapist with whom he shares therapeutic space.[36]

Substitute the word "Jesus" for the word "therapist" again, and we are forcefully reminded of the truth that, after necessary regression, we make every timid move forward in the presence of Jesus. He was with Nicodemus, and later Nicodemus was with him. In his presence Nicodemus had permission and the support to face a deep question about himself.

The libido is often more active in the early stages of depressiveness, with, for instance, a longing for sexual pictures, whereas in deeper depression it is often quite suppressed and lying under the surface and there is a distinct lack of interest. We are not being judgmental, but descriptive, of how we work when depressed. Maybe it is not too far-fetched (though for some it will be) to think these thoughts about Nicodemus. It is certainly not damaging, and it illuminates the way Jesus draws near to

---

35. Cox, *Structuring the Therapeutic Process*, 206–12.

36. Cox, *Structuring the Therapeutic Process*, 193–94.

him and interprets the heavenly to him, even to him. When we meet the woman at the well, she will be less resistant, and Jesus will draw near to her as well, and interpret the heavenly to her also.

Nicodemus is stepping out of line socially, and also personally. He finds it hard to step out beyond his comfort zone and look inside himself. So do we all!

> Where objective knowing is passive, subjective knowing is active—rather than giving allegiance to a set of methodological rules which are designed to deliver up truth through some kind of automatic process, the subjective knower takes a personal risk in entering into the meaning of the phenomenon to be known.[37]

We have to learn often to investigate ourselves creatively, and to share what we are, and to take risks with ourselves. Our reluctance to talk about ourselves is often cultural and personally learned, often through hard knocks which have prompted us to suppress our vulnerability; both sources of resistance overlap.

Call to mind a childhood influence on you—for good, and then one for ill.

Can you recall a life event which trapped you, or shaped your personality?

2e. The New Birth

Jesus' remark was not naïvely simple, nor was Nicodemus's response. It is a feature of human living that a breakthrough recurs frequently for all of us. Often it is a creative moment, a moment of intense affect. A breakthrough occurs in personal life, in literature, music, art, science, theology, and in love. It sets the tone, the depth, the meaning of subsequent life. It is a powerful new beginning. The previous life is not meaningless, and the subsequent experience is still frail and doubting and exploratory. But the change is there.

37. Smail, *Illusion and Reality*, 152.

Every such growth point will be related to many areas of what went before. One of these areas will relate to "mother." Erik Erikson in *Young Man Luther* analyzes substantially the complex development of Martin Luther, both as person and theologian. The dominance of his father is a major factor, but Martin Luther also had a mother! The relationship was fraught in childhood—she once caned him "till there was blood"—but he could not avoid the nurturing he got! His breakthrough occurred as he lectured on the Psalms, and of course as he read Romans 1:17, "the just shall live by faith." The Word set him free—sort of! He had to learn to receive it with a "deep passivity," a "feminine" quality. We remember that he "spoke of an attitude of womanly conception—*sicut mulier in conceptu.*" It is an active passivity; "all our partial as well as our total functioning is based on a metabolism of passivity and activity." "The theology as well as the psychology of Luther's passivity is that of a man in the state of prayer, a state in which he fully means what he can say only to God, 'I have sinned against You.'" "In two ways, then, rebirth by prayer is passive: it means surrender to God the Father; but it also means to be reborn *ex matrice scriptura nati*, out of the matrix of the scriptures." The origin of the word "matrix" is Late Middle English (in the sense of womb), from Latin, "breeding female," later "womb," from *mater, matr*—"mother."[38]

> 'Matrix' is as close as such a man's man will come to saying 'mater'. But he cannot remember and will not acknowledge that long before he had developed those wilful modes which were specifically suppressed and paradoxically aggravated by a challenging father, a mother had taught him to touch the world with his searching mouth and his probing senses. What to a man's man, in the course of his development, seems like a passivity hard to acquire, is only a regained ability to be active with his oldest and most neglected modes. Is it coincidence that Luther, now that he was explicitly teaching passivity, should come to the conclusion that a lecturer should feed his audience as a mother suckles her child? Intrinsic to the kind of passivity we speak of is not only the memory of having been given, but also the identification with the maternal giver . . .

Luther said, "the glory of a good thing is that it flows out to others." Erikson considers that in the Bible Luther at last found a "mother" "whom he could acknowledge: he could attribute to the Bible a generosity

---

38. *Oxford English Dictionary.*

to which he could open himself, and which he could pass on to others, at last a mother's son." This active passivity is distinctive.

> Meaningful implications are lost in the flat word passivity—among them the total attitude of living receptively and through the senses, of willingly 'suffering' the voice of one's intuition and of living a Passion: that total passivity in which man regains, through considered self-sacrifice and self-transcendence, his active position in the face of nothingness, and thus is saved.

I find the latter part of the sentence almost ambiguous. I kept it in because in the word "nothingness" it expresses where Luther often found himself, with both existential and learned anxiety. But he was saved by a gift, not by merit; "regains" must mean "is restored to," not "earns by his own effort." Yet he put in plenty of effort! It is the old conundrum: "by faith alone," keeping the "cycle"[39] flowing from status to work, and not reversing it, and not reinforcing the depressive position. Luther, anxious, depressed, and obsessional, spent much thought on "faith and works" and out of his insecurity was led to the security of faith as a gift, to the "passion" of the cross.[40]

Nicodemus is resisting owning his mother, or rather, in Object Relations terms, the "mother" in him. The "active" man could not let himself be "passive," as a little child. We marvel at the subtlety and depth of Jesus' insight as to where new beginnings come from, a reconciliation with the inner parts of ourselves, or "objects." Then Jesus himself, in the last week, exemplified an "active passivity."

2f. Birth–Rebirth

It is vital that we are sure that we do not dismiss this syndrome, this syndrome of birth and rebirth, as just a nice idea, a metaphor, or model only. It is all of these, but they point forward to real change in people's lives. Ann Belford Ulanov, a Jungian analyst and Professor of Psychiatry and Religion at Union Seminary, in *The Functioning Transcendent* describes analytical work with three women, Jean, Sara and Sophie, during which time she herself married and then became pregnant. In different ways each woman

39. See Frank Lake's model above in "Introduction 2: Understanding People," heading 6.

40. All quotations from Erikson, *Young Man Luther*, including Luther's Latin, 201–3.

felt criticized by her mother, remained "the little girl," suppressed great anger, missed out on mature relationships with people, the masculine in particular, and critically lacked self-worth. But they discovered through relating to a woman, and a real baby-to-be, that they could identify the transference (infantile, submissive, and aggressive) which they put onto a real mother sitting in front of them and onto a real baby-to-be. They could identify their intense resistance to entering the womb, the matrix from which they were trying to emerge, and to being "born again." Gradually they could come to a new sense of self and of self-worth, and to the ability to be a person, to be a woman, in their own right.

Ulanov wrote of the process of insight and recovery: "Each now really saw just how caught up she had been in her mother–daughter complex. This awareness set in motion her ego's birth from its womb-like containment in the matrix of the unconscious. This 'birth' constellated in each woman a sense of her rebirth as an adult female." With this "new emergence of her ego, each woman was able to cut her ties of psychological identification with the mother archetype" and to see herself as a person in her own right. And "With the emergence of a sense of self, each woman could perceive others differently." Jean "no longer found it suitable to alternate between mothering and being mothered." Sarah "now discovered that she also had identified with my unborn baby, whom she saw as receiving a secure mothering that she herself had been denied."

All three had reacted negatively to the pregnancy. But each could see that they could no longer, need no longer, be mothered by the analyst. She need no longer be the saving maternal figure. "Each had to nurture this new attitude to self and world just as a mother must slowly bring up a new born child, and each found herself capable of doing so, in spite of all the anxieties, uncertainties, and fears, so much like those which confront all who give birth."[41]   It is quite realistic for a needy man, in a transference relationship,[42] through oscillating attraction and rejection of a father figure, a "manly" figure, to be put in touch with the fear of intimacy. Hence Nicodemus's puzzled resistance to a man who puts him in mind of a mother figure, to entering the womb again, and to envisioning being "born again," and so moving to a new sense of self.

It is possible/probable that he varied in his response to Jesus as father figure (difference of age and status being subsumed into the transference

---

41. Ulanov, *Functioning Transcendent*, 84, 86, 90, 96, in the chapter "Birth and Rebirth," 75–96.

42. The positive and/or negative feelings we have towards a helping person.

relationship), a figure who was charismatic, learned, distinguished, perceptive. He secretly moved backwards and forwards in this relationship till he realized Jesus had a (loving, heavenly) Father himself. Then he is freed to act maturely and even protectively (7:45–52). He now has mature respect for this man and sees him for who he is and not through limiting transferential eyes. Despite the shock of the rebirth image, he can, we presume, face the issue of renewal within his own life. Through the presence in front of him of this man, he is able not to back off from recognizing in himself the simplicity and profundity of the move he can make within himself to go beyond his resistance. He can defend Jesus legally, care for his body, and enter, not a womb, but a tomb and with great courage go through the constriction of a narrow entrance, as in the birth process, to a place of death (19:38–42).

It is *totally extraordinary* that Jesus should identify the way human beings psychodynamically move from old pain, old reaction patterns and inhibitions, from the repetitions that sabotage relationships and personal growth, with the imagery of birth and rebirth. This was long before so many modern writers in the psychodynamic literature refer to the metaphor and symbol of birth, to repetition of primal experience in the process of self-discovery and healing, as a powerful model of breakthrough into healing and growth.[43]

Jesus' metaphors are unbelievably profound and arise in his relationship with the persons he meets in a helping role. He knows his own countertransference[44] and keeps a balance between the realities of rejection and acceptance in others[45] and the impact within himself. He accepts people in their need and knows their potential for rebirth. His place within himself is secure, through "good enough" mothering, with his ability to "hold" others' transference and his own countertransference, and to relate appropriately to each person and to each stage of their growth.

---

43. For example, the Canadian Jungian analyst and daughter of a minister, Marion Woodman, in *The Pregnant Virgin*, has "birth" and "rebirth" and primal experience used as a model to describe the fundamental stage in personal psychic growth on at least 74 pages out of 183!

44. The strong positive and/or negative feelings we have towards a person we are helping.

45. For instance, the man weak for thirty-eight years, and the blind man, Mary, and Thomas and their need in the resurrection experience, chapters 5, 9, and 20–21.

2g. The Past and the Present in Us

"Whenever a baby is born, it is a kind of summing up, a culmination of everything that has ever happened before. His parents and grandparents live on in him, and not only they but all the forgotten generations are, as it were, incarnate in the new-born child." So it is not a new idea to "think of the birth of Jesus as an emergence rather than as a breaking in from outside"[46] The "shadow side"[47] of this is that we do learn, ingest, copy, and live out the personality patterns of those who have gone before. Jeremiah, following the Old Testament sense of the connectedness of the generations, perceived this clearly[48] ("the fathers have eaten sour grapes, the children's teeth are set on edge"), but he saw it in the context of a new covenant, of heart religion, of each responsible for self, and each knowing God (Jer 31:27–34). The easing of the transgenerational burden occurs when we own our own pain and release it, thus renewing our inner patterns. The one who enables this renewal, who can start us off afresh, is Jesus.

Erikson coined the phrase "the metabolism of the generations." Luther was imprisoned in his past vis-à-vis his parents, yet substantially created the future for those who followed. We digest the past, and create new sustenance for the next step. One of the restorative joys of Christian worship is that we do this psychically when we take Holy Communion (John 6). "Each new being is received into a style of life prepared by tradition and held together by tradition, and at the same time disintegrating because of the very nature of tradition." "[T]he social process does not mould a new being merely to housebreak him; it moulds generations in order to be remoulded, to be reinvigorated, by them." The energy of the ego is "transformed into action" (within the self and toward others), "into character, into style—in short, into an identity with a core of integrity which is to be derived from and also contributed to the tradition."[49] The individual and also society can synthesize old and new in a new integrity. But there is huge resistance. Individually we see it in Nicodemus. Jesus is aware of it, and knows its bitter taste as he meets entrenched opposition

---

46. Taylor. *Go-Between God*, 89–90.

47. "Shadow side" is not derogatory, but descriptive. We have material within us which is less acceptable to us or disowned, mainly in the unconscious, the "darker" side of our personalities, from which we often project our negatives out onto others. Growth comes when we allow openness, and integrate our shadow into our whole personality.

48. Exod 20:5; Num 14:18; Deut 5:9.

49. Erikson, *Young Man Luther*, 247–48.

(e.g., chapters 7–8) and oppression, the role of tradition against the radical innovator. What pains he had to bear!

> Share your insight, and own precisely a specific way in which your personality reflects the role of "mother" in you.
>
> Share your insight, and own precisely a specific way in which your personality reflects the role of "father" in you.

> Get in touch with the tensions in your group, or your church community, over "but that is how we have always done it" and the need for and suggestions for change. Share as carefully and as realistically as you can *your* feelings, without judging or naming anyone. Own your own dilemma.

3. John's First Discourse, Theological Reflections: 3:16–21

And the greatest of these is verse 16. Henry James's novel *The Author of Beltraffio* tells a macabre and tragic story of a writer and his wife fighting over their sickly son. She wanted to keep the boy with her, and his father wanted him to go to the gate to say goodbye to a friend. "Will you choose?" The child replies, "I don't think I can choose." "We'll probably kill this child before we've finished with him—by fighting for him." And it came true. Compare this with the love of a heavenly Father! God so loved—he gave his son unreservedly. This is John's powerful image and metaphor.

Two worlds meet, earthly and heavenly (v. 12). "Johannine dualism tends to be spatial in its imagery."[50] In a post-demythologizing age, I do not actually like talk of heaven as up and earth as down. Nor do I like the implication that up is fine and spiritual and Godly, and down is not. I want the earth to be the Lord's.[51] Something of this ambiguity we recognize in John's use of the word *cosmos* as both the property of God,

50. Brown, *Gospel*, 1:132.

51. Ps 24:1

the God-created good world, and also as the alien realm of evil, identified with humankind, which is separated from him. Here the reference is to the things of the earth, *Gaia*, which are just different from the heavenly, which are not part of that which, coming from above, transmutes the earthly into a greater insight, richness, rightness. We should listen to the language again and find a new way of hearing it.

"Dualism" is both the difficulty and the opportunity. If we lose the pejorative classification "dualism" and choose a more neutral word, say, "opposites" or "complementarities" or "polarities" or "pairs," where there is some connection or relationship implied or even asserted between them, then the list of traditional ("dualistic") terms in chapter 3 can be counted as one of the insights into the way John is using binary elements in his language. Thus, beginning at 3:2 and throughout John, we have pairs: comes by night (*nuktos*)/comes from God (and 3:21 comes to the light, *phos*); knowing/not knowing; born/old; water/spirit (*pneuma*/wind); entering the womb/entering the kingdom; flesh/spirit; whence/wither; seeing (3:11)/not seeing (3:3); earthly *(epigeia)*/heavenly; trusting/not trusting; ascended—descended; eternal life/perishing; being condemned/being saved; judgment (*krisis*)/belief; light (*phos*)/darkness (*skotos*); not receiving/gift; bride/bridegroom; coming from above (*anothen*)/of the earth (*Gaia*). John thinks in binary categories.

It does not fit these pairs to assert "that reality is of two distinct and irreducible kinds," as though they exemplify a strict metaphysical dualism. They better suit "a qualified dualism between God and the creation, whereby an irreducible difference is related through an indissoluble bond." The created world and humankind within it is touched with chaos, with evil, with the possibility of non-redemption; but it is still created, still has the mark of the divine on it, is populated by those made from the earth (*gē*), into whom spirit has been breathed and who live in his image and by grace. This Christian qualified dualism "is historically dynamic, providing both difference and relation"[52] These pairs, expressed as positives and negatives, in different order, call Nicodemus, the first readers, and us ourselves to a coalescence, a synthesis of higher and lower within ourselves. We earthlings can be new made! "For God so loved the *cosmos* that he gave . . ."

---

52. Rouner, "Dualism," in Richardson and Bowden, *New Dictionary*, 166.

Will you now share, as nearly as you can, the highest moment in your life when you felt loved?

What anchors hold you in your place in the world?

What is of *Gaia* includes how we draw truth from air and water, birth and life, and how people change and grow. We often deeply resist the notion of remembering the past input into that process. This is understandable, because we are living organisms and defend against pain. It is also strange because (it could be argued) it is memory which makes us distinctively human, and because forgiveness (the entry point for Christian life) is the way of dealing with our history, or at least the negative parts of it. Forgiveness simply means living with grace-adjusted history. It is the prime Christian experience! Yet how much do we resist reowning the past, reclaiming and repatterning it? We resist the pain of disclosure and thus miss the chance of syntheszing the material which remains held within us.

If we do not understand this earthly way we work, how can we understand grace? If we can't or don't reown the past, then grace is not able to work within us. This is a description of how things are, not a moral chiding. It is an offer, not a condemnation; it sets us free. If you, a teacher, or a minister, or priest or . . . , and you understand how you work inside yourself, and the need to reown the past, and the capacity you have to reown the past, then grace, the heavenly stuff, is simply able to operate more fully within you. And it is going to be possible through the lifting up of Jesus; trust will then mean life. So often in life experience up to now, trust, in others or ourselves, has meant damage or hurt, and we have learned to defend against it. But God so loved the *cosmos* that he gave a gift, his own son, that whoever trusts him should not perish but have *zoen aionion* (3:16).

In these activities of sharing something of ourselves, it is more than common for the speaker to have "a deep-seated fear that disclosure will take from him that which he wishes to retain."[53] We are protected by our own "self-care system,"[54] but there are many times when, if we wish to grow, we must break through by sharing what is there. The listener needs to be a presence who empathetically waits with "freely hovering attention," who makes the gift of their presence to the other by witnessing what is said, and being aware of his or her own reactions, of transference and countertransference.

Share as honestly as you can what holds you back from telling your story, from talking about your Self. Why do you hesitate, or censure and conceal what you are like?

If you are listening, how does what you hear affect you? What happens to you in the process?

The wind of the spirit blows with an energy of its own. We need to understand this. There is as much energy available as we need. Grace is the energy of God in action within us. Even a teacher of Israel can learn that birth is from above, somehow by relating to the one descending from above. He can see a new realm, ruled by reowning the origins of his personality. This is the work of the spirit, the *pneuma*. It leads to life.

It may be your conversion experience, or it may be another moment of renewed faith, or worth. How much did that experience involve a sense of being loved, however simply demonstrated?

The dualist split sometimes runs quite deeply within us. Someone who had been psychodynamically depressed for many years said, "If only I could get nearer to God I would be less depressed." It is the same as saying, "If only I was less depressed I would be nearer to God." The reply goes firmly and kindly like this: How can you suggest that you are not

53. Cox and Thielgaard, *Mutative Metaphors*, 181.
54. Kalsched, *Inner World*, throughout.

near enough to God? You may *feel* that you are not, but in fact you are. Our darkness not only affects our knowing but our affect, what we feel, as well.[55] God is near enough to you for every purpose? How dare we suggest God is not near to us! He is as near as we need. He works in us as we are, depressed or not. It must be so. He cannot just work in the bit that is not depressed!

Surely he works in the whole of you. You are one person, and therefore God is at work *in the depression*. That is where he works—else how can it be changed? You cannot do it all yourself. He works in the darkness, in the depressive material. The depressive material is not something alien come in from outside. It is part of you, and the way through it—easier said than done—is somehow to integrate it. It will be changed in you when you see yourself as depressed, not as having some separate entity like an alien incubus in you. Then you can see God working in all of you. What a relief! He works in the negative so that even the sense of what is negative changes. You have not only changed your view of yourself, but you have changed your theology. You do not have to get rid of your depression before you can get near to God!

"Nor yet do thou say, 'I must do something more before I come to Christ.' . . . Oh do not set him a time! Expect him every hour. Now he is nigh. Even at the door!"[56]

Do you have any sense that God in his spirit is working in the shadow side of your personality? What would it mean for you to think of renewal as coming in the negative side of your personality?

The discourse of verses 16–21 is the author's commentary. There are many threads of the tapestry showing—love, cosmos, gift, Son, life, believe/trust, judgment, darkness, light, true.

---

55. Williams, "Dark Night, Darkness," in Wakefield, ed., *Dictionary*, 103–5.
56. John Wesley, *Great Thoughts*, 20–21.

4. Judgment

Nicodemus came by night (*nuktos*), which has more than the literal import. Maybe John was indicating the darkness out of which he came to the light that was Jesus. The word for "darkness" is *skotos* or *scotia*, as in 1:5, and it has negative connotations.

The gift of Jesus so expresses God's love (*agapao*) that to trust him means that you will not perish (*appollumi*). God sent (*apostello*) the Son not to judge (*krino*—implying condemn) the *cosmos* but that the *cosmos* may be saved (*sozo*) through him. The reassurance is complete; the person who trusts in him is not condemned. The judgment is that not to trust means to be part of the darkness, to share love for the darkness, life without Jesus, where one's inner world is moving away from the light of Jesus. If one is involved in a praxis of evil things (the "second-rate" in classical Greek), one hates light (*phos*) and does not come (*erchomai*) to it. This is what men (*anthropoi*) do, lest their works (*erga*) are exposed.

By contrast, he who does the truth has his works (*erga*) made manifest, open, that is, they are worked (*ergazomai*) in God. An intrinsic judgment simply exists in the order of things. It is a moral universe where the core value is the gift of love, seen in Jesus. Trusting (believing) this is trusting (believing) heavenly things (v. 12). "Doing truth" (v. 21) is a powerful phrase describing, surely not moral effort only as the focus, but the energy of grace working within our core being to change the patterns of our personality so that we do not *need* to do evil, and so that we love the "unbearable lightness of (God's) being" within us.

This experience involves repentance and forgiveness, though these familiar words should not impose a pattern on us. Repentance "means, in essence, discovering something about yourself, something positive, not negative . . . that you have more to you than you dreamt or knew . . ."[57] Thurneysen writes of the place of moral judgment in the role of the caring pastor,

> who has to proclaim the forgiveness of sins as his sole message. Does not the forgiveness of sins in itself mean that there is a Word which sovereignly stands over against all human evil and all human good, a Word which reduces the contradiction of good and evil, as seriously as it is to be taken in its place, to a relative contradiction, since the forgiving Word includes the evil and the good, the unrighteous and the righteous, and

---

57. Williams, *True Wilderness*, 81–82.

transfers them to a new ground beyond good and evil? Does not forgiveness in itself mean that our good cannot redeem us, but our evil not condemn us either? What saves us is the mercy of Christ alone, and what condemns us is our overlooking and forgetting this mercy . . . The pastoral conversation must . . . accept and work out the ethical conflict, and not 'counsel' it away. It must lead to utter frankness. But it will only hold forth a solution when it does not seek this solution on the same ground on which the conflict arose and exists, namely on the moral ground. The pastoral counsellor, directed by the Word of God, must know, and remember throughout the whole conversation that moral conflicts can not be worked out morally.[58]

We may add that his mercy is meant for us even before we come to the point of forgiveness. The poet Samuel Taylor Coleridge offers a reminder of this wisdom: "Christianity is not so much the gift of forgiveness to those who repent, but the gift of repentance to those who sin." When deeply troubled, it is the gift of repentance that opens the heart.

What does the "gift of repentance" mean to you? Can you remember a time when the ability to repent was the significant moment? Who gave you that gift?

The unhappy person needs the possibility of drawing near to someone appropriately. The listener hears and holds the disclosure, *for the time being*, that is, as an empathic transitional object. The novel *Gilead* by Marilynne Robinson about Pastor John Ames was described by a broadsheet newspaper review as "having a lot of theology in it." It shows him towards the end listening to the life story of Jack Boughton, the wandering sheep of his best friend's family, who had badly hurt him and that family. As John Ames listens, there is a change in him, losing his resentment, and at the bus stop he can give the gift of his blessing to Jack as Jack leaves the town and finally goes away. "And grace is the great gift. So to be forgiven is only half the gift. The other half is that we also can forgive, restore, and liberate, and therefore we can feel the will of God enacted through us,

---

58. See Thurneysen, *Theology of Pastoral Care*, 135, 142; quoted in Lake, *Clinical Theology*, 336, italics added.

which is the great restoration of ourselves to ourselves."[59] The one doing the truth comes to the light! (3:21)

D. T. Niles, Methodist minister, one-time secretary of the South East Asia Christian Congress, preached at the World Student Christian Congress in Edinburgh 1958 on the theme that we come in Easter week to meet Christ and we meet him as Judge; the importance of having a judge.

> I was returning home after office one day years ago, and my little son was sitting on the doorstep waiting for me. He followed me into the house, and stood by as I was talking to my wife. After a little while he suddenly blurted out, "But Mama, why don't you tell Papa what I have done?" So I looked at him, and I looked at my wife, and I said, "What has he done?" She smiled and said, "He broke the jam pot today." There he was, sitting on the doorstep with that jam pot on his conscience; and the only person who could remove it, who could set him free, had to come. Father had to come; the thing had to be confessed; he had to say something. I said to him, "That is all right. We'll buy another jam pot. It doesn't matter." The thing was over. If at the end of a day I could not get down on my knees by my bed and confess my sins to my Father—the things which I have done consciously, which I ought not to have done; the many deeds I have done unconsciously I ought not to have done; if I could not say to somebody, "God be merciful to me a sinner"—life would become unbearable. And life has become unbearable for countless men and women of our times. They have no judge; they refuse to have a judge; they have got rid of Jesus Christ.[60]

God judges with love. He is "the mild Judge and Intercessor both"; he comes to "temper Justice with Mercie."[61] To suggest that God's love and justice vie with each other is our projection. Wrath and mercy, judgment and love go together. They are inseparable. You cannot have one without the other. For humans they are consecutive, but not for God.

> Throw away thy rod,
> Throw away thy wrath:
>   O my God,
> Take the gentle path.

59. Robinson, *Gilead*, 183.

60. Maury, ed., "Life for the World," 232.

61. Milton, *Paradise Lost*, 10:77–78. "Mild" meant "gracious, merciful." See Watson, "Charles Wesley," 289.

Then let wrath remove;
Love will do the deed.[62]

"[T]he rude mind with difficulty associates the ideas of power and benignity." There is only "a shadowy conception of power that by much persuasion can be induced to refrain from inflicting harm"[63] With God they are contemporaneous. Luther learned this as he moved from an oppositional experience to an inclusive one. He moved from "I knew Christ as none other than a stern judge, from whose face I wanted to flee, and yet I could not" and "Christ was for me not a mediator, but a judge"[64] to "And now, as much as I hated this word 'Justice of God' before, so much the more sweetly I extolled this word to myself now."[65] In this sense, the church is under judgment, always failing and always being renewed, *semper reformanda*. The combination is called "grace." Love and justice meet in Jesus and are one, the grace of our Lord Jesus Christ. "[H]e does not resolve the paradox with a form of words—instead, he dies: he takes the struggle, the ambivalence, into the silence of that terrible death and *God* brings the synthesis out of it . . . He is the at-one-ment, the synthesis."[66] Luther's reality about both our humanity and our life in Christ is that we have both the light and the darkness in us. We are *simul justus et peccator*, at once justified and sinner, and yet we are in Christ. This has implications for pastoral psychology and for pastoral theology.

In a caring activity, can you identify the moment when you find yourself splitting into judge and reconciler, when you suddenly feel judgmental, allocating right and wrong, needing to condemn? Or offering and *embodying* grace?

What features in another's life are the ones which spark off your judgmental feelings, or your inclination to be kind and forbearing?

---

62. George Herbert's poem, *Discipline*.

63. Eliot, *Silas Marner*, ch. 1 of the folk religion of a rural community, 53.

64. Quoted in Rupp, *Righteousness of God*, 145. See Jenson, "Martin Luther's 'Sin Boldly' Revisited," 2–13. See Williams, *Wound of Knowledge*, 142–58.

65. Rupp, *Righteousness of God*, 122.

66. Holloway, "Preaching," 412.

In this spirit we may run with William Law (1686–1761), though he seems almost to dispense with "wrath" all together; we need to keep it (as I think he actually does) but in the context of the joy of the love of God.

> It is a glorious and joyful truth . . . that from eternity to eternity no spark of wrath ever was or ever will be in the holy triune God. If a wrath of God was anywhere it must be everywhere; if it burned once it must burn to all eternity. For everything that is in God Himself is boundless, incapable of any increase or diminution, without beginning and without end . . . God considered in himself is as infinitely separate from all possibility of doing hurt or willing pain to any creature as He is from a possibility of suffering pain or hurt from the hand of man. And this, for the plain reason, because He is in Himself, in His Holy Trinity, nothing else but the boundless abyss of all that is good, and sweet, and amiable, and therefore stands in the utmost contrariety to everything that is not a blessing—in an eternal impossibility of willing and intending a moment's pain or hurt to any creature.[67]

There is, of course, another side to God's passibility, namely, his capacity to be wounded for us, to be identified with us, and also to "wound" us so that we grow. Charles Wesley, in the intensity of the spiritual experience of longing for the cure that love can give, could sing, "Deepen the wounds thy hands have made / in this weak, helpless soul."[68] He knows that the hurt we need to know if we are to grow is worked in us by God. For Wesley, "the depth of perfect love" was inclusive of the love felt for us, the love which seems to hurt so that we do grow, the love we offer back, and the love we give to others. "Perfect love" embraces all. The sensitive pastoral heart will know it as well and will be a present help. It would be strange if we claimed a skill and a gift, of empathetically suffering with another, which God himself did not have! For both God and humans, we claim with Vanstone in *The Stature of Waiting* that "man must see his dignity not only being a point of activity in the world but also in being a point of receptivity: not only in his manifold capacity for action but also in the many facets of his passibility; not only in his potential for 'doing' but also in his exposure to 'being done to.'"[69]

67. In Handley et al., *English Spirit*, 153.

68. *MHB* 556; Hildebrandt and Beckerlegge, eds., *Works of John Wesley*, 7: 528 (no. 359).

69. Vanstone, *Stature of Waiting*, cited Cox and Thielgaard, *Mutative Metaphors*, 181. Thus reflecting the anomaly sensed in God, who grieves us yet has compassion, and yet does not will grief for us; e.g., Lam 3:32–33.

Share an experience when you felt judged and continued to feel imprisoned in the judgment. Be clear about what was happening to you. Identify if there was a previous experience of being judged which the later one recapitulated.

Share an experience of being judged with love, where you felt freed by the judgment. Does it turn on you trusting, and/or on you being trusted? How much more is it possible in the presence of Jesus?

Can you identify in you this sense that God wounds you and thus you have to grow?

Try to identify in yourself that hurt which is good for you as you seek to grow in personality and in spirit, and which is the work of God's spirit, and share it with your partner.

Do not blame God for what he is not doing, nor yourself for what you are not doing, but trust his work in you!

He who does the truth (*aletheia*)—what is genuine, not hypocritical, and in the Old Testament "keeps faith"—comes (*erchomai*) to the light (*phos*), the very opposite of "hating" the light. He has chosen to move away from the radical evil he is capable of. This is not a picture of two groups predestined, the baddies and the goodies, but of the hope and possibility of transfer. That is what judgment effects. Why else a notion of beginning again, or being "born again," or regeneration? "[T]he idea is that Jesus brings out what a man really is and the real nature of his life. Jesus is a penetrating light that provokes judgment by making it apparent what a man is."[70] The light of Jesus shows brilliantly what a person really is: not just how bad, but how bad and how good. It will be made open, apparent (*phaneroo*), not latent, that his works (*erga*) have been worked (*ergazomai*) in God. That is the only "place" a human can do them!

70. Brown, *Gospel*, 1:148–49.

5. John and Jesus: 3:22–30

This passage contains narrative, dialogue, and discourse about Jesus, and
John the Baptist relating! John's text works at many levels and with many
connections. In the tapestry of the text, the stitches, threads, and loops
of meaning are manifold. Great themes and words of all kinds dip in and
out of our view. This is often the effect of the narrative or of a commentary by John, often from the mouth of Jesus. So now these verses refer
both backwards and forwards. Firstly, there is geographical shift with
two tiny scenes; Jesus spends some time with the disciples and baptizes,
and John is baptizing in a place of many waters. Our reading minds are
conscious we have just read of water and spirit, and our knowing minds
that we will read of the water of life in chapter 4. We already realize what
a key motif water is. We might in our modern way focus on the number
of candidates for baptism, but not on the quantity of water! They are near
such abundance (John 2:1–11)! It is from heaven, from above, that we
have what we have.

So we have moved back to John the Baptist, strangely, to a "wedding" where he is the best man (*philos*) who stands (*histemi*) and listens
to the bridegroom, which is what Jesus has become, and rejoices with
joy (*chara chairei*, "with joy rejoices") because of the voice (*phone*) of
the bridegroom. Therefore, his joy has been fulfilled (*pleroo*). "It must be
that that one increases [*auzano*] but I am to be made smaller [*elatoo*]"
(cf. 2:10, the "worse" wine, *elasson*). The disciples' relationship with Jesus
decreased and increased as ours does! It may be a mature judgment on
oneself to say, with John the Baptist, "I am not . . ." as a starting point!

A candle decreases while it gives light. Have you a recollection of
facing a time when you had to yield up to another your project, work,
skills, role, status? How was it being selfless *and* yet being perceptive
of what is happening to you? What feelings did you have?

John the Baptist is clear about his relationship to Jesus. It was a common and strong pattern in Greek and Hebrew experience for there to be
an affectionate relationship between teacher and "beloved disciple," the

older and the younger. John was not put out by the fact that Jesus is also baptizing and all come (*erchomai*) to him.

This second pointing by John to Jesus has arisen out of an incipient anxiety amongst his followers. They address John as "Rabbi" and use the same pointer to Jesus as John did, "Behold" (3:26), and they know he is the one John witnessed to. They feel confusion, concern, competition. They are a human group wondering where their boundaries are. Does their circle include Jesus or exclude him? is their question. Is he a competitor, and if so, what are we doing? Is he outside us or inside us?

The questions of any human group are: What does what is done by the other mean? Does he do it properly? Does he have authority to do it? Do we stop him? Do we join him? The dilemma classically analyzed by Mary Douglas is between *Purity and Danger*.[71] Human groups, large and small, define themselves so as to remain true to their purpose. They then fulfill it by seeking to remain pure and define their boundaries and internal qualities. Any people failing are extruded. It's a natural process and works itself out in moderate or extreme ways.

Recapitulate an occasion when you were conscious of wishing to defend your group, community, or institution by expelling those who disagreed with its belief or practice. What has happening inside you?

Recall an occasion when you were thrust out as the one not fitting in.

You are not discussing the rightness or wrongness in either case, but revealing the inner world of your experience of inclusion or extrusion.

The context is thus a discussion about "purifying" (*kathaireo*), and not surprisingly it is with a "Jew" (3:25). The writer's gift of hope—there were many waters (a strong symbolic theme throughout)—is dashed for the readers by the caveat that John had not yet been thrown into prison, confined within a tight and unbreakable boundary.

What purifying (catharsis) is needed for a person to have God purely within? The old water jars have been replaced. What is the best wine? How do people change? What transmutes human nature (earthy

---

71. Douglas, *Purity and Danger*.

as it is) to something finer, or rather synthesizes it with the divine, the earthy with the heavenly? No one can receive anything unless it is given from heaven. John's permissible negative definition of himself was "I am not [*ouk eimi ego*] the Christ," but he *is* the one having been sent before him (*apostello*) like a best man (vv. 27, 28). This opens the way for a vivid image. The best man rejoices, for Christ is the bridegroom. And the bride? Surely the Johannine community would feel confirmed as the church. And the change happens in people because Jesus penetrates with his purifying, his catharsis, and creates new life.

Thus John, the author, prepares us for the unfolding answers in each chapter up to chapter 15 to the question: How does Jesus get into us? How does he give himself to us?

6. Life

In 3:31–36 we are not sure who is speaking. The editor or author or Jesus or the Baptist recapitulates and emphasizes how it is. This summary is not merely descriptive; it has a cutting edge. There is a qualitative distinction between what is from above and what is of the earth, but to trust in the Son, who joins the two in himself and in Spirit, is to have that quality of life which is eternal. Every word is pregnant with meaning.

The one coming (*erchomai*) from above (*anothen*) is over all; the one being of (*ek*) the earth (*ge*) is of (*ek*) the earth and speaks of (*ek*) the earth. The word *ge* speaks of what is created and does not have the negative connotation *cosmos* sometimes has. But to be of the earth is to remain attached to the earth. The way one speaks will be "earthy," not in the rude or rustic sense, but without the sense of being from above. Missing that dimension, to which the Baptist witnesses, is to be with those who do not receive his witness. What Jesus has seen (*orao*) and heard (*akouo*) he bears witness to (*martureo*), and no one receives his witness. Whoever receives his witness attests, sets his seal, that God is true (*alethes*). (See 6:27, the only other use in John, where God "seals," accredits, attests Jesus as his purveyor of food which endures to eternal life.) For the one God sent (*apostello*) speaks the words of God, for he gives the Spirit without restriction, "not by measure" (*metron*), not in six jars containing two or three measures (*metretes*, 2:6). God does not measure out a quantity of himself, of his spirit, to define what Jesus is, or will be or do on the earth.

He is not a quantity, a fluid, a dose, but a presence. What a liberating offer; there is enough for each, enough for all.

The unfettered intimacy of the relationship is expressed simply. The Father loves (*agapao*) the Son and has given (*didomi*) all things into his hand. He is accepted and sustained (Lake's model). There is a consequence. The one trusting (present tense) in the Son has life eternal (*zoe aionios*); the one not obeying the Son will not see (*horao*) life (*zoe*), but God's wrath (*orge*) remains on him. "Remain" is that favored Johannine word *meno*. "Wrath" is only used here in John and is presumably similar to "judgment," the permanent presence of the judging God in the life of the one who distrusts/disbelieves, which because it is a judgment-with-love gives him or her hope. See Charles Wesley's hymn of incarnation and atonement:

> And can it be that I should gain
> An interest in the Saviour's blood?
> Tis mystery all . . .
> Tis mercy all . . .
> Tis mercy all, immense and free;
> For, O my God, it found out me!
> No condemnation now I dread;
> Jesus, and all in Him, is mine![72]

A good friend who read this noted, "This was my 'conversion' hymn on 19 April 1964."

This is a description of *what is*. This kind of writing about "judgment" we so often hear as an ethical threat; it is extraordinarily difficult to hear it in a neutral way. But that is what is meant. It is not a crude picture of God condemning. The one who does not trust, who disobeys (*apeitheo*, John's only use), who is literally "unpersuaded," who is the opposite of being "persuaded," who does not trust the Son, shall not see life.[73] Compare 3:18: the one who does not trust is judged already; this is how things are. We live in a moral universe but a description of it is not merely a moral threat but also a moral promise. It behoves you to be born anew, from above (3:7). Then you will see life!

---

72. *STF* 345; *H&P* 216; *MHB* 371.

73. *Peitho* is frequent in the NT, though never in John; for "to persuade," see, e.g., 1 John 3:19, the only use in the Letters.

Do you find it easy to trust? What happens in you, to you, as you seek to trust? What process do you go through? What pains and joys occur in you? This refers to trusting others, and to trusting God. What is the effect of trusting?

"Eternal life" means quality, not quantity. It refers to a type of life, not its length, nor only that which goes beyond death. I remember as a teenager knowing that what it meant was the heightened sense of existence I was experiencing in Christ. It was not a nominal thing. It does not come through baptism, though that symbolizes it.

The reality of our condition persists naturally! Speaking of Luther's stance, Gordon Rupp writes, "The guilt of original sin may have been remitted in baptism, but 'the misery of infirmity' remains, as a 'weakness in the memory, a blindness of intellect, or a disorder of the will, and as a dolour of conscience' which are only gradually healed by grace, in the inn where Christ, the Good Samaritan has placed us."[74] Though not intended, that neatly encompasses a psychodynamic invitation and a Christian insight. And, of course, "eternal" life does not come through a psychotherapeutic experience only. That gives the experience, but not fully till there is a sense of the presence of Jesus in it. It is a quality of being, sensitive of God, touched by him or her, the inner witness, heart religion, the inner world patterned in Christ, and thus in tune with one's "true self." It's a communion experience, of abiding (remaining, *meno*) in Christ. But this anticipates, for instance, John 6 and 15.

Can you see in yourself any point in your life when you felt the judgment of God, but were able to realize, or move on to, a sense that that was not condemnation but forgiveness or "justification"? Justification is God's free acceptance of you.

Do you have a sense of being touched freely by a "heavenly" influence in your life?

Where do you get *your* truth from?

Share your answers to all the questions.

74. Rupp, *Righteousness of God*, 153.

Part of the case for John being the "Pastoral Gospel" is that it could be argued that whenever Jesus meets an individual, they are in need, and sometimes at the greatest point of need; then he ministers to them and they are changed. Everyone has to come to terms with himself or herself in the same moments as they meet Jesus.

> Seek we then ourselves in ourselves; for as
> Men force the sun with much more force to pass,
> By gathering his beams with a crystal glass;
>
> So we, if we into ourselves will turn,
> Blowing our sparks of virtue, may outburn
> The straw, which doth about our hearts sojourn.[75]

We keep that in balance with Charles Wesley. "I cannot wash my heart"[76] We cannot do it ourselves, and are totally dependent on grace, "so measureless is God's gift of the Spirit" (3:34, NEB). It is in the dark that we find him, as Nicodemus did, and with Charles Wesley wearing Jacob's coat, we will say, "With Thee all night I mean to stay, and wrestle till the break of day."[77]

We need to keep a balance between "dark" as bad, not God, and "dark" as the sphere where God works. After all, God created the dark! We need to let him own the dark in us. The artist Rembrandt expects the viewer to explore the dark so as to feel the impression of the light, to receive the full message, say, of the human face, or of the presence of Christ. "[T]his is a technique of balance which demands that the viewer explore the darkness and shadow as much as the light, for they are in their complementarity, responsible for the beauty of the work." "God has entrusted darkness into human hands."[78] So it is with our human beauty in Christ. In Christ we trust ourselves to the darkness, the darkness in God, the darkness we do not want to flee from (Ps 139:7–12) "[W]ise Nicodemus saw such light / as made him know his God by night . . . There is in God, some say, / a deep but dazzling darkness."[79]

---

75. Donne, *To Mr. Rowland Woodward.*

76. *MHB* 564, v. 5.

77. "Come, O thou traveler unknown," v. 1, *MHB* 339; *H&P* 434; see Gen 32:26–32.

78. Bird, *Divine Heart*, 99–100, 118.

79. Henry Vaughan, "The Night."

But Thou art Light and darkness both together:
If that be dark we cannot see,
The sun is darker than a tree,
And Thou more dark than either.

Yet Thou art not so dark, since I know this
But that my darkness may touch Thine.
And hope, that may teach it to shine,
Since Light thy Darkness is.[80]

7. Heartfelt Religion

John Newton had known heartache, despair, and degeneracy. His mother
died when he was seven; he went to sea at eleven; deserted, recaptured,
disrated, profane, slaver (though sensitivity to that came later). Hardships "for about the space of eighteen months" made him "captive and a
slave myself . . . depressed to the lowest degree of human wretchedness."
In a huge storm he heard himself saying to the captain, "almost without
meaning, 'If this will not do, the Lord have mercy on us.' This (although
spoken with little reflection) was the first desire I had breathed for mercy
for the space of many years." Providentially, he felt, he had been "delivered out of deep waters." He was "on every . . . side surrounded with black
unfathomable despair." His conversion was a "faltering gradual process."
A composite of physical weakness, of listening to and reading evangelical
Christian leaders, of self-reflection, and of the release of tears led him
to the point when he felt that "notwithstanding all my vileness I was
made free from sin by the spirit of Life in Jesus Christ, what a wonderful instance am I, both of the riches and the freedom of grace." He was
convinced that "doctrines of grace are essential to my peace."[81]

Conversion, we must note again, is both a beginning and a continuance. There is a sequel, often fraught, though the reality remains. "Conversion does not signify an end to the chaos of human experience; it does
not make self-understanding suddenly easy or guarantee an ordered or
intelligible life."[82] "Conversion is a beginning, not an end, an entry into a

---

80. George Herbert, "Evensong."

81. Brooks, *Hymns as Homilies*, 99–122.

82. Rowan Williams, quoted by Gordon Wakefield in the *Methodist Recorder*
(reference lost).

perilous and confused world."[83] But it does change lives and personality. We must also note again that in the Methodist strand of Pietism affect and reason went together, at least in Wesley's thinking. Rationalism, if cold, dry, and empty of feeling, was eschewed but not reason. The experience of so many was a felt experience, focusing on "deep piety and holy life," where the emphasis was on rebirth as the prime mover. "[F]eeling is given a new importance in the religious revivals of the period, among Pietists, Methodists and Chasidim."[84]

It is true that the conversion accounts of this period, and later, follow a stylized pattern, but even so the writers of their autobiographies were recounting life-changing experiences which remained with them all their days.[85] What is not often realized is that some conversions happened quickly, but what was common was that the journey from first "awakening" to "conviction" of sin lasted a long time, with much personal doubt and distress till peace was found. Tom Albin has studied 555 early Methodist biographies, 1725–1790 (Methodism is the most biographized church ever!). The essential nature of the heart/mind/spirit experience of Methodism meant that 57 percent of people joined a society *prior* to new birth, and the mean time between awakening and new birth was 2.4 years. That experience of nurturing continued in the process of sanctification (sometimes a moment, and often much longer), all sustained in the Society and small group, Band and Class meetings. All that time they would be *in* the Society. They did their searching and their breakthrough *within* the Society, with their regular Christian fellowship, *within* the church. *Growth* was normal and Christian![86] And then conversion was the fulcrum around which the whole of life evolved. "Conversion became not a moment in one's life, but the key to interpreting the meaning of one's life from beginning to end."[87] The work and journey to that point of new birth occurred in a very high percentage of people actually *within* the Christian group. A new sense of what the church is is provided.

Amazing grace!

83. Williams, *Wound of Knowledge*, 70.

84. Taylor, *Sources of the Self*, 302.

85. For an extensive survey, see Hindmarsh, *Evangelical Conversion Narrative*. For a commentary on the early Methodist experience, see Mack, *Heart Religion*; and Goodhead, *Crown and a Cross*. For a nineteenth-century study, see Wilson, "Conversion Among Female Methodists, 1825–75." In general, see Routley, *Gift of Conversion*.

86. Albin, *Empirical Study*, 275–88.

87. Hindmarsh, *Evangelical Conversion Narrative*, 322.

Tell your biography to someone who does not know you. Be aware of what you are selecting and of what you are leaving out or censoring. It is quite useful to have a time limit, say, of five minutes each. When you have finished, the other says what they appreciate about you in one sentence, "What I appreciate about you is . . ." When you have listened carefully and attentively to your partner, you say what you appreciate about her/him.

John 4

A Picture of Trust

Though we are clumsy disciples may we meet you as the woman did,
and be your people.

1. Trust and the Image of Water

"THE STORY OF THE Samaritan woman is remarkable for the clarity and completeness of its presentation of the revelation process in the Fourth Gospel."[1] This has sometimes been perceived as an erotic account, and if not that, it certainly catches our emotions. It is a powerful narrative to which we respond with affect as well as thought. Within all the various responses is the overwhelming sense of how special Jesus is. We long for him. "Come thou fount of every blessing."[2] Or Charles Wesley's "Jesu, Lover of My Soul":

> Plenteous grace with thee is found,
>   Grace to cover all my sin,
> Let the healing streams abound,
>   Make and keep me pure within.
> Thou of life the fountain art;
>   Freely let me take of thee;
> Spring thou up within my heart,
>   Rise to all eternity.[3]

In chapter 3 we were made aware of what resistance to the love of God shown in Jesus means in general, and in particular how resistance by a man to the need to reconnect with his earliest experience was used by Jesus to explain the means whereby new life comes. Nicodemus found it hard to conceive of going back to dependent infancy. Creative regression is out of his ken. Such resistance symbolizes both our reluctance to experience new birth (rebirth, literally in French, *renaissance*) and our unwillingness to get in touch with, for instance, the early identities contained and preserved within us. We resist knowing our own kin within ourselves, our internalized "objects."[4] How hard it is to trust, being old (3:4). Making contact with mother, even figuratively, through a journey back into the past, is nerve-wracking.

If that is how Jesus deals with a man, how will he deal with a woman? How does he help us, man or woman, to make contact with a living woman, with a real woman? Jesus shows us how. He now models a way of meeting a real woman, where barriers are already in place, and of how to

---

1. S. M. Schneiders "Women in the Fourth Gospel," in Stibbe, ed., *Gospel*, 132.
2. Robert Robinson, *H&P* 517.
3. Charles Wesley, *H&P* 528.
4. See footnote 36 in "Introduction 1" and footnote 42 in "Introduction 2."

live with her needs. And this becomes the context for understanding how it is that our own needs can be met.

Jesus exemplifies how, in any early stage of a meeting with another, certainly in a pastoral encounter, what is critical is the establishment of basic trust. "[A]nd such trust can only be established where there is minimal fear of an incursion and invasion." If we monitor our intonation, even the statement by Jesus in verse 18, "You have had five husbands . . . ," need not be read as a threat. The woman certainly did not respond as if it was. In Conrad's powerful entry into the human spirit in *The Heart of Darkness*, he portrays an encounter which perfectly describes this meeting: "And the girl talked, easing the pain in the certitude of my sympathy; she talked as thirsty men drink."

Jesus bridges the space between cultures by creating trust. "The potential space between baby and mother, between child and family, between individual and society or the world depends on experience which leads to trust. It can be looked on as sacred to the individual in that it is here that the individual experiences creative living."[5] This was a moment of creative living par excellence for this woman!

One reflection is necessary here. One connecting motif of chapters 1–5 is water: the water that purifies, the water that cleanses, the water that quenches thirst, the water that heals, the water that symbolizes God. It is a dominant motif in the Gospel. It points to Jesus. It is very clear that it is not just the physical effects of water of which the text is speaking. It is more than suggestive of an infinitely richer life through Christ, which is inexhaustible and creates wholeness of spirit, healing of the inner person. This we cannot achieve for ourselves. It is a gift. It is a gift of love and is received by trust. "Trust heals people."[6] It is the work of God.

Ever since New Testament times, Christians have found it possible to bridge the gap between the literal and the metaphor. The metaphors water, spring, and fountain are everywhere in Christian biography. George Whitfield (1714–1770) writes autobiographically:

> One Day, perceiving an uncommon Drought, and a disagreeable Clamminess in my mouth, and using Things to allay my Thirst, but in vain, it was suggested to me, that when Jesus Christ cried out, 'I thirst' his sufferings were near at an End. Upon which, I cast myself down on the Bed, crying out, I thirst! I thirst! Soon after this, I found and *felt* in myself that I was delivered from

5. Winnicott, *Playing and Reality*, 135.
6. Williams, *Meeting God*, 35.

that Burden that had so heavily oppressed me! The Spirit of Mourning was taken from me, and I knew what it was to truly rejoice in God my Saviour . . .[7]

He could hardly avoid singing psalms, "but my joy gradually became more settled, and . . . God has abode and increased in my Soul (saving a few casual Intermissions) ever since." In later editions of his journal he took out the "I thirst" so as to avoid any messianic pretensions. But we need the water. Thomas Cooper wrote, "I felt my heart hopen [*sic*] within me and like a fountain of water run from it and in that moment I felt such Love, peace and joy . . ."[8]

Charles Wesley says, "I cannot wash my heart . . ." I cannot do it myself. He links what happens in us, as we shall eventually see John does, to the cross and the blood of Christ. It is a yearning application of St. John's (and Old Testament) language and thought, moving through the steps of longing to the realization of impossibility; but the empty jars are filled; feebleness is the starting point for restoration and "renaissance," now, today. "A man must know what it is that he has to receive from God, a knowledge which is at one with the realisation of his own poverty."[9] We have prior knowledge but need the recognition in the encounter for the revelation to be real.[10]

> Father I dare believe
> Thee merciful and true:
> Thou wilt my guilty soul forgive,
> My fallen soul renew.
>
> Come then for Jesu's sake,
> And bid my heart be clean
> An end of all my troubles make,
> An end of all my sin.
>
> I will, through grace, I will,
> I do, return to Thee;
> Take, empty it, O Lord, and fill
> My heart with purity.

7. Quoted in Hindmarsh, *Evangelical Conversion Narrative*, 107, italics added.

8. Quoted in Hindmarsh, *Evangelical Conversion Narrative*, 134.

9. Bultmann, *Gospel*, 180.

10. Bultmann, *Gospel*, 62–65.

For power I feebly pray;
Thy kingdom now restore,
Today, while it is called today,
And I shall sin no more.

I cannot wash my heart,
But by believing Thee,
And waiting for Thy blood to impart,
Thy spotless purity.

While at Thy Cross I lie,
Jesus, the grace bestow,
Now Thy all-cleansing blood apply,
And I am white as snow.[11]

What does it mean to trust? How does Jesus give himself so that we trust, and believe in him and who he is? How will he get into our minds so as to deal with that very element in us which longs to trust and yet does not (the hysteric)[12] and that element in us that finds it hard to trust and avoids it (the schizoid)? Painful yearning transmutes into distrust. Can he draw near one who overcompensates for the need to trust closely by being too intimate (the hysteric)? Can he draw near one who keeps people away (the schizoid)? Can he keep his boundary, his integrity, and yet give himself? Can he cross boundaries, with safety? Can he do this in broad daylight? In this story he crosses the boundaries of gender, of race, of religion, of sexuality, of nationality, and in such a way that true faith encompasses them all and creates a new community of trusting people, the Samaritans.

Do you find it easy to trust? Share experiences of trusting and being let down.

Share experiences of trusting and enjoying a rich relationship.

Which parts of your personality are operating, and which parts of your personal history are operating?

---

11. Charles Wesley, *MHB* 564.

12. "Hysteric" is the position of need for contact and of separation anxiety and "schizoid" is used in this work as the opposite, the avoidance of contact and commitment anxiety. See above in "Introduction 2" under heading 6b, "The Interruption of the Dynamic Cycle."

2. The Setting: The Journey

The scene with Nicodemus was a one-off. It was *sui generis*. Even though the discourse was repetitive, the new birth motif was distinctive, and has lodged itself impressively and uniquely in Christian sensibility. Having shown Jesus' impact in Galilee and Judaea, John now recalls his ministry in Samaria. Chapters 3 and 4 contain "intentionally contrasted episodes."[13] The scene in John 4 is a type scene. His readers will recognize the style of scene from previous literary knowledge. "In John, however, conventional elements are treated unconventionally."[14] Out of this will come truth which is distinctive, and which will be all the more striking for being unexpected. The reader will journey through the scene with the characters and experience the shock of the new with them. Ian Ramsey, in the phrase "mysterious situations whose language cannot be straightforward," points to the shock of a sequence of disclosures conveyed in the language. "Here is a disclosure which has only been evoked when 'thirsty Jew' becomes strange water purveyor, becomes 'prophet', becomes 'Messiah', becomes 'I . . . speaking . . . to you.'"[15] Here is an encounter with the non-Jewish world where the writ of Jesus is also meant to run.

It is a pattern in John that the connection between the thinking, the revelation of each chapter, can be spotted in the formula, "If he deals with so-and-so in this way, how does he deal with so-and-so?" "If he shares himself, gives himself in this way to . . . , how does he share himself, give himself to . . . ?" This provides a clue to the developmental step involved as we pass from one chapter to the next (even allowing for the artificiality of chapters), which answers the question "How does he give himself to us?" with a new piece of information and new insight each time. If he deals with a man in this way, how does he deal with a woman? If with a shy man, how with a forward woman? With named, with anonymous; with depressed, with hysteric; with anti-libidinous, with libidinous? How does he move from a somebody to a nobody with a body? "The Samaritan woman is Nicodemus's mirror opposite."[16] Her sexuality is overt. Jesus draws attention to it. She is known for it (maybe) in her community. Certainly in the mind of the commentators!

13. Neyrey, *Gospel*, 88.

14. Culpepper, *Anatomy*, 136.

15. Ramsey, *Religious Language*, 123–26.

16. Koester, *Symbolism*, 48.

What surfaced in the disciples' minds? The type scene begs the question. Isaac, Jacob, and Moses met their brides at a well; in the case of the first, Abraham's servant prays that the first maiden whom he meets and begs a drink from will be the one![17] Maybe they were suddenly, unexpectedly, very anxious. Is it possible that Jesus can relate to her in such a way as to reveal more of how he gives himself to her, gets into her, penetrates her?

Possibly in the background, as awareness dawns on them as to the significance of this Jesus they are following, they feel echoes of Yahweh's relationship with Israel in Hosea. God first castigates his people for their lewdness and apostasy, but then they change in their relationship to him; in that day you will call me "my husband" (Hos 2:16). Part of the immediate background that we should remember was the strong belief that a woman should have no more than three husbands,[18] and in any case should not talk with a man in public unless is was a close relation, and above all should not discuss theology with him, certainly not with a male Jew.

Chapter 3 starts with what Nicodemus, a man, knows; chapter 4 with what the Lord "knows"—that is, what he "learned" (aorist of *ginosko*)—that Pharisees had heard about his ministry, the prompt for the journey north. The next reference to "knowing" is verse 22, a watershed (a suitable word in this story) in the dialogue, "You worship what you do not know; we worship what we know" (*oida*—have discovered and know; "I am in possession of previously acquired knowledge"[19]). But then *she* becomes the knowing one; "I know that Messiah is coming" (*erchomai*) (4:25). So she and her community are more not-knowing than Nicodemus but have a residual knowledge of the coming Messiah. This is a field ripe for harvest for Jesus. He can work with this when it is through an encounter with her as a person. What a model for ministry!

This geographical shift to Samaria involves a transitional state (4:4). The event is transitional in more ways than one. It is so for Jesus, the disciples, the woman, the Jewish/Samaritan mentality, the early church, and the reader, and it is transitional physically, psychologically, and theologically. Real change occurs. It is not just a pretty picture.

The journey north to Galilee and south to Jerusalem would often avoid the unclean, despised, ignorant, and even dangerous Samaritans.

---

17. Gen 24:10–49; Gen 29:4–14, Exod 2:15–22.

18. Koester, *Symbolism*, 49.

19. Moule, *Idiom-Book*, 16.

Pilgrims going south would cross by the fords of Jordan below Lake Galilee, travel down the east side of the river, and cross back near Jericho and go literally up to Jerusalem and return so. It was far shorter (and quicker; three days according to Josephus) to go north out of Jerusalem past Anathoth (Jeremiah) and Shiloh (Samuel), to journey with several steep climbs up and down through the Judean heights, and then to climb through the hills towards Samaria, with its Herodian temple and amphitheatre and Hellenized buildings. Beyond there, after the foothills, the flat Plain of Esdraelon would give way to the escarpment before Nazareth. A stopping place would be some way before Samaria, the well of Sychar, not far short of modern Nablus. At this deep well, a deep cylinder cut one hundred feet into the rock, Jesus was at the source of his history, of his nation's life, in touch with his ancestors, Jacob and Joseph, who was buried here (Josh 24:32).

He has been traveling through this rather hostile territory, but in the middle of it he finds the source of his own tradition. Jacob was a very ambiguous character, who cheated his brother, sucked up to his mother, deceived his father, wanted life for himself. He got the woman he wanted, stole the household gods from his father-in-law, and yet saw a ladder set up from earth to heaven and communication taking place upon it; and, when quite rich, but needy and fearful, he wrestled with himself/a man/ an angel/God, all night, was reconciled to his brother, and was chosen by God to give his name to the nation. He gave (*didomai*) this plot to his son Joseph, another ambiguous, narcissistic daydreamer, who thought he was at the center of the universe. Yet he too was used by God. There is hope for us all, though limping along! The gift of one flawed character to another is the starting place for a transition.

Can you describe a transition that you have been through? It may be, say, decorating a room in your home, having an operation, losing someone, moving house or church, a shift in faith. How did it feel, and how did you get through, and how did it change you?

3. The Setting: Samaria

Jesus comes (*erchomai*) to a city of Samaria called Sychar, near the field Jacob gave to Joseph, "and a fountain of Jacob was there" (4:5). A bucket is let down on a rope and comes up with fresh water from a running spring. Wearied as he was with his journey, Jesus sat down by this deep man-made well at the crossroads of the north/south ridge (beneath the Mount of Blessing and the Mount of Cursing), and the east/west route from the Jordan Valley to the city of Samaria itself, and on to the west coast. It has been known by Christians since the fourth century. It is watched over by a solitary monk who lifts water in a bucket and gives it to the traveler, in an uncompleted chapel beneath Mount Gerizim, on which the Samaritan remnant still worships. It is a symbolic place. What was in Jesus' mind? A sense of God himself springing up through the ambiguity of human nature, and of how he could convey the experience to arid humanity? He comes to the source of what *was*, and it is converted to what *is*. He sits by the well and knows *he* is the "water." It is in his own depths that the connection will be made between earth and heaven. "Jacob and Jacob's well were pointing to the reality which was the centre of his own self-consciousness, that out of his flesh the spirit was springing, and through his human personality the love of the father was flowing."[20] The gift of one person to him, and of his own person to another would be the catalyst that would transform that other and her community.

Do you have a place which "contains" your history, your heritage, a link with your ancestry, your beginnings? What does it mean to you? How are you affected when you go there and sit and reflect? This kind of question is not just for reminiscence, though that can often be therapeutic, but to enable you to identify your *feeling* in the past, and now in the present, about the experience, and how it affects you.

It was about the sixth hour (noon, we think, according to the Jewish mode; according to the Roman, it could be 6:00 p.m., the time for eating and socializing, hence the quick gathering of the Samaritans and the common sense of staying overnight). The next time John uses the phrase

20. Verney, *Water into Wine*, 55.

"sixth hour" is at 19:14; standing on the pavement before Pilate; Jesus has just been asked about his source, his origins, "Where are you from?" This is immediately prior to the crucifixion, where again he would be alone and fatigued and cry, "I thirst" (*dipso*). Nothing happens by chance in John. It is too well written. The reverberation is intended. The text forces us to think to the end. The hour is not yet, but it is coming, and it is about him giving himself, pouring himself out completely, about emptying himself. [21]

However, in the meantime, "a woman of Samaria comes [*erchomai*] to draw water." There is an ample supply of water here as well as where John is baptizing. Jesus says to her, "Give [*didomain*] me to drink." "One of his pleasures, thirsty,/Was to ask a drink/ at the hot farms . . ."[22] There is an encounter[23] across the bounds of racial and sexual prejudice. Both are alone as individuals. He meets her, not with "Are you saved?," but with a request for her to give him a gift. He reverses the complaint of the people against Moses, their projection onto him, "Give us water to drink" (Exod 17:1–7). He makes himself vulnerable. His first move is to expose his need and his trust of her (4:7). It is a primal need from infancy on!

How do you ask for what you need?

At the end of a very tiring day for both, after the evening meal, a wife says to her husband, "Would you like a coffee?" "Oh, yes," says the husband.

Time passes and no coffee appears. In the Care and Share Group that evening, she is visibly upset. After gentle questions, "He never does anything for me when I need it. I've worked hard as well." Leader, "Did you ask him?" "Yes, certainly." "What did you say?" "Well, I said very clearly, 'Would you like a coffee?'" Leader to him: "How did you hear that?" "I thought she was going to make me one!"

A very moving exchange then followed when, quite hesitantly at first, *she learned to get in touch with her need to be cared for*, to shape her words accurately, and actually to ask unambiguously for what she needed! "I need you to look after me for once."

Try again! How do you ask for what you need?

---

21. Compare Phil 2:7.

22. Thomas, "The Fisherman," in *Selected Poems*, 102.

23. In psychodynamic language the neutral word, a "confrontation."

What do you *feel* about the man needing to read non-verbal signals?

(Be aware the roles may have been reversed for reasons of confidentiality!)

It is the first cry of the child, the babe, "Give me to drink." It is going to be the last cry of Christ on the cross. How strange that he sees in her the symbol of receiving water from the well. She carries none of the purity symbolized by the water. She is struck by that: "What," she says, "you a Jew ask a drink of me a Samaritan woman?" In modern jargon, it's a double whammy. It is the only occasion in the Gospel when Jesus is called a "Jew." The author adds a note: "For Jews have no dealings with"—do not associate with, do not share vessels with, have no sexual intercourse with—"Samaritans" (v. 9).

Some Pharisees were known as "the bruised and bleeding Pharisees" because when they saw a woman they closed their eyes, and walked into the walls and corners of the narrow streets! We should not underestimate the strength of the purity laws. A senior lecturer at a British University did a house exchange with a member of staff from the Hebrew University of Jerusalem. He phoned him just before, saying, "Please treat the house as yours: car in the garage, keys on the hall stand, use anything in the kitchen, pots and pans and so on." The reply was, "Oh! No, that's all right, we shall bring our own." They brought all their own cooking utensils from Israel so that they would not be contaminated by those of a lecturer in Hebrew and Old Testament studies here!

Share a moment when you were given a gift by a woman, or by a man, when you might have thought you would have been the provider. How did it feel?

How did it feel if it was on the level or/and if there was an imbalance, or a flippant, or flirtatious, or erotic element to it? Share the beauty, the tenderness, the risk, the generosity, the ambiguity of that moment.

The offer of new life begins (4:10). "If you knew [*oida*] the gift [*dorea*, acc. *dorean*] of God and who says [*lego*] 'Give me to drink,' you would have asked him and he would have given [*didomain*] you fresh water [*hudor zon*]." No wonder she was confused; the riddle is that "fresh water" has a double meaning. It means "fresh" as opposed to still or stagnant water, but it is also the "living water" that creates and sustains life. To walk in a Greek vineyard to this day and request some grapes, to be given a bunch and then to offer to pay, might well be met with *dorean*. It is a free gift.[24] "Let one who is thirsty come, let one who desires take the water of life [*zoe*] for free" (*dorean*, Rev 22:17) .

How strange that Paul (at least from the Reformation onwards) should be alone linked with the free gift of God. John also is the theologian of the free gift. You say to God, "How much?" and he says, "It is a free gift! If you knew who gives the gift, you would look at me with knowledge as I look at you, and you would see that I am the source, the fountain, the well of the water of life, of *zoe*. You would expose your need to me, trust me as I trusted you. Something would have happened inside you." She, like Nicodemus, is resistant, but willing to go along with it. She is in a relationship with this strange man who offers fresh water. "[I]t seemed fresh water at her thirsty lips to speak without fear to the one person whom she had found receptive."[25]

Share a moment when you were in need and someone else fetched a drink for you. What sense did you have of the value of that moment?

Where and when, in what situation, and from what person in your life do you find living water for yourself?

Living water for your faith?

She is willing to chat, speculate, argue; it is a good point of entry for new insight into the one we wrestle with. The wrestling of one flawed character with her shadow,[26] with a man, with God, in broad daylight is a good turning point. "Sir [*kurios*], you have no pail to draw with and

24. Verney, *Water into Wine*, 55.

25. Dorothea Brooke in Eliot, *Middlemarch*, bk. 4, ch. 37, when she can't speak to her husband, but can to a friend.

26. See chapter 3, footnote 47.

the well is deep. Whence ([*pothen*] do you get that fresh water?" "[T]he question about the *pothen* which is central to the whole of Johannine theology."[27] (At 2:9 the master did not know whence, *pothen*, the water turned into wine had come from.) "Are you greater than our father Jacob?" (4:12). Ironically, the readers know the answer is "Yes." Her tease (if that is what it is) is met with his reassurance. Everyone who drinks of this water, this H2O from the earth, will thirst again, every few hours, but whoever drinks of the water "I shall give" (*ego didomai*) will not thirst "unto the age" (*aion*, ever). As in chapter 3, Jesus has plunged into the metaphorical. But the water which I shall give will become in him a fountain of water springing up, leaping, bubbling up to eternal life (*zoe aionios*). No pail water, no jar water this, but a quality of life which lasts. The transition is from the literal to the meaningful, to the symbol, from the earthy to the heavenly. Then, if only we knew how she said the words in verse 15 requesting the water and never having to fetch water again! If only we knew!

Even the water of the tradition, of their origins, Samaritan and Jew, runs out, like wine at a wedding. Even if the community was then, and now is, sustained here at this well, you will keep coming back for more. There is more, there is an inner spring, welling up. The "I" of Jesus will meet the raw material in her, in ourselves, and will flow through her, through us. The process goes on between the thirsty teacher and the thirsty pupil, both believing in each other. What is drawn out of the woman is a new spirit, for what is drawn out of the one who gives is not words only, but the very spirit of the man, and that water is a new kind of awareness, of consciousness, now and into the new age. From a believer's heart water will also flow and share water afresh (see 7:38).

If she thought she could play ideas with this interesting stranger, she was mistaken. There is a shift into the depths of *her* spirit and *her* history in verse 16. He said to her, "Go and call [*phoneo*] your husband, and come [*erchomai*] here."

I have interpreted her switching off the subject to talk of worship as her avoiding painful personal issues. But that may be my projection, symptomatic of my tendency to avoid the personally awkward. Do I need to learn that that is part of my personality, is the text reading me at this point? Another interpretation is possible. "Since she perceives Christ as a prophet, the woman shifts the dialogue and turns it toward the ultimate

27. Van Tilborg, *Imaginative Love* (page reference lost).

existential issue: God."[28] She asks about a crucial and divisive matter. So I learn that *it may be* that it is my projection that she is deflecting interest from herself. Do I do that? Do I turn from Christ when he comes too close to my person? If I do, then do I thus project my world into hers? Or perhaps not? The learning point is that I need to observe myself and learn who I am from my encounter in the text of John with the woman, and with the woman's Jesus.

What sort of woman do you think she was? Answer that question first, and then the second question.

How much of that answer comes from you, and not from a (supposedly) clear message in the text?

---

4. The Pattern of Jesus' Thought

It will help us to understand John's structure, and thus the impact of his writing, and the intended impact of the encounter, when we realize that there is a common rhetorical pattern in many of the meetings he describes between Jesus and others, both individuals and groups. These patterns are patent in the preceding and succeeding chapters.

One is a *literary* pattern—of *statement, leading to misunderstanding, leading to clarification, leading to response.* John (Jesus) uses this to show how his interlocutors and groups grow, or not, as the case may be, in understanding, in "knowing," in the Johannine language. Jesus makes a statement which is not understood, so he enlarges, explains, interprets,[29] so as to clarify and so as to lead to a climax or enlightenment. This is seen in the dialogue with the Samaritan woman, and with the disciples, but also, for instance, though with more of a struggle, with Nicodemus. It is often double meanings which do not flexibly sink into the consciousness of those with whom he is talking which actually provide the catalyst for developing insight. "But Nicodemus is not in any way enlightened; on

---

28. Fotiou, "Transformation of Existence," 329.

29. Luke 24:37, *hermeneuo*, from which we get the word for the interpretation of text, "hermeneutic."

the contrary, he appears to be utterly obtuse."[30] Need we be that hard on him? Neyrey would like him to have the same strong faith as he has! Is it that we as readers warm more easily to a seductive woman? If that is what she is!

This literary pattern appears in 4:7–15 and again in the discourse with the disciples 4:31–38, with statements respectively at verses 7, 10, and 32; with misunderstandings at verses 9, 11–12, and 33; and with clarification at verses 10, 13–14, and 34–48. The movement turns on double-meaning words, "give," "drink," "water," and "food," so that progression takes place in the woman's response. "[U]nlike night time Nicodemus, who stalled from the start, the noonday woman is successfully catechised and transformed from one 'not in the know' to one who 'knows the gift of God,'" at least so as to ask the question, "Can this be the Christ?" Jesus commends her twice (verses 17 and 18). "Her enlightenment continues."[31] She "sees" (*theoreo*) that Jesus is a prophet.[32] She is both an individual and a representative character where much of the language is intended symbolically.

Share an experience of hearing but not understanding, and then of hearing with an explanation, and then of insight coming—about yourself, or a point of faith or belief.

Share the *feeling* attached to each stage of the process.

Another pattern is *cultural*, that of *challenge and riposte*. One person challenges another with the shape or force of a comment or question. The other responds, even sharply, we may imagine. Neyrey has Jesus challenging Nicodemus (3:3) and the latter's riposte is with his question (3:4). (Or it is possible to see Jesus making a statement and the reply being a challenge, and so on?) We need not agree with Neyrey's judgment that "He ridicules Jesus' teaching by reducing it to literal absurdness." Then a second challenge (3:5), the riposte, is Nicodemus's acquiescence in "not knowing" (3:9). We can actually make this analysis without asserting Nicodemus's "mockery" four times, "obtuseness," "hopelessness" twice,

30. Neyrey, *Gospel*, 78.
31. Neyrey, *Gospel*, 91, 92.
32. Compare 9:17, the blind man.

and "ridicule," none of which are in the New Testament text! Even Jesus is seen to be "utterly dismissive of him"! Was Jesus ever that?[33] We need to be aware, as we draw near to the well woman, how we put our own emotional loading into the text.

The forensic, adversarial style suggested by the phrase "challenge and riposte" is exemplified in the snappy dialogue in modern soaps, and in TV news commentary interviews. In the schoolroom, the office, the home, or in public life it is sadly the modern way, as though aggressiveness leads to truth. Our consolation is that Jesus endured it also. In the Gospel it is most apparent in Jesus' encounter with "the Jews."[34] Here in chapter 4 the pattern is clear, but we may choose to hesitate from making it so cut and thrust. Either Jesus makes a challenge at verse 7 and the woman makes a riposte (verse 9), or Jesus makes a claim and she challenges him, and so on, alternating. We do need to note that each exchange *can* in fact be read with a gentle intonation and a mild judgment by the reader! John (Jesus) uses the style to convey the journey of faith and knowledge. In this way, Jesus gets himself into us.

> When you are confronted, how do you react and what happens to you?
>   When you have to confront, how do you manage? And how do you feel? Do you collapse inwardly, or become assertive? Are you able to be both kind and firm?

An overall pattern reflecting social and *rhetorical* practice of the time is stronger still and also pervades the Gospel. Here the words are *praise or encomium*, and *blame or vituperation*.[35] The words positively applaud one's own group or position, and negatively summarize the view one group has of another. They reflect perceived or projected divisions in society, and the rhetorical practice of praise of one's own, say, in a funeral oration, and on the other hand the demonizing of the enemy. We see in the Gospel a genre which uses the attacks on Jesus and the distinctive Johannine view of him to elevate his status and prove who he is. "We are then interpreting the Fourth Gospel accurately as the ancients would

33. Neyrey, *Gospel*, 79.

34. In chapters 7 and 8, "the Jews" being the temple authorities and the Pharisees.

35. Neyrey, *Gospel of John in Cultural and Rhetorical Perspective*, 3–28.

have heard it."[36] John is writing in praise of Jesus, an encomium as understood, reassuring for insiders, but fully aware of the vituperation heaped on him from outsiders. Negatively, he came from Galilee—can any good come out of Nazareth? He is of an ordinary family with no schooling; a deceiver, lawbreaker, and blasphemer; and deserving of death. Positively, he comes from his heavenly Father and abides in him; he is uniquely a son; taught by the Holy Spirit; and called a rabbi; courageous, loyal, and true; greater than Moses and Jacob. He died for love and truth, a shepherd who lays down his life, his *psyche*, for the sheep, and this is the ultimate paradox, giving the lie to all human judgment; his death was glorious and was not the end. Just so have the Johannine community and later Christians been reassured and confirmed in their faith.

When you are being praised, can you hear it and avoid being shy, bashful, regressive, dismissive, embarrassed? Feelings? Share your answer to all the questions.

When you suffer vituperation, can you hear it without imploding, projecting back, swallowing the judgment, or hating the speaker? Feelings?

What happens to you and how do you handle it when people criticize the church, or scorn the faith, or swear by God or Jesus?

What would be your simple word of praise for Jesus? Start your sentence, "For me you are . . ." Write or share.

5. Our View of a "Shady Lady"

This section addresses the issue of how we as readers "see" the woman. Here is a window of interpretation which importantly leads to the way the text helps us to see ourselves. We do not necessarily set out to interpret texts in a particular way, and thus it is imperative that we face the implications of our own judgments. Our interpretations reflect who we are and what we want. This is a "readerly" approach where we focus on our "reader response" and then understand it from a psychodynamic point

---

36. Neyrey, *Gospel of John in Cultural and Rhetorical Perspective*, 27.

of view. If we want the text to read us, then we need the courage for, and openness to, self-reflection. It is our projections that speak for us; they vividly speak for who we are, and knowing who we are is a work of grace. God is in both the cerebral and affective response we make to his word!

So proposers of models and interpreters of text show themselves in their writing, as we do in ours! A simple illustration compares Melanie Klein with Donald Winnicott. Klein had a bitter early experience of life and wrote into her writing the astringency of the paranoid-schizoid position and projected it onto her clients. "Her life of loss and turmoil, is reflected in the grim picture she paints of her special area: the early months of infancy . . ."[37] Winnicott was brought up in a secure Methodist home with good-enough mothering and fathering and kind people around him, and wrote this kindness into his theorizing and his practice. This does not mean necessarily that either of their theories is right or wrong; each has to be evaluated, as does happen, over many years, and with many perceptions of their worth. All authors write themselves into their text.

Bultmann seems to have an instinct for understanding the hysteric experience, but is he not judgmental of the woman? How does he know these things about her? "Man is made aware of the unrest in his life, which drives him from one supposed satisfaction to another, never letting him attain the final fulfilment until he finds the water of life, of which 'one drink for ever stills the thirst.'" The water which we drink once and which satisfies our need forever is an intensely attractive object, but when we step back we know it to be an illusion, and that we have the insight and strength to be "dis-illusioned" (Winnicott). Just maybe she is wise enough to know the irony in what she is saying. She had a good relationship with Jesus. He had already got through to her. Then Bultmann adds, "This unrest is portrayed by the woman's disturbed past and her unsatisfied present state. Perhaps one may go so far as to say that the married life of the woman 'who reels from desire to pleasure' portrays not only the unrest, but the aberrations of the desire for life."[38] How does he know that that is what she is like? It is only the process of reflecting on *our* response and perception that allows *us* to gain insight.

---

37. Gomez, *Introduction*, 29.
38. Bultmann, *Gospel*, 188.

Will you share any way in which you are aware that you "reel from desire to pleasure," or would like to, and the sense of lack of fulfillment in it?

As you share, you will be heard and not judged.

To be realistic, what we must also say is that it is not the case that "one drink forever stills the thirst." Living with the hysteric need for acceptance and satisfaction is a lifelong process, however much conversion, or continuous drinking of the life of Jesus, gives satisfaction and assuages the pain of separation anxiety. Ultimately the process of sanctification is a process, however much the one-off drink satisfies us and does profoundly change us. We, like Luther's church, are "always needing to be reformed."

Share something of your own hysteric need for attention, for avoiding separation from others, for intimacy, for having to manipulate others, and the struggle not to manipulate others.

Try and own yourself in these dimensions.

A more balanced assessment is suggested by S. M. Schneiders, who asserts that the woman's "irregular marital situation" has been focused on by exegetes and preachers, but they have written "very little of the clear indication of her apostleship, and virtually nothing of her role against the implicit disapproval of the male members of the community."[39] Commentators "either idealize her as a bride or they condemn her as a whore."[40] Some commentators are quite restrained in describing her, or avoid it altogether. "Not many readers of the story will dare say that all manner of attraction between the man and the woman is absent." "The Samaritan woman is a loving woman."[41] "She had had a tough life, not a tawdry one." As for the sixth man, "We just do not know. The only ones who do know are Jesus and the woman, and such knowledge produces recognition and

39. In Stibbe, *Gospel*, 134.
40. Stibbe, *John* (Readings), 69.
41. Van Tilborg, *Imaginative Love*, 183, 188, though "love" is not defined.

insight, not repentance and incrimination."[42] With a cultural reference, Neyrey asks, "How are we to think about this woman?" [43] The answer, in cultural terms of the day, is Gentile, unclean, sinner, female.

So how have *we* thought about her? For instance, "Are the different readings of John 4 merely reflections of the gender of the commentators?"[44]

5a.

How do some of the projections show negatively? This story certainly excites us!

Projection makes her the woman we need, or desire, or reject. The negative judgment on her is ancient, even in the Greek fathers, and even if followed by a more benign view of her. Chrysostom: "See how he constructs the woman's faith. See how little by little he raises her soul onto heavens [*sic*], without being embarrassed because she is a prostitute but serving her salvation." And then she is the first missionary, and "proclaimed the Christ before his passion and resurrection." She is beatified by the church with the name Fotini, Greek for "Enlightened."[45]

Here is a list of examples of the views held:

- Zahn: "immoral life, which has exhibited profligacy and unbridled passions for a long time."[46]

- Hoskyns: she is "outraged" because it was Jacob who gave the running water; "the disorders of her domestic life are laid bare"; "necessary that Jesus should lay bare the woman's sin"; and he "laid bare her conduct" ("bare"—quite a metaphor!) (and the natural question is, where to go for forgiveness—to which high place?).[47]

42. Spencer in Green, *Hearing the New Testament*, 310.

43. Neyrey, *Gospel of John in Cultural and Rhetorical Perspective*, 164.

44. Neyrey, *Gospel of John in Cultural and Rhetorical Perspective*, 144.

45. Fotiou, "Transformation of Existence," 329–31. Fotini—linked to *phos*, light.

46. Zahn, 1921, cited in Moore, *Bible in Theory*, 85.

47. Hoskyns, *Fourth Gospel*, 242.

- Brown: "markedly immoral" and a doer of "evil deeds."[48]

- Schnackenburg: "wayward."[49]

- Dodd: "loose . . . living."[50]

- Olsson: "of low morals."[51]

- Culpepper: "she has a shameful past."[52]

- Duke: "five times loser . . . currently committed to an illicit affair."[53]

- Beasley-Murray: "immoral life."[54]

- Eslinger: "coquettish," "coy," "lascivious," "brazen," "carnal." She makes "sexual advances" to Jesus.[55]

- Okure: "quarrelsome and annoying," "telling the truth, but with her tongue in her cheek, because she wants to get rid of Jesus."[56]

- Staley: "exposed her bawdy past."[57]

The woman is presented "realistically" and shows "indignation" and "sarcasm," and the Greek text is even added to—"you haven't *even brought* a pitcher," "pragmatic celerity," "garrulousnesss," "reluctant and laconic confession"—and yet she comes to represent "the true disciple."[58] Jean Vanier calls her a "broken" woman—thirteen times! She "feels rejected and ashamed." "She responds with vivacity"—not flat, nervous, ashamed, curious, searching, but vivacious—"her usual vivacity." She is "fragile," has a "negative self-image," "lost all trust in her own goodness." "In trusting her, [Jesus] uplifts her and gives her back her self esteem." (There is no suggestion that there is a sexual connotation to "he uplifts her," but we need to be aware!) She is "wounded"; "Such people who are already ashamed of themselves"; "poverty and feelings of guilt"; "lonely

48. Brown, *Gospel*, 1:171, 177.

49. Schnackenburg, *Gospel*, 433.

50. Dodd, *Interpretation*, 313.

51. Olsson, cited in Moore, *Bible in Theory*, 85.

52. Culpepper, *Anatomy*, 136.

53. Duke, 1985, cited in Moore, *Bible in Theory*, 85.

54. Beasley-Murray, *John*, 61.

55. Eslinger, "Wooing of the Woman," 171, 172–78.

56. Okure, 1988, cited in Moore, *Bible in Theory*, 85.

57. Staley, 1988, cited in Moore, *Bible in Theory*, 85.

58. Stibbe, *John* (Readings), 66–67.

and guilty"; "anguish"; "the most broken and lonely of women . . . banished." The wonder is that "It is he, the Broken One, who will awaken us in love and give us new life."[59] Neyrey speaks of her "lack of sexual exclusivity i.e., her shamelessness"; "no maiden, but a sexually seasoned woman." (This is partly a description of her status as lacking "honor.")[60]

For Marsh, "the woman's individual matrimonial maladjustment" is not dealt with because she is a symbol of the poverty of Samaritan religion.[61] The central question is whether the words in verse 18 should be taken literally (as most of the mainline commentators do) or figuratively—the infidelity of Samaria. Many of the commentators simply assume that the Samaritans also had the rule of not having more than three husbands, which may not have been the case.[62]

How do they know all these things, all differing, but with a common pattern of condemnation? What a catalogue of speculation!

What are you *feeling* as you hear these comments?

5b.

We may add perceptions about her attitude.

- "She raises a surprising and mocking question to Jesus."[63]
- Giblin says she "mockingly asks for the lasting eternal water" and is "humouring Jesus with a tinge of sarcasm"; "she is not asking *seriously* for the kind of water he has been talking about" (original italics). "The reader should readily perceive that there is no communication here on the level of religious dialogue." (Did John write all this for us to think that?) Jesus "pretends" that her "apparent request is genuine." "Jesus' ploy in probing for a moral nerve . . ."

---

59. Vanier, *Drawn into the Mystery*, 89–100.

60. Neyrey, *Gospel of John in Cultural and Rhetorical Perspective*, 156.

61. Marsh, *Saint John*, 214.

62. For the importance of the Samaritan context, see Maccini, "Reassessment of the Woman at the Well."

63. Moloney, *Belief in the Word*, 135.

(Did Jesus ever behave like that?) "[S]he is not married and never was, her 'confession' implies a moral confession about this stranger's prophetic knowledge and rebuke concerning a sinful way of life" (Did Jesus "rebuke" her?)[64]

- Beasley-Murray: "The woman's misunderstanding becomes crass."[65]

- Dodd sees the rejoinder "Sir give me this water" as "evidently intended to indicate a cross inability to penetrate below the surface meaning."[66]

- But the issue of the statement at verse 18 is whether it is a simple statement of fact or a suggestion of Jesus' power to know people, which Maloney and Barrett call "supernatural."[67] Surely the whole of his life was supernatural, and natural also! The woman is affected; having called Jesus an "insulting name" ("Jew"), she now changes to "Sir."[68]

- Eslinger has pushed the boundaries of interpretation. "The reader's recognition of the double entendres, all of which have sexual overtones leads to the belief that both characters are engaging in a bit of verbal coquetry." "[H]e, as the Word become flesh, responds to her coquetry with a sexually suggestive offer of his own 'living water.'" The woman digresses "in a last ditch attempt to maintain her respectability, which Jesus has not shown the slightest concern to attack."[69]

- Scott asserts that she moves from no faith to incomplete faith; she has opened herself up to Jesus' "Wisdom." She is the recipient of revelation, having started with a "shady background" and as a "shady lady."[70]

- Koester: "At best her story is tragic, at worst it is sinful."[71]

How do they know all these things?

---

64. Giblin, "What Was Everything He Told Her She Did?," 148–52.

65. Beasley-Murray, *John*, 61.

66. Dodd, *Interpretation*, 313.

67. Maloney, *Belief in the Word*, 148; and Barrett, *Gospel*, 235.

68. Maloney, *Belief in the Word*, 139.

69. Eslinger, "Wooing of the Woman at the Well," 169, 176, 179.

70. Scott, *Sophia* (page reference lost).

71. Koester, *Symbolism*, 49.

5c.

There are more moderate opinions; for instance, the transition from a focus on herself to talking about worship "is not an attempt to steer Jesus' questioning away from her personal secrets."[72] It simply raises the age-old debate between Samaritans and Jews.

But even when the voices are moderate, the interesting question still is, "How can writers vary so substantially in their perceptions of the same text?" "All the writers whose work is assessed here are responding to the same text . . . Yet each has his or her own point of view . . ." If one or two have "blinkered vision," "how are we to account for the remarkable divergences of the rest?"[73] "Tiny differences in perception may have great consequences."[74] The puzzle is not just over what sort of a woman she is, and in particular is not just over whether verse 18 is meant literally or figuratively. How can so many readers read, into the words of a neutral text, an *intonation*, and thus read into it a prejudicial view in the case of the woman, and sometimes even in the case of Jesus? How can they put meaning into the characters' mouths and minds? It is quite extraordinary, but unfortunately all too common. No! Fortunately, the double meaning and hidden depths of the text, with its "purposeful ambivalence"[75] and "two-world" approach, is bound to stretch us; *hence we need to understand at depth our own reactions to it.* While dedicating the highest brains to it, we still must let it mirror who we are. It is worthy of that! Our sexualizing of this story, for instance, indicates our own needs, but there is also salvation in it!

In the wider picture, "John" has been regarded as a Pauline, a philosopher, a mystic, as Gnostic, as poetic, as "spiritual," as Greek, and latterly to more general acceptance now, as Jewish. In the more focused experience of each piece of text, we must realize that we put a diverse construction on things which spring out of our own personalities.

How do you see her now?
    Has your awareness of your own interpretation changed?

---

72. Moloney, *Belief in the Word*, 148.

73. Ashton, "John and the Johannine Literature," 259.

74. Ashton, "John and the Johannine Literature," 263.

75. Ashton, "John and the Johannine Literature," 261.

We started this chapter with a simple question. If Jesus was brusque with a good woman, his mother, how will he deal with a bad woman? We are redeemed in a very mixed up world! It will help to look at how the text "reads" us.

6. How the Text Reads Us

What motivates us to make such dogmatic assertions about the woman? Why the need to be so judgmental? Whoever we are, we will recognize that each one of us does in fact respond, even in the microcosm of reading one small part of the text! Verney writes clearly from personal experience and wants an integration of flesh and spirit, for them not to pull in opposite directions. "[G]radually John's Gospel, and especially this conversation with the woman of Samaria, began to open up an answer." In what is the first occurrence of "I am," "Jesus is affirming both sexuality and spirituality . . . he is offering to give us back the wholeness of flesh and Spirit which we long for and have lost."[76] The disciples wondered or marveled that Jesus was speaking to a woman; "they were shocked."[77] We may well be "shocked" at our own judgmentalism. We are made conscious of the risk of taking sides, for or against the woman, in our hasty reading of the text!

Have you been read wrongly? Have you been conscious of being marginalized and even ignored in a conversation and left out of speaking in public, or seen as an object, not as a person? Feelings and impact on your ongoing sense of worth?

One of the psychodynamic connections that we may make to bring the impact of this chapter home and make it practical is that the existential encounter with Christ involves knowledge of oneself, self-awareness. To know God is to know the self and, coexistent with that, to know the self means to know God. Some commentators make the connection. "His meeting with the Samaritan woman is, at the simplest, a story about

76. Verney, *Water into Wine*, 53–54.
77. Brown, *Gospel*, 1:167.

moving from ignorance to disturbing self-knowledge."[78] Her process has been likened to Jung's process of "individuation."[79] She "progresses from appearance to reality and from falsehood to truth."[80] We may have a "stubborn refusal to make a biblical text say more than its author meant it to say," according to Brown.[81] But we do just that! Even Brown asserts (in the context of whether the story has historical plausibility), "if we analyse the repartee at the well, we find quite true-to-life the characterization of the woman as mincing and coy, with a certain light grace . . ."

How does he know that that is what she is like? Because he has that woman in his head, his ideal woman, his desired woman, whom he spurns, but to whom he is attracted, whom he must reject. He is in good company! We all have an ideal woman, or man, in our heads. John Milton, in the opening scene in Paradise, visualizes Adam and Eve:

> Two of far nobler shape erect and tall,
> God-like erect . . . though both
> Not equal, as their sex not equal, seemed;
> For contemplation he and valour formed,
> For softness she and sweet attractive grace;

Even after three marriages, he still has his ideal woman in his head:

> She as a veil down to the slender waist
> Her unadorned golden tresses wore
> Dishevelled, but in wanton ringlets waved,
> As the vine curls her tendrils, which implied
> Subjection, but required with gentle sway,
> And by her yielded, by him best received,
> Yielded with coy submission, modest pride,
> And sweet reluctant, amorous, delay.[82]

---

78. Grayson, *Gospel*, 40.

79. "Individuation" is not a state of being, but a life-long process of *becoming*; of becoming oneself, becoming who one really is and wants to be. It involves recognizing the parts of ourselves which initially we repudiate, and then finding a way of using them to become more our true self. We develop a personality that is more whole, less fractured, less self-sabotaging. It is not an easy process. We need to withdraw our projections onto others, to reconcile our unconscious with our consciousness. We move toward self-acceptance, and having an image of self with less self-deception. In theological terms, it is "sanctification" and is the work of the Spirit of Jesus.

80. Ashton, "John and the Johannine Literature," 265.

81. Brown, *Gospel*, 1:vi.

82. Milton, *Paradise Lost*, bk. 4.

What a mixture of chauvinism, decency, dream, and desire!

Brown also sees that the key characters in chapters 3, 4, 5, and 9[83] "are—to a certain extent—foils used by the evangelist to permit Jesus to unfold his revelation."[84] They certainly act as foils to unfold us to ourselves so that we may receive the revelation about ourselves in the light of how Jesus deals with each one. The point is that, firstly, the text is open to interpretation, and, secondly, the only way to monitor our interpretive judgments is to be self-aware. We are going to do the one and we have to do the other, and share our judgments with our brothers and sisters in Christ.

Share boldly an attempt to describe your ideal woman. (We can do this as men or women. Then when that is done, we can move to the next prompt.)

Share boldly an attempt to describe your ideal man.

Stephen Moore emphasizes the need, the desire of Jesus that the Samaritan woman should desire what he has to offer. Along with the psychological approach, there is a feminist one as well arguing against a literalist reading of verse 18,[85] and, while feminist critics use exactly the same *methods* of reading as non-feminist critics, they may inject different judgments and thus avoid the negative judgments of her character made by some others. Could, for instance, the number simply be a symbol of the woman's great need? Moore cites commentators' words: "profligacy and unbridled passions," "a tramp," "an illicit affair," "bawdy past," "immoral life." He reflects that commentators who readily accept the figurative meaning of "fresh water" take the five husbands plus one other literally, rather than as a suggestion that she was hitched to the five gods of the Samaritans. Thus the text "turns the tables on the critics."[86] By this we mean that, in trying to interpret the story, we perform in the same way as characters within it! "The reader not only reads about, but

---

83. Nicodemus, the woman at the well, the ill man by the pool, and the man born blind.

84. Brown, *Gospel*, 1:175–76.

85. Five husbands, and the sixth is not!

86. Moore, "Are There Impurities," 85–86.

undergoes, the experience of misunderstanding Jesus."[87] In psychodynamic terms, it is a form of projective identification, in that we ingest the
emotion or affect of those taking part in the event. We do this with both
fact and fiction.

From a literary point of view, Felman has expressed the feature
crisply.

> The scene of the critical debate is thus a *repetition* of the scene
> dramatised in the text. The critical interpretation, in other
> words, not only elucidates the text but also reproduces it dra-
> matically, unwittingly *participates in it*. Through its very read-
> ing, the text, so to speak, acts itself out. As a reading effect, this
> inadvertent "acting out" is indeed uncanny: whichever way the
> reader turns, he can but be turned by the text, he can but *per-
> form* it by *repeating* it.[88]

Again, in discussing the conflict of interpretations, she writes,
"Reading here becomes not the cognitive observation of the text's plu-
ralistic meaning, but its 'acting out'. Indeed it is not so much the critic
who comprehends the text, as the text which comprehends the critic."
She quotes Barthes, "irony is what is immediately given to the critic: not
to see the truth, but . . . to be it."[89] In John's terms, "seeing" the truth is
also a reality that includes *being* it. If we let the text "dwell on us" as well
as giving ourselves time to dwell on the text, we may drink the water of
life frequently.

Just as the characters in the Gospel who meet Jesus, including the
disciples, have to wrestle with the structure of pairs of literal and figurative meanings, so do the readers. These binary complementary comparisons abound: light/dark, knowing/not knowing, spirit/flesh, heavenly/
earthly, birth/rebirth—Nicodemus could not quite manage the leap to
the metaphorical. Here commentators have managed to see water/water
and food/food as having double meanings, so the irony has been un-
packed and significance perceived. But not when it comes to verse 18;
husband/five husbands has been taken literally, and the superiority of the
male observers over the "immoral woman" sustained.[90]

---

87. Vanhoozer, in Green, ed., *Hearing the New Testament*, 278.

88. Felman, *Literature and Psychoanalysis*, 101, italics original.

89. Felman, *Literature and Psychoanalysis*, 115.

90. See 7:53—8:11, The woman taken in adultery.

The moment of disclosure comes, in the Gospel, when the inter-locutor realizes that half of a pair is to be understood figuratively. Maybe the woman did, and in verse 15b she is not so stupid as she is made out to be, and begins to sense there is more here than meets the eye; she grasps the irony. The reader has the same task exactly.

A positive view is that "she sheds her 'public sauciness' and is wel-comed into Jesus' private world." She does not have a formal role but "she functions as a mediating figure in spreading the news about Jesus to the Samaritans."[91] The outsider becomes an insider and what she now knows is in the core of her being and therefore able to be shared. She becomes in a positive way part of the "gossip network" around Jesus, no longer a marginal person. Those who hear her ask Jesus to stay (*meno*) with them—John's word, which conveys more than just staying the night. In like manner, we "stay" with Jesus and he "stays" with us.

What have you learnt about yourself as you read this story?

Can you share an experience of discrimination? What was the pain? How then did you try to relate to the person or group who discrimi-nated against you?

7. An Integration

In the light of all these reading of her, we need to go back to Verney's desire for an integration of lust and love, of desire and desire satisfied, of flesh and spirit. It is possible! "They trembled as their lips / Welded holy and carnal in one flame."[92] The difficulty in even using such words in that way is that they appear as binary opposites, when what we want and need is for them to be complementary, "wedded" together, integrated, part of our human relating; that is what is intended for us. If we interpret

91. Nerey, *Gospel of John in Cultural and Rhetorical Perspective*, 170–71.
92. Brown, "Port of Venus," in *Collected Poems*, 22.

narratives either with our own erotic desire or with our own withdrawal
from a sensuous world, this story can help us!

7a.

R. S. Thomas is well aware of the fact that Christians share the same ener-
gies as everyone, even in church. In "Chapel Deacon"[93] he asks, "Who
put that crease in you soul, Davies . . . ?" How can you be two people at
the same time? "Who taught you to pray / And scheme at once, your eyes
turning / Skywards, while your swift mind weighs your heifer's chances in
the next town's / fair on Thursday?"[94] And then the poet asks, "Are your
heart's coals / Kindled for God, or is the burning / Of your lean cheeks
because you sit / Too near that girl's smouldering gaze?" "Who taught you
your deft poise?" But that is how we all live, balancing the "the pull" in
all directions. Not one dimension can be eradicated; it is about synthesis.

Thomas's poem "The Woman"[95] is enigmatic and we could read it
either way: either that God wipes his hands of the physical, or that he
is intimately concerned with our sexuality, and that our living with it is
shared by the pain Christ feels for the human condition. It is a commentary on the Adam and Eve story. "So beautiful—God himself quailed /
At her approach; the long body curved / Like the horizon. Why had he
made / Her so?" She leans towards him and suggests a compromise (. . .
ing situation). "How would it be . . . if instead of / Quarrelling over it,
we divided it / Between us?" God gets the credit for "its invention" but
leaves "the ordering of it" to her. "He looked into her / eyes"—the contact
between every man and every woman, especially with mother—"and saw
far down the bones / Of the generations that would navigate / By those
great stars"—the ability to create, in response to a certain look—"but the
pull of it / Was too much." So the compromise, "Yes, he thought, give
me their minds' / Tribute, and what they do with their bodies is not my
concern." But this dualism, it is suggested, is ameliorated by the suffering
of Christ, his identity with us, costly for God. "He put his hand in his
side / and drew out the thorn for the letting / of the ordained blood and
touched her with / it." In R. S. Thomas the common reference is to the
crown of thorns, and here to the piercing of the side of Jesus (a powerful

93. In Thomas, *Collected Poems*, 76.
94. Shades of Burns's poem "Holy Willie's Prayer!"
95. In Thomas, *Collected Poems*, 330.

image in John 19:34; 20:20, 25, 27). Then, not a threat if we detach ourselves from the creation myth,[96] "Go, he said. They shall come to you for
ever / with their desire, and you shall bleed for them in return." That, in
general, is how things are! But have we a rapprochement here?

We are not equating this (mind for God and body for human) with
the difference between "flesh" and "spirit"; the former, at least in St. Paul,
is meant to indicate, not the body or our dwelling in the body, but the
corruption of bodily desire and practice. The things of the "spirit" include
the right use of the body; bodily desires are integrated or synthesized. So
Jesus, not an unfeeling person, could encounter this woman, remain in
his own maturity, and draw hers out of her.

Three insights are helpful here.

i. The psychodynamic concept which helps is *transference*, and its cor-
    ollary, *countertransference*: the attraction or dislike, mild or moder-
    ate, we feel to those helping us or to those in a role of power or
    leadership; and the feeling, positive or negative, the helper or leader
    has to the person being helped. The engine of transference is projec-
    tion. The happening in us of transference or countertransference is
    quite "normal."[97] "The phenomena of transference are all around
    us."[98] What matters is that we are aware of what is happening, to
    cease treating someone as if they were someone else, for instance a
    parent of long ago, and not to act out our fantasies of how wonderful
    or how horrible they are. The shady memories, often in our uncon-
    scious, may start even before we have words to express them, so that
    the lovers in an affair, say, often feel that here is the answer to all
    needs, the one who has always been waited for, the perfect antidote
    to all doubt and emptiness. "The transference-countertransference
    field carries the agony that words cannot capture because injury
    occurred before words did."[99] Hence the loving couple are able to
    gaze wordlessly into each other's eyes. No wonder the disciples were
    scared! We need to withdraw our projections, even from God and
    Jesus, and certainly from fellow human beings.

96. Gen 3:10–19.

97. See above in "Introduction 2: Understanding People," under heading 7, "The
Need for a Model or Models."

98. Hinksman in Lynch, *Clinical Counselling*, 95.

99. Ulanov, *Finding Space*, 69.

Identify and share a time when you felt immensely attracted to someone, knowing that you were transferring old needs onto a new person.

Identify and share a time when as a helper you felt attraction
to a person you were helping, and you knew the need to keep your
boundary and not to act out your feeling.

Identify and share a time when you felt very negative toward
someone, knowing that you were transferring old needs onto a new
person.

Identify and share a time when as a helper you felt very negative
toward a person you were helping, and you knew the need to keep
your boundary and not to act out your feeling.

ii. We need to recognize (with Klein, for example) that antagonism and
aggression to mother are common features of the attitude of a baby
to its mother. This is present even when we have had "good-enough
mothering" (Winnicott). Such an attitude, often strong enough to
be called "hatred," is recapitulated also as a feature of toddlers, and
teenagers, and people in a "mid-life crisis." We recapitulate earlier
moods and attitudes throughout life. We do this into adult life and
part of our growth process has to be a reconciliation of the tensions
in our relationship even to those we love. Primal dislike of "woman"
is transferred into current relationships. But we know instinctively
that such attitudes are shameful, and even unwise—mother gives us
her supplies or we die—so they are suppressed, repressed, and then
projected out onto a woman later in life. We need a "bad" woman
to condemn (see 7:53—8:12). Rather than recognize this bitterness
in our own lives, we project it out onto another target, whom at the
worst we will try to discredit or even destroy. Hence the deluge of
disapprobation directed against the woman at the well. Archetypal
feelings are very strong.

Share honestly memories you have of dislike of your mother or mother figure early in life, or as a teenager, or now. Allow others to express empathy towards you.

If you think you have nonesuch, share any negative feelings you have of your home situation, then or now.

We have used the word "object" of that idea, that notion, that we have inside us corresponding in part to a real "object" or person outside us. This sphere of understanding is called Object Relations.[100] It focuses always on the centrality of relationship between people and inside people. Here we focus on the relationship between Jesus and the woman, and that makes us aware of the tensions within her, of her conflicting "objects" within. Is this man to be trusted or isn't he? Somehow he has got through her defenses and put her in touch with herself. She is pulled both ways. "Relationship is conceived not as an easy process, but as an ambivalent expression of both our incompleteness and our autonomy. We are drawn by our need for affiliation to connect with others in the elusive shared phenomenon we call rapport, while the equal imperative to preserve our individuality fosters distance, conflict and estrangement."[101]

Share your perception that the idea of a person you have inside you is not necessarily an accurate picture of the person.

Share an experience you have of meeting another person and feeling an oscillation between both attraction and rejection.

iii. A further insight or model that helps us to realize the power of aggression to the "woman" is based paradoxically on the realization that she is attractive to us. This reflects Freud's "Oedipal complex." It is a very useful insight, for instance, in observing the closeness of a boy teenager to his mother and aggression toward or avoidance of

100. See footnote 36 in "Introduction 1."
101. Gomez, *Introduction*, 200.

or dislike of father. The child wants to "seduce" mother and "kill" father. In *Oedipus* this happened literally. But it is not nice to want these things! So we suppress the shame of lust for mother; she ceases, has to cease, to be a sexual object. Hence Nicodemus's withdrawal. So the teenager gets exceedingly angry with her and "rejects" her! But the strong desire surfaces later, either properly in a loving sexual relationship or as a projection onto a desired object, and, of course, in both together. Hence the overwhelming view of the commentators of what this woman at the well is like! And in order not to fall for her we distance her by spurning and condemning *her*. It is *our own* growth that is needed.

Jesus had integrated in himself anything that was in him of these attitudes, and so could keep a level relationship with her. Lord, let me be like you! This discussion raises very fascinating psychodynamic questions about his humanity. He really was one of us?[102] We need also to note that the presence of an erotic element is present in many relationships along with genuine love, closeness, and respect, and is not necessarily bad. So maybe he was attracted to her; he was a man after all! But he was such a full, mature man that he could hold all the elements of human relating together. Mutual attraction is permissible and enjoyable; it is what we do with it that is critical!

Share memories of attraction to your mother or mother figure which you were just conscious of rejecting.

7b.

We also need an awareness of what the attractive woman is feeling. In *Adam Bede*, the open-minded (and we would now say, "ecumenical") rector, Mr. Irwine, genuinely wants to find out what motivates the Methodist preacher, Dinah Morris. He asks in a kindly and searching way questions about her conviction. "And you never feel any embarrassment from the

---

102. This is a crucial theological question and these christological issues underlie much of this writing.

sense of your youth—that you are a lovely young woman on whom men's eyes are fixed?"[103] She replies a shade naively that she doesn't think people take notice of that and the rough miners treat her with great respect. Adam Bede thinks she is "over-speritial [sic]"; later she weeps over her physical desire for him, and they marry. She moved in that direction, the well woman in the opposite way! Both make their witness to the presence of Jesus! "When beauty of form and of soul truly come together in a single figure such as Dinah Morris . . . we behold something very special."[104] This is George Eliot's deep conviction.

In *The Mill on the Floss*, Maggie, spirited, beloved daughter of the miller, oscillates between guilty renunciation and seeking satisfaction. Philip, who loves her genuinely, remarks "that every rational satisfaction of your nature that you deny now, will assault you like a savage appetite."[105] She had to learn that a denial of egoism does not require a denial of selfhood. But she was severely tested. Eliot leads her on a balancing act between "passion" (for the attractive Stephen) and duty (to all she has learned and deeply values in her home life). She wrestles with longing and obligation, as George Eliot did in her own life and thought. She translated Spinoza just before writing her main novels and his categories are traceable in hers.[106]

In John 4 we have focused on the relationship between Jesus and a woman, and between ourselves and the woman, and we have seen how we can write in our own script without checking it against the text or against our own psyche, and without balancing our own reactions even to the commentators! Jesus held the balance. That is his gift to us. We may have our attractions and can hold them in the tension between our desire and what we may not have. If we can't, they often end in tragedy. The community of the church has many such strong feelings. For instance, Phyllis Mack, in a very balanced way gets under the surface of early Methodism, from a historical aspect, in chapters on "Men of Feeling: Natural and Spiritual Affection in the Lives of the Preachers" and "Women in Love: Eros and Piety in the Minds of Methodist Women."[107] Frank Lake has a realistic chapter examining "Infatuation and the Divine."[108]

103. Eliot, *Adam Bede*, 136.

104. Hodgson, *Theology*, 50.

105. Hodgson, *Theology*, 72.

106. Hodgson, *Theology*, 11–12.

107. Mack, *Heart Religion*, 83–170.

108. Lake, *Tight Corners*, 162–71. See Ulanov, *Healing Imagination*, ch. 5, "The

The disaster is in the illusion that the beloved object carries a divine presence. The task for the individual who is illicitly in love is to honor "the God bit" but to advance no further towards a supposed fulfillment. This requires great honesty, and huge integrity in the sense of being brave enough to explore all the antecedents of why *this person* becomes the beloved, and to withdraw the projections which skew the relationship into something it is not meant to be. It needs the "intentionality" (Rollo May) to live with gratitude, mutual respect, and honor afterwards. Jesus stayed on the level with the woman at the well and she was transformed and could live with herself afterwards, as did Mary Magdalene, and Thomas and Peter, and so can each one of us. We need to interpret what the idealized image consists of, which for the time being rests in the (m)other. Finding the true self is hard work but it is the work of the Spirit of Jesus. It is being able to say, or to hear the message, though full of pain, "Do not touch me" (20:17). Let the love of the other provide the source of a new idea, that we are loved and that *we do not need* to act it out. "We are our new idea; it permeates our being. Held in its containing presence . . . its possibility inspires us, makes us feel life."[109] We hark back to our infancy and to the nurturing (m)other and the space between, where we create our formulations of her and of God.

> God comes into our world through woman. In daily religious experience, God goes into us through this female element, wooing us into shared life, much like a mother with her infant. We take this gift by coming into ourselves, our own self that communicates this incommunicable core of being that we experience both as our own and as addressing us. From this source springs our resilience to survive and go on growing . . . the mystery of God dwells at the core of us.
>
> Without this feminine mode of merger and dependence that produces the basis for self-discovery, we do not partake of the sacred in life. We long for, hanker after . . . the priceless gem, to feel real, supported by the real. When subjective and objective realms meet and mix, then life feels worthwhile, indeed worth everything. The female element originates this. That fact gives it a special place in theology.[110]

People Who People Our Imagination," 73–92, for the creative use of our imagination in sexual fantasies.

109. Ulanov, *Finding Space*, 69.

110. Ulanov, *Finding Space*, 74. Ulanov writes this in a chapter called "Female and Male," with the subheadings "The Female Element of Being," "The Male Element of

> How do you hold together your sensuality and your need to relate
> without objectifying the opposite, or your own sex?

7c.

Pastorally, when helping a person through an illicit strong attraction,
make sure you contact/visit them. Do not avoid them. Listen carefully
and long to what the value of the relationship is to the person to whom
you are listening. Offer reassurance that what is said will not be passed
on to anyone else and certainly not to other parties involved, that you are
not a messenger for anyone. Honor the strength of feeling and stay with
the feelings, even if you feel it is all wrong. Be very aware of what *you* are
feeling; that is, be very aware of your own countertransference—anger,
disgust, jealousy, admiration, censure, regret. Honor "the God bit" and
the love that really is there. Appropriately make it clear that the person
does have a choice. Assert that "you can live without her/him." Affirm the
person's courage, their ability *to observe* what they are doing and wanting,
and that they can get through without having what they desire. Allow the
person to say what choices he/she has. Give affirmation which is not soft
or sentimental, but concerned, loving, and firm. Ask what is right.

    N.B.: Make it clear appropriately that you may have to be a repre-
sentative of a church disciplinary pattern and that you may have to act
in a disciplinary way. Articulate clearly that you are genuinely concerned
and caring, *and* (not but) that you do have also to be a representative and
honor the ethos of the institution. Oscillation between the two positions
is possible, and say that you will indicate very clearly when you move
from one to the other.

7d.

Elisabeth Moltmann-Wendel counteracts the way in which Christianity
has been dominated by a male perspective by asserting that "Psychoanalytical research has demonstrated that Jesus was the only man not

---

Being," and "Theology in the Feminine."

dominated by the animus."[111] (Perhaps not the only one!) She sees him as "a man who integrated and brought to maturity the masculine and feminine attitudes which are to be found in any human being. As a result he was capable of entering into a more absolute partnership with women."[112] Scott interprets Jesus as containing the Sophia principle, the wisdom of God. In Jewish history and thought, Sophia was always feminine:

> [T]he femininity of Jesus Sophia is to be seen in the consistent emphasis on women as his main dialogue partners, the principle foils for major Christological events, and the paradigms of discipleship for the [Johannine] community. Here something of a balance is maintained between the maleness of Jesus and the femaleness of so many of the main Gospel figures.[113]

Surely this is because Jesus maintains a balance between his animus and anima. Just as Jesus lived in this boundary area, so do we, if we are carers, helpers, counselors, ministers.

> [T]o flee from this boundary area is to close oneself to that complexity of feeling, reason, intuition and sensation that so often constitutes the confusing terrain where clients risk losing themselves but also have the opportunity of discovering the nature of their own unique identities. I have come to love the male and female in myself and increasingly value the boundary territory where the two converse with each other with serenity.[114]

Are you conscious at different times of objectifying the opposite sex, that is, of turning the other into an "object"?

Are you conscious at different times of taking sides in the polarities you perceive in yourself, or in the objective sexualization of men and women and children in the media?

111. Both women and men have both animus and anima. They are strictly not the element of maleness in a woman and femaleness in a man, but are the image of woman held within a man and the image of man held within a woman. Perhaps here Moltmann-Wendel is saying that Jesus is not dominated by his masculinity but is able to feel and use his feminine side.

112. Moltmann-Wendel, *Women Around Jesus*, 3.

113. Scott, *Sophia*, 250.

114. Thorne, *Counsellor as Prophet*, 7.

Are you conscious at different times of the tension between, on the one hand, the virgin image of Mary the mother of Jesus, and on the other hand, the untouchableness of Mary Magdalene?

How do you keep a balance?

What is happening to you when you find yourself looking at someone as a "sex object"? Share as bravely as you can.

What is happening to you when you feel someone looking at you as a "sex object"?

Projections of longing for the ideal are common in life, and so are projections of rejection and condemnation. This is as true for characters in literature, including the New Testament, as in real life. Sometimes infatuation or fancies are resolved by common sense; otherwise they can be painful and even tragic, like, say, leaving work and family "to be with," or attempted murder so that "no one else can have," the beloved. Awareness of self can in fact prevail.

Rudyard Kipling announced, "I am going up to Simla . . . to make love to Mrs Edge!!!!" But his mother, Alice, pointed out, "I shan't hinder you but she's a yellowish green just at present and like a daguerreotype only shows in certain lights. It doesn't show much for your taste." "That sort of thing is fine if you don't care deeply about the woman"—which in this case Rudyard didn't. But if you are uncertain about yourself, which Rudyard was, it can be excruciating. Then he conceived another distant passion and later reflected, "She has the face of an angel, the voice of a dove and the step of the fawn. I worshipped her blindly till I found out she was the Cantonment Chaplain's daughter. My love was proof against this also and I said; I will go and listen to her Papa on Sundays." He went twice, "for I saw that she was lovely and hoped peradventure that her Papa might have been drunk." He showed his notes of the sermons to his father who said, "My son—there must be hereditary insanity in that family. Avoid it." "And I avode [sic] for I was of the same opinion as my Papa."[115] The disciples at the well did not need to be alarmed—Jesus was not uncertain about himself!

---

115. Flanders, *Circle of Sisters*, 215. The sisters were daughters of Rev. George and

Attraction comes and goes! It is often an accurate guide, but sometimes not, because it may come out of inner need only, or be contrary to other obligations, to others, or to one's "true self."

See if you can share an experience where you have longed for someone and did not "have" them, maybe even after a "brief encounter."

7e.

Two poets can help. They struggle, as we all do, with the balance between *having* and *not having*. John Clare, the Northamptonshire poet of nature, spent his last twenty years in the Northampton General Lunatic Asylum, and still wrestled with the longed for real and the imagined unreal. In 1844, while there, he wrote "A Vision." It all starts with despair, yet the longing remains.

> I lost the love of heaven above
> I spurned the lust of earth below
> I felt the sweets of fancied love
> And hell itself my only foe.
>
> I lost earth's joys but felt the glow
> Of heaven's flame abound in me
> Till loveliness and I did grow
> The bard of immortality.
>
> I loved but woman fell away
> I hid me from her faded fame
> I snatched the sun's eternal ray
> And wrote till earth was but a name.
>
> In every language upon earth
> On every shore, o'er every sea
> I gave my name immortal birth,
> And kept my spirit with the free.[116]

Mrs. Hannah Macdonald. Their father and grandfather were Methodist ministers. They were Alice Kipling, Georgiana Burne-Jones, Agnes Poynter, and Louisa Baldwin.

116. Clay, *John Clare*, 120. John Clare used minimal punctuation.

Clare felt desolate, without love. Patty, his wife, and his children never came to visit him, so he was sustained by "fancy," his fantasy. It was especially of Mary, whom he had loved from school days on. "[I]f I could but gaze on her face or fancy a smile on her countenance it was sufficient." Defenses are used by all of us to avoid pain, especially the pain of loss. They have a logic which is to be respected as part of the build of a person's personality. We respect the defense, against the pain, of fantasizing or "fancy" and his awareness of what it avoided. "O Mary sing thy songs to me / Of love and beauty's melody / My sorrows sink beneath distress . . ."[117]

Try and identify a fantasy which you use as a defense, and also identify that which you are defending against. Share as honestly as you can. Own your own need, even if, and especially if, there is no simple answer for it.

Clare exemplifies perfectly the hysteric experience, the loss of actual love, the continued longing for it, turning that natural or felt need into an imaginative projection, to outsiders seeming unreal, and yet enabling him to continue with a loving life, and a reconciliation of need and want in some form of maturity and worth. Did Jesus know something about this? Did he long for what he could not have? Like his life, for instance, or the love of a woman?

Share as honestly as you can the ache, the heartache, of not being with the person you once wanted or still want to be with.

Then somehow get hold of the way you have kept your sense of dignity and worth and carried on. Share that with some thanksgiving.

The defense of sublimation, avoiding the pain, we also respect; it was Clare's writing that saved him and kept his spirit "free." An imagined Mary was his muse. There is a touch of heaven that we feel even in "fancy."

117. See Foulds, *Quickening Maze*, 43.

Mary's memory sustained him for the rest of his life. "[T]hese dreams of a beautiful presence a woman deity gave the sublimest conceptions of beauty to my imagination." So he wrote the dreams down "to prolong the happiness of my faith in believing her my guardian genius."[118]

We should note that there is a difference in usage and of substance in the two spellings of "fantasy" and "phantasy." When I watch a film or read a book, I enter into it, and then it is easy to have a (conscious) fantasy that I am the hero, the batsman, the lover, the aristocrat, the rescuer, the scholar, or the star and so on. That narrative I create is a *fantasy*, but it reflects the *phantasy* I have running in my psyche about my longed-for self-image, my sense of who I am, or would like to be. It is like an underlying motif and describes the content of the continual flow of unconscious mental life.[119] So the escapist fantasy gives me a very valuable insight to what is happening underneath the surface in my psyche. It alerts me to part of my stream of unconsciousness, which in itself inhibits or enhances who "I am." So for John Clare, fantasizing about his Mary was built on a lifelong image or idea of the *ideal* girl/woman he had in him. So he longed for her and for women to be like her. For all his love for his wife Pat, she had not met his phantasy.

Share as honestly as you can one of your own fantasy journeys. Share how you identify with a character and then invent your own scenarios and language, how you aggrandize yourself or belittle yourself.

What does such material tell you about your inner phantasy in the area you are imagining?

The poet R. S. Thomas can align our (unconscious) desires with the biblical text in a suggestive way. The erotic is part of God; misuse of the erotic is not. Ann Griffith was illiterate, yet seventy of her stanzas survive. She was a fruit of the eighteenth-century revival in Wales. She created poetry that has been acclaimed. She died in 1805 at the young age of twenty-nine. In R. S. Thomas's *Later Poems* God wants to be part of her life, part of her, and needs *her gifts to him*, so that he can be true to himself.

118. Clay, *John Clare*, 9–11.
119. See Gomez, *Introduction*, 51–52.

So God spoke to her,
She the poor girl from the village
without learning. 'Play me,'
he said, 'on the white keys
of your body. I have seen you dance
for the bridegrooms that were not
to be, while I waited for you
under the ripening boughs of
the myrtle. These people know me
only in the thin hymns of
the mind, in the arid sermons
and prayers. I am the live God
nailed fast to the old tree
of a nation by its unreal
tears. I thirst, I thirst
for the spring water. Draw it up
for me from your heart's well and I will change
it to wine upon your unkissed lips.'[120]

R. S. Thomas links the water of chapter 4 with the images of chapter 2. Transformation is what he is about. God *holds together* the schizoid element in us, "the thin hymns" and "arid sermons and prayers" which are the very opposite of "affect laden"—they represent the schizoid intellectual defense—and the needy, touching, visual, hysteric element in us, the need to touch and be touched, to kiss and be kissed.

God knows our need. He shares our need. He draws near to us, owns his own need, is stretched by the tension, and through our gift to him, by his transforming presence, enables *us* to sustain natural unmet needs, or needs perceived to be unmet. Here is a live God nailed fast to humanity. It is the offering of the water from our "heart's well" that enables the change in us, enables us to carry on when need, real or perceived, is not met. For sure, the woman can be sensual without being immoral. And so can the man.

Do you have any sense of God being involved in your sensual nature?
Or in the unfeeling part of your nature?

---

120. Thomas, *Later Poems*, 65.

Albert Schweitzer concluded *The Quest for the Historical Jesus* with the image of a well. Looking down into "the well of Jesus' history," we may see only the reflection of our own faces, narcissistically. If that is all, we end up "thirsty." "The reader at the well, in order to be nourished, must draw from and drink of the text." Our response should be "a creative echo to the text."[121]

Paul Tillich faced much suffering, "non-being," literally, in Nazi Germany, and in his own psyche. Yet with the "courage to be,"[122] he faced life in the intimacy of Jesus' presence living in us. He wrote a letter to a loving woman friend. "We need each other—others' [plural] warmth in a world which is colder than human nature demands—at least my nature. Give me your warmth. Don't stop giving it to me even if I am swallowed up by darkness, cold and silence."[123]

> Write a letter to the person who is that one similarly close for you.
>   Share with a partner as much as you wish. Honour the person who fulfils that role. (You do not have to send the letter!)

How much more can we say to Jesus, *Give me your warmth, your light, your water, your bread, your abiding, your life!*

> Remember and share a moment when you were profoundly grateful for a drink of water.
>   Remember and share a moment when Jesus refreshed you.

The novels of Marilynne Robinson have a lot of theology in them! The wandering Lila has ended up in Gilead. She is really the Magdalene figure. One day, without knowing quite why, she knocks on the door of the pastor, John Ames, who is the Jesus figure. He has been a widower for many years and he is apologetic for the state of the house. He is surprised.

121. Vanhoozer, in Green, *Hearing the New Testament*, 283.
122. See Tillich, *Courage to Be*.
123. May, *Paulus*, 103.

"Hello. Good morning. Please come in." "She didn't know then that it would have embarrassed him to have her there, a woman alone with him, a stranger. But he didn't want her to leave, she did know that. 'Can I get you a glass of water? I could make coffee, if you have a few minutes.' . . . the mystery of her presence . . ." They did marry![124]

8. So We Are Able to Worship

4:19–24. There is no need to go to Gerizim or Jerusalem to worship. This is more radical than it appears. Brueggemann points out that claims to exclusive truth can lead to exclusivity. The Israelites' insistence, in the growth of and adherence to monotheism, on "only Yahweh" leads to "only Israel" having the Torah, and being particularly privileged (Deut 4:5–8). "Thus what purports to be a theological affirmation of "only Yahweh" turns out to be a claim, in rather blatant ways, for "only Israel." "The inescapable problem, of course, is that Israel (and belatedly the church) is never simply a theological entity, but it is always a socioeconomic-political entity, alive to issues of power, and therefore endlessly capable of committing overt ideological claims for itself."[125] Jesus holds to the truth in his own heritage, but with the greatest clarity. He is aware of this tendency and its damage (damage, for instance, between Samaritans and Jews, and prospectively in human history) and announces a simplicity of faith that transcends the "political" status quo of any faith community.

> Do you have a sense in your own religious community of claims to power, or a restriction on styles of worship? Share how it affects you and how you live with it.

Jesus' truth, which is a pointer to true worship, transcends Zionism or any other—ism that locates proper attention to the Father in only one "special" place. Local sites are "dispossessed."[126] Jesus "declassified" sacred

---

124. Robinson, *Lila*, 28.
125. Brueggemann, *Texts That Linger*, 89–92.
126. Hoskyns, *Fourth Gospel*, 236.

and, we would say, "secular" space; "there is *no* 'holy land.'"[127] Indeed, his body becomes the temple (2:19–22) and the group, the Christian church, and a person's body, is called a "temple." John is very sensitive to place; Galilee is safe while Jerusalem is not; Jesus only "remains"—that powerful word and sensation (*meno*) in John—in the former and even in Samaria, never in Jerusalem![128]

In this "foreign" place, Samaria, Jesus points to the presence of the Father and the possibility of opening the heart to him. "The hour is coming and now is." The "end" hope is "realized" because true worship consists in the orientation of oneself to the Father himself. The Greek *proskuneo*, "worship," is to bend or turn oneself towards the one worshipped. That is done within the ambit of spirit and truth because the Father reaches out for us. This we can now know. "Nicodemus was challenged to reach beyond the categories he could control,"[129] and we learn that if we allow ourselves to do that—from above, in the spirit—then we live in the light and do the truth (3:3–5, 21). Spiritual birth leads to spiritual worship. Overwhelming testimonies of the converted testify that worship is no longer formal; with the experience of great joy goes a freedom in worship.

Will you share a memory, distant or recent, when you felt a freedom and inspiration in worship?

Do you have a sense of some place that it is special, even "sacred"? What do you mean by that, and how does it feel, and how do you tally that with the belief that all space is sacred and belongs to the Father, and that we can worship him anywhere?

Do not answer that some places are "more sacred" than others!

---

127. Neyey, *Gospel of John in Cultural and Rhetorical Perspective*, 70, italics original.

128. Neyey, *Gospel of John in Cultural and Rhetorical Perspective*, 65–67.

129. Moloney, *Belief in the Word*, 152.

9. Confession of Faith?

4.25–26. She has become a knowing woman; old knowledge is combined with new by the presence of Jesus. She says (*lego*) to him, "I know that Messiah is coming, the one being called the Christ." He says (*lego*) to her, "I am he speaking to you." It is a most significant moment of new revelation. Jesus speaks about himself in the first-person singular. The water jar is left behind (4:28). A casual note, unlike John, or a strong symbol? The past is past; the future becomes the present; eschatology, the end time, is now realized; hope is immanent when we hear the word of Christ, "I am . . ."

> When you say, or said, to Jesus, "You are the Christ," what does, or did it, mean to you? Make confession of your faith—to each other or to the whole group.
>
> Has the sense of Jesus speaking to you been realized in your life?

10. Talking of Jesus

4:27–30. The tête-à-tête is ended. The disciples were full of wonder that he was chatting (*lalo*) with a woman, but they were inhibited from asking what he was "seeking." I wonder what they thought! In fact, he was seeking a drink and a relationship! But why with her—was there intonation that stressed "her"? *It was Jesus asking for help and then his knowledge of her* which changed her. Interestingly, she was not such an excluded person as to be outside the "gossip network" of the city, the *polis*. Normally women would only speak to women, but here, spreading information, her informal communication is obviously to the men, or "people," some possibly her kin, but maybe not, in which case her enthusiasm for Jesus breaks through social barriers. Having been an outsider (perhaps), "Here she functions as a mediating figure in spreading the news about Jesus to the Samaritans."[130] She says (*lego*), "Come and see" (*horao*)—in John the classic invitation to discipleship, to following Jesus.

130. Neyrey, *Gospel of John in Cultural and Rhetorical Perspective,* 168–70; *Gospel of John,* 55, 96.

The subplot of the disciples' reappearance reminds us of how they react and how *we* react. Verses 27 and 31 earth us in reactions to this event. The disciples had their fantasies, of what a woman like this might mean, not only in practical terms for the future of Jesus, but in terms of their own response to her. They also could see her as both tempting and forbidding.

Many years ago, at a meeting of the Institute of Religion and Medicine, a voluntary organization and fellowship to promulgate understanding, the sharing of ideas, and cooperation between doctors and clergy, ministers and laypeople, a senior consultant-looking doctor appeared with a young wife half his age or less. *Our projections* saw her as the second wife after the breakup of the first family. She was stunningly beautiful, striking, with fair hair, reserved, possessed. He was well known and was greeted by the others. But not a single person in the room spoke to her the whole evening! Much too dangerous! She "belonged" to him, for now! Taboo! Too ambiguous by far to get into conversation with. Dumb blonde, desperately attractive and deadly dangerous. Consultants, doctors, clergy, all inhibited!

A young mother went with her two children and her mother to a Christian holiday home by the sea, where everyone always talked with each other. Her husband had to work elsewhere that week. She was acutely distressed as the week went on that no one spoke to her, neither the men of her own age, nor the women. They saw her as a young widow. She was taboo, to men not wanting to engage with a "single" attractive woman, and to women because they wanted to avoid the threat of death, of losing their man! Our defensive projections have a lot to answer for!

The disciples were nervous and projected their anxiety, fear, and longing onto Jesus. What on earth was he doing talking to her? But Jesus could hold her in his arms (metaphorically) and yet keep her appropriately at arm's length. His presence affirmed or confirmed her. Martin Buber:

> . . . identified confirmation as one of the key elements in dialogue. Confirmation is grounded in an acknowledgement of otherness. As I enter into dialogue with the other, I accept her uniqueness and particularity and struggle with her in the release of her potential as a person. Confirmation depends on a capacity for *inclusion*. Inclusion, or 'imagining the real', is the attempt to grasp the thoughts, feelings, and wishes of the other while maintaining one's own concreteness and particularity. Through

inclusion one is able to catch hold of otherness. This grasp of the particularity of the other is the first step in confirmation.[131]

Jesus could hold both himself and herself in dialogue. He could "include" her and yet keep his own particularity.

The disciples were not "imagining the real" but had a fantasy, of what they could do with her, or of what she could do to them, and projected that onto him. Many modern commentators are the same, but project onto her! Or am I the only one who is fantasizing? The text seems to be reading me!

The role of fantasy, or "phantasy" as described above, develops early in infancy. When food is needed, imagining the breast or mother as present occurs, especially if there is the slightest delay in her coming to meet a natural need, or when to the needy one she *seems* to be delaying. She is desired and may be experienced both as seductive and persecutory, desperately attractive *and/or* dangerous. It is a matter of survival. "Mother" is not only an external object, but is shaped as an internal "object" as well.[132] In meeting its vital needs, the infant learns to distinguish between the reality that is out there and the phantasy in here. As we grow, "the infant structures are submerged below the level of the adult psyche, but they remain functionally active in shaping motivations. When the adult psychic structures fail to maintain the individual's psychic integration . . . the dormant infantile psychic structures will re-assert themselves."[133]

There is a dissonance between being an adult and the pressures to perform as a child in phantasy and sometimes in action. Phantasies endure. To relate, say on a social occasion, to an attractive or unattractive person needs *an awareness of* the rush of internal objects, our phantasies of "woman" or "man" which skew our attempts to relate to *her as she is or him as he is*. In some internal way we turn the person into what we want them to be or don't want them to be. Jesus, being well individuated, is both nourished by the "external" woman, and is able to transfuse his phantasies into a warm, real, not phony, relationship with her. This work in himself is done in relation to his Father's work in him. What an illustration for the disciples of what their future ministry can be like and how his people should be!

131. Pembroke, *Art of Listening*, 31, italics original. He usefully addresses Buber's insight into I-Thou relations in the affirmation offered pastorally to others, 31–47.

132. See footnote 36 in "Introcution 1" on Object Relations.

133. Sturdee, in Mace, *Heart and Soul*, 38.

> Share what you are *feeling* as you read or hear this material.

So we are not despising fantasies as such; they serve a useful purpose so long as we self-reflect on them. The comedian Ronnie Barker, as Fletcher in the sitcom *Porridge*, speculates longingly on all the things he is going to do on his day out of prison. But, says his cellmate, young Godber, "You aren't having a day out." No, says Fletcher, "But dreams is freedom!"

> Share some of your secret dreams or fantasies or projections if you can. Non-judgmentally, but so as to inform yourself about yourself, especially about your needs. Allow others to hear what you need.

We experience here the sheer value of dialogue. The situation was clearly pastoral. We are made, as child or adult, in such a way that when we are not in the presence of someone who is open to us and to our experience, we remain unconfirmed in our being. We develop a sense of self and the ability to make sense of our experience when the other is a *real* presence. "No abstraction [e.g., ideas of "worship" or "Messiah" or "water"] can stand independently of the concrete situation in which human beings meet and try to understand one another. The therapeutic dialogue as a particular case is a meeting of two people embedded in their histories, who see the world and each other through their histories. They cannot do otherwise. Yet in their meeting the horizon of each may be expanded, if they are open"[134]

We create a sense of self when someone else is open to us; otherwise we lack "the creative potential for meeting." Intersubjectivity is then a possibility. If we are subject to, or compliant with, the world of one who is not open to us, we resist open relating so as to maintain the status quo. We "reduce the world to the terms of the other." This reduces mutuality, the ability to share, and to grow.[135] That Jesus does not do this is the

---

134. John Wheway, in Mace, *Heart and Soul*, 117.
135. John Wheway, in Mace, *Heart and Soul*, 117.

theme of the Gospel. Jesus is open to the others; the conversation, despite the perspectives of many commentators as above, is mutual, and hence the woman blossoms, the people gather round, and disciples have opportunity to grow.

We are now aware of what John is aware of, namely, what Jesus is totally aware of, that, "the root of human alienation lies not in economics or politics but in personal life itself, at the intimate level where each person faces (or avoids facing) his own inner life, and is involved in relationships with other individuals on the basis of recognising them (or directly refusing to recognize them) as beings with the same kind of inner life."[136] That quotation expresses succinctly a key theme of John's Gospel!

4:31–38. In the interim, John deepens the narrative again and he prompts us to join with the disciples in acknowledging that Jesus is nourished by doing what his Father wants. For this he has been sent. "Food" is a metaphor—Jesus did not actually stop eating! "You must sit down, says Love and taste my meat: / So I did sit and eat."[137]

The "harvest" is another metaphor. It looks forward. To be involved in the activity of reaping, the fruit of hard work in the seasons of the year, is life, and leads to joy in the team working at doing God's will (4:36). "The ordinary meanings for temple, birth, water, a well, and food have been transcended to speak of the transformation worked by the presence of Jesus, so now the term 'harvest' becomes an image used by Jesus to speak of the newness of life, the eternal life, which he has come to bring."[138] We would also add that the ordinary meaning for "husbands" has been transcended, with important consequences for commentary.

Is this kind of teamwork your experience of membership and attendance in the Christian community in which your discipleship is practiced?

---

136. John Wren Lewis, "Loves Coming of Age," in Rycroft, ed., *Psychoanalysis Observed*, 106; quoted in Ulanov, *Healing Imagination*, 164.

137. George Herbert, "Love bade me welcome."

138. Moloney, *Belief in the Word*, 164.

> What are the difficulties *you feel* in cooperation, or lack of it, in your church?
>
> Or in any other groups to which you belong?

There is a colleagueship in Christian work, so we only see the beginning, or the fruit. Paul uses the same metaphor (1 Cor 3:6). God gives the "growth"—the same word as at John 3:30, John the Baptist on Jesus, "He must increase." "We are God's field."

> What have you sown? What have you reaped? How does the growth happen?
>
> Share when you know you have benefited in life or in your Christian life, from the labor of another.
>
> Explore issues for you of dependence, obedience, second-hand knowledge, being delegated to, enjoying what others have worked for; and the feelings associated with your own sense of identity. Share perhaps shame, gratitude, indebtedness, irritation, being not in control, uncertainty, bewilderment, fear, irrelevance, thankfulness or admiration.

4:39–42. The woman won over a whole group to Jesus; indeed, over the two days she presumably brought Judeans and Samaritans together in one group. (It is still one of the most intractable political/peace problems of our own times!) The Samaritans came to trust because of the *logos* she spoke to them. How surprising is that! It is a significant phrase because Jesus' "priestly" prayer is not only for those near to him, "but for those who trust through their word." There is already envisaged an extension of himself through the *logos* of his followers (17:20). It is the privileged ministry that we all have. Then, "When the text says 'they asked him to stay with them' (4:40) we should understand 'stay' [*meno*] as a characteristic Johannine term indicating close affiliation with and loyalty to Jesus, namely membership in his circle (1:28–29; 5:28; 8:31; 12:46; 15:4–7)."[139]

139. Neryey, *Gospel of John in Cultural and Rhetorical Perspective*, 169.

We witness the founding of the Samaritan church. Then many more believed because of his *logos*, not just because of her talk (*lalia*). Augustine's comment on this was, "First by reputation, then by his presence."[140] Now it is they who are the knowing ones. We may believe because we hear about Jesus, and also because his word abides in us—now we "know" (*oida* as in 4:10, 22, 25) "that this is truly [*alethes*] the Savior of the cosmos."

It is a very strong factor in our history that people become Christian because they have been listening. The people said, "We have heard for ourselves." Talk may have profound effect on the knowledge of willing or unwilling listeners. The coming to faith through oral, and not written, experience is remarkable in Christian history. The caring and sharing groups of early Methodism, called Class Meetings and the Bands, led many to faith through listening to others talk about their experience. John Wesley's "Speak your experience" was more than giving a testimony to your religious experience, but rather a sharing of "what God had done for me" in relation to personality and the course of life. It was a relation of life experience to answers found in Christian experience. People joined the groups *before* they were converted because they were seeking. The thousands of conversion narratives of the seventeenth, eighteenth, and nineteenth centuries related an awakening and assurance of faith through conversation.

David George (1743–1810), the black Baptist minister, traveled to Freetown with ex-slaves from Nova Scotia, where they had migrated to from across America. The governor of Sierra Leone, Zachary Macaulay, a close friend of Wilberforce and the Clapham circle, met David George and wrote in his journal:

> Ask either one or the other [Methodists] how he knows himself to be a child of God, and the answer from both will be pretty much in the style of David George, 'I know it,' not because of this or the other proof drawn from the word of God but because (perhaps) twenty years ago I saw a certain sight or heard certain words or passed though a certain train of impressions varying from solicitude to deep concern & terror & despair & thence again thro fluctuations of fear & hope to peace & joy & assured confidence.[141]

---

140. Moloney, *Belief in the Word*, 169.

141. Quoted in Hindmarsh, *Evangelical Conversion Narrative*, 331.

Sometime after David George was converted by the spoken word, he realized he needed to learn to read. "I can now read the Bible, so that what I have in my heart I can see again in the Scriptures." He said his people met in groups "to hear experiences." "In talking about what he had 'in his heart' . . . he was talking about his *feelings* . . . The heart strangely warmed by the spoken word came first."[142]

Can you relate your own journey in faith, especially perhaps its beginnings, to a time of listening?

How does it feel to have a sense of belonging through experience shared?

The sharing of experience is what will happen in the group you are in, and your life and your faith will be deepened.

The oral communication of the faith founds churches and Churches and movements. For instance, eighteenth-century narratives of conversion were individual but not individualistic, because they came about through painful honesty in small groups. Troubled seekers needed and experienced not only a new heart but also a new family, a new community functioning in new groups of Christians. "When such people were converted, they felt that they were born again not in isolation, but into a new family of brothers and sisters."[143] They also paralleled their story in the story of God's revelation to and guiding of his people. "[F]aith is not a self-generated or autonomous reaction, but a relationship that is generated in response to Jesus. As people are brought to faith, they are moved to act according to the pattern set by Jesus, whose own actions are congruent with what he sees his father doing."[144] So, for instance, for David George and the ex-slaves, "Come ye who are heavy laden," and the song of Miriam, and the exodus, were "organising motifs" for conversion, for crossing the Atlantic, and going ashore in Sierra Leone.[145]

So Jesus, through the painful honesty of a woman, and through contemplation of the religious history of both Samaritans and Jews, creates a

---

142. Hindmarsh, *Evangelical Conversion Narrative*, 331–32, original italics.

143. Hindmarsh, *Evangelical Conversion Narrative*, 344.

144. Koester, "Rethinking the Ethics of John," 93.

145. Hindmarsh, *Evangelical Conversion Narrative*, 332

new community, the Samaritan church. The analysis of person and past is seen, for instance, in his mysterious but direct approach to two on the Emmaus road and his interpretation (*hermeneuo*) of the Scriptures. He also "stayed" with them, and "they said to each other, 'Did not our hearts burn within us while he talked (*lalo*) to us on the road, while he opened to us the scriptures?'" (Luke 24). The interpretation of the text and the interpretation of the living text, the living human document, what goes on inside people, always go together as we come to faith and continue in faith. "Opening up" the person and "opening up" the texts are both essential. This is the central message of this book, this text!

> When you began to trust in Jesus, or as you continue to believe, how were you, how are you, "opened up"? Share bravely!

> How does it feel to have a sense of sharing in God's story of redemption?

What the Samaritans know is that "this is truly [*alethos*] the Savior of the world." This is a political as well as a theological statement. John uses the word "world" (*cosmos*) over eighty times of the created world and of the alienated world of humanity. Why this phrase, "Savior of the world," here? It is only used once more in the whole New Testament (1 John 4:14), but the word "Savior" is used of eleven Roman emperors in the first century.

This is the culmination of the series of affirmations of the identity of Jesus. Salvation is *from* the Jews, but is *for* all who worship, not bound to Jerusalem or Gerizim. They used to worship what they did not know, now they worship what they know. It can be argued that the woman is both an individual and a representative of the Samaritan people. The dialogues with her, as with Nathanael, Nicodemus, and the man born blind (chapter 9), alternate between singular and plural forms of address ("you" in Greek is sometimes plural). Samaria was colonized by five Assyrian nations, and the capital, Samaria, was renamed by Herod as Sebaste (the Greek name for Augustus). It was colonised by six thousand foreigners, and later Shechem, near Sychar, was turned into a Roman city. The issue in the region was always whether to compromise or resist. The Johannine community would be well aware of this chequered history, about which "the Jews" had strong feelings,[146] and would need to know afresh that the Samaritan Christians now have no king other than Jesus, that their truth comes through him, and that he comes from "above." The "Savior of the world" title truly belongs to him.[147]

As a group share where you feel compromise with or resistance to the civil power is required. Are there limits to your willingness to comply with the requirements of the State?

In what sense for you is Jesus the Savior of the world?

---

11. The Second Sign

4:43–54. Capernaum, on the west shore of Galilee, was the scene for John's choice of a second sign (*semeion*), though the conversation was held at Cana, to which Jesus has come after two days (cf. 2:1). Jesus is on the move again and meets an official, perhaps an officer of King Herod, who had heard that Jesus was coming; he perseveres in favor of his little boy, and he trusts the *logos* of Jesus, and the result is that he and his household believe, trust. The present tenses give a feeling of immediacy; "Go, your son lives."[148] The official is also an *anthropos* and a father. When the fever breaks at the moment Jesus speaks, they see a sign. Do we need to see a miracle here, or did Jesus hear enough about it to know that some fevers do break and the patient recovers? The man now knows (*ginosko*), and knew there was a connection with Jesus at a particular "hour." For each one of us, the "hour" of Jesus is now.

---

146. See Jeremias, *Jerusalem in the Time of Jesus*, 352–58.

147. This paragraph tries to summarise the argument in Koester, "Savior of the World," 51–52.

148. *Zao*, to live, be alive; *zoe*, life.

12.

John, especially in chapter 4, is the book of gift, knowing and gift, of gift and knowing!

> Jesus the gift divine I know,
> The gift divine I ask of thee;
> That living water now bestow,
> The Spirit and Thyself, on me;
> Thou, Lord of life the Fountain art;
> Now let me feel Thee in my heart.
>
> Thee let me drink and thirst no more
> For drops of finite happiness;
> Spring up, O well, in heavenly power,
> In streams of pure perennial peace,
> In joy that none can take away,
> In life which shall for ever stay.
>
> Father, on me the grace bestow,
> Unblamable before Thy sight,
> Whence all the streams of mercy flow;
> Mercy Thy own supreme delight,
> To me, for Jesu's sake, impart,
> And plant Thy nature in my heart.
>
> Thy mind throughout my life be shown,
> While listening to the sufferer's cry,
> The widow's and the orphan's groan
> On mercy's wings I swiftly fly,
> The poor and helpless to relieve,
> My life, my all, for them to give.
>
> Thus may I show the Spirit within,
> Which purges me from every stain;
> Unspotted from the world and sin,
> My faith's integrity maintain;
> The truth of my religion prove
> By perfect purity and love.[149]

In that Charles Wesley hymn, which catches the feel of chapter 4 perfectly, "Note . . . how from this starting-point we arrive, by natural

---

149. Charles Wesley, in *H&P* 318.

transition, at the concrete details of practical Christianity."[150] The life-giving spring enables him to minister and empowers his ministry. And note how many of the John words are there and how Charles Wesley's Christian is both engaged with "the world" and yet keeps his/her own integrity. It signifies the experiential religion, the "experimental piety" of the eighteenth century, carrying the "nature" of God in the heart.

"Come. And whoever wants, may take the water of life [*zoe*] freely [*dorean*]" (Rev 22: 17).

---

150. Franz Hildebrandt, (one of the founders with Martin Niemoeller and Dietrich Bonhoeffer of the German Confessing Church under Hitler), *Christianity According to the Wesleys*, 37; *MHB* 605 or Hildebrandt and Beckerlegge, eds., *Works of John Wesley*, 7:521. I actually prefer the early alternative to line 15, "streams of goodness." Hildebrandt knew all about "the concrete details of practical Christianity," living under Hitler. He came to the UK, became a Methodist minister and a scholar of Wesley's hymns, ministering in London, Cambridge, and then in Scotland as a minister of the Church of Scotland. See Cresswell, *Dr. Franz Hildebrandt.*

Bibliography

Books which give an introduction to John and books which give a guide to a psychodynamic approach are marked with an asterisk (*). Several of the older books will be out of print, but they are included in the hope that many will still have places on the shelves of online booksellers and are thus possibly available.

Albin, T. R. "An Empirical Study of Early Methodist Spirituality." In *Wesleyan Theology Today: Bicentennial Consultation*, edited by T. Runyon, 275–88. Nashville: Abingdon, 1985.

Aichele, George, et al. *The Postmodern Bible: the Bible and Culture Collective*. New Haven, CT: Yale University Press, 1995.

Alter, Robert, Frank Kermode. *The Literary Guide to the Bible*. London: Fontana/ Harper Collins, 1997.

Anderson, Linda. "Historians of the Self." Ch. 1 in Anderson, *Autobiography*. 2nd ed. London: Routledge, 2011.

*Anderson, Philip, and Phoebe Anderson. *The House Church*. Nashville: Abingdon, 1975.

Ashton, John, ed. *The Interpretation of John*. London: SPCK, 1986.

———. "John and the Johannine Literature: The Woman at the Well." Ch. 17 in *The Cambridge Companion to Biblical Interpretation*, edited by John Barton. Cambridge: Cambridge University Press, 1998.

———. *Studying John: Approaches to the Fourth Gospel*. Oxford: Oxford University Press, 1994.

———. *Understanding the Fourth Gospel*. Oxford: Clarendon, 1991.

Augustine, Saint. *Confessions*. Translated by R. S. Pine Coffin. London: Penguin, 1961.

Ballard, Paul, and Stephen R. Holmes. *The Bible in Pastoral Practice: Readings in the Place and Function of Scripture in the Church*. London: Darton, Longman & Todd, 2005.

*Barclay, William. *The Gospel of John*. Edinburgh: St. Andrew, 1955.

Barrett, C. K. *The Gospel According to St. John*. 1st ed. London: SPCK, 1955.

———. *The New Testament Background: Selected Documents*. San Francisco: Harper, 1987.

———. *New Testament Essays*. London: SPCK, 1972.

Bartlett, David. "Interpreting and Preaching the Gospel of John." *Interpretation* 60:1 (January 2006) 48–63.

Barton, John, ed. *The Cambridge Companion to Biblical Interpretation*. Cambridge: Cambridge University Press, 1998.

Bash, Anthony. "A Psychodynamic Approach to the Interpretation of 2 Corinthians 10–13." *JSNT* 24:1 (September 2001) 51–67.

Bauckham, Richard. *God of Glory: Major Themes in Johannine Theology*. Grand Rapids: Baker Academic, 2015.

———. "Historiographical Characteristics of the Gospel of John." *NTS* 53:1 (January 2007) 17–36.

———. *The Testimony of the Beloved Disciple: Narrative, History and Theology in the Gospel of John*. Grand Rapids: Baker Academic, 2007.

Beasley-Murray, George R. *John*. Word Biblical Commentary 36. 2nd ed. Nashville: T. Nelson, 1999.

Bieringer, Reimund, Didier Pollefeyt, and Frederique Vandecasteele-Vanneuville, eds. *Anti-Judaism and the Fourth Gospel*. London: Westminster John Knox, 2001.

Bird, Cathy. *The Divine Heart of Darkness: Finding God in the Shadows*. Durham: Sacristy, 2017.

Blackwell, John. *The Methodist Class Leader, or, The Duties, Qualifications, Difficulties, and Encouragements of a Class Leader Considered with an Account of Class Meetings*. 1818.

Bonhoeffer, Dietrich. *Letters and Papers from Prison*. Edited by Eberhard Bethge, translated by Reginald H. Fuller. London: Collins, Fontana, 1959; London, SCM, 1953.

Boyd, Robert D. *Personal Transformations in Small Groups: A Jungian Perspective*. London: Routledge, 1991.

*Bragan, Kenneth. *Self and Spirit in the Therapeutic Relationship*. London: Routledge, Kegan & Paul, 1996.

Brant, Jo-Ann A. *Elements of Greek Tragedy in the Fourth Gospel*. Peabody, MA: Hendrickson, 2004.

Brodie, Thomas L. *The Gospel According to John: a Literary and Theological Commentary*. Oxford: Oxford University Press, 1993.

Brooks, Peter Newman. *Hymns as Homilies*. Leominster, Herefordshire: Gracewing Fowler Wright, 1997.

Brotton, Jerry. *A History of the World in Twelve Maps*. London: Penguin, 2013.

Brown, George Mackay. *Collected Poems*. London: John Murray, 2005.

Brown, R. E. *The Community of the Beloved Disciple*. London: G. Chapman, 1979.

———. *The Epistles of John*. Anchor Bible. London: G. Chapman, 1982.

———. *The Gospel according to John*. 2 vols. Anchor Bible. New York: Doubleday, 1966, 1970.

*———. *The Gospels and Epistles of John: A Concise Commentary*. Minneapolis: Liturgical, 1988.

Brueggemann, Walter. *Texts That Linger, Words That Explode: Listening to Prophetic Voices*. Minneapolis: Fortress, 2000.

Bultmann, Rudolf. *The Gospel of John*. Translated by G. R. Beasley-Murray. Oxford: Blackwell, 1971.

Burkett, Delbert. *The Son of Man in the Gospel of John*. JSNT Supplement Series 56. Sheffield: Sheffield Academic, 1991.

*Campbell, Alastair V. *Rediscovering Pastoral Care*. London: Darton, Longman & Todd, 1981.

Carr, Wesley. *The Pastor as Theologian: The Integration of Pastoral Ministry, Theology and Discipleship*. London: SPCK, 1989.

Carter, Warren. "The Prologue and John's Gospel: Function, Symbol and the Definitive Word." *JSNT* 12:39 (1990) 35–58.

Casement, Patrick. *Further Learning from the Patient: the Analytic Space and Process*. London: Routledge, 1990.

*Christian, Carol, ed. *In The Spirit of Truth: A Reader in the Work of Frank Lake*. London: Darton, Longman & Todd, 1991.

*Clark-Soles, Jaime. *Reading John for Dear Life: A Spiritual Walk with the Fourth Gospel*. Louisville: Westminster John Knox, 2016.

Clay, Arnold. *"Itching After Rhyme": A Life of John Clare*. Tunbridge Wells: Parapress, 2000.

———. *John Clare: The Peasant Poet*. Tunbridge Wells: Parapress, 1999.

Clemo, Jack. *Selected Poems*. Newcastle-on-Tyne: Bloodaxe, 1988.

Coggins, R. J., and J. L. Houlden, eds. *A Dictionary of Biblical Interpretation*. London: SCM, 1990. See all articles on "criticism," including David K. Miell, "Psychological Interpretation," 571–72.

Collins, Raymond F. "From John to the Beloved Disciple." *Interpretation* 49:4 (October 1995) 359–69.

Conrad, Joseph. *Heart of Darkness*. London: Penguin, 1973.

Cope, Lamar. *Faith for a New Day: The New View of the Gospel of John*. St. Louis: CBP, 1986.

Cordingly John. *Disordered Heroes in Opera: A Psychiatric Report*. Edited by Claire Seymour. Woodbridge, Suffolk: Boydell Brewer, 2015.

Countryman, L. William. *The Mystical Way in the Fourth Gospel: Crossing Over into God*. Valley Forge, PA: Trinity, 1994.

Cox, Murray. *Structuring the Therapeutic Process: Compromise with Chaos: The Therapist's Response to the Individual and the Group*. London: Jessica Kingsley, 1988.

———. *Transferring the Untransferable*. 1991 Frank Lake Memorial Lecture. Lingdale Paper 18. Church Westcote, Oxford: Clinical Theology Association, 1983.

Cox, Murray, and Alice Theilgaard. *Mutative Metaphors in Psychotherapy: The Aeolian Mode*. London: Tavistock, 1987.

———. *Shakespeare as Prompter: The Amending Imagination & The Therapeutic Process*. London: Kingsley, 1994.

Cresswell, Amos. *Dr. Franz Hildebrandt: Mr Valiant-for-Truth*. Leominster: Gracewing, 2000.

*Culpepper, R. Alan. *Anatomy of the Fourth Gospel: A Study in Literary Design*. Philadelphia: Fortress, 1987.

*———. *The Gospel and Letters of John*. Nashville: Abingdon, 1998.

———. "The Plot of John's Story of Jesus." *Interpretation* 49:4 (October 1995) 347–58.

Culpepper, R. Alan, and Fernando Segovia, eds. *The Fourth Gospel from a Literary Perspective*. Semeia 53. Atlanta: Society of Biblical Literature, 1991.

Davies, Margaret. *Rhetoric and Reference in the Fourth Gospel*. JSNT Supplement Series 69, Sheffield: Sheffield Academic, 1992.

Davies, Oliver. *A Theology of Compassion: Metaphysics of Difference and the Renewal of Tradition*. London: SCM, 2001.

Davis, Derek Russell. *Scenes of Madness: A Psychiatrist at the Theatre*. London: Routledge, 1995.

Davis, Mark. *Walking on the Shore: A Way of Sharing Faith in Groups*. Chelmsford: Matthew James, 2002.

De Boer, M. C. "Narrative Criticism, Historical Criticism, and the Gospel of John." *JSNT* 15:47 (1992) 35–48.

DeYoung, Patricia A. *Relational Psychotherapy: A Primer*. New York: Brunner-Routledge, 2003.

Dodd, C. H. *Historical Tradition in the Fourth Gospel*. Cambridge: Cambridge University Press, 1963.

———. *The Interpretation of the Fourth Gospel*. Cambridge: Cambridge University Press, 1953.

Douglas, Mary. *Purity and Danger: An Analysis of Concepts of Pollution and Taboo*. London: Routledge, 1966.

Drury, John. *Music at Midnight: The Life and Poetry of George Herbert*. London: Penguin, 2013.

Eliot, George. *Adam Bede*. London: Penguin, 1985.

———. *Middlemarch*. Oxford: Oxford University Press, 1996.

———. *Silas Marner*. London: Penguin, 1967.

Elliott, Charles. *Memory and Salvation*. London: Darton, Longman & Todd, 1995.

Erikson, Erik. *Young Man Luther: A Study in Psychoanalysis and History*. London: Faber, 1972.

Eslinger, Lyle. "The Wooing of the Woman at the Well: Jesus, The Reader and Reader-Response Criticism." *Journal of Literature and Theology* 1:2 (September 1987) 167–83. Reprinted in Stibbe, ed., *The Gospel of John as Literature*, 163–82.

Felman, Shoshana. *Literature and Psychoanalysis: The Question of Reading Otherwise*. Baltimore: John Hopkins University Press, 1989.

*Fenton, John. *Finding the Way Through John*. London: Mowbray, 1988.

Ferguson, Ron. *George Mackay Brown: The Wound and the Gift*. Edinburgh: Saint Andrew, 2011.

Fiumara, Gemma Corradi. *The Other Side of Language: A Philosophy of Listening*. London: Routledge, 1990.

Flanders, Judith. *Circle of Sisters: Alice Kipling, Georgiana Burne-Jones, Agnes Poynter, and Louisa Baldwin*. London: Norton, 2001.

Fotiou, Stavros S. "The Transformation of Existence: Christ's Encounter with the Samaritan Woman According to John 4:4–42." *Expository Times* 124:7 (April 2013) 329.

Foulds, Adam. *The Quickening Maze*. London: Jonathan Cape 2009.

Freud, Sigmund, and Josef Breuer. *Studies on Hysteria*. Translated by James and Alix Strachey, edited by Angela Richards. Pelican Freud Library 3. London: Penguin, 1974.

Frye, Northrop. *Anatomy of Criticism: Four Essays*. Princeton, NJ: Princeton University Press, 1990.

*Gerkin, Charles V. *An Introduction to Pastoral Care*. Nashville: Abingdon, 1997.

Ghiloni, Aaron J. "On Writing Interdisciplinary Theology." *Practical Theology* 6:1 (2013) 9–33.

Giblin, Charles H. "What Was Everything He Told Her She Did?" *NTS* 45:1 (1999) 148–52.

Glas, Gerrit, et al., eds. *Hearing Visions and Seeing Voices: Psychological Aspects of Biblical Concepts and Personalities*. Dordrecht: Springer, 2007.

Gomez, Lavinia. *An Introduction to Object Relations*. London: Free Association, 1997.

Goodhead, Andrew. *A Crown and a Cross: The Rise, Development, and Decline of the Methodist Class Meeting in Eighteenth-Century England*. Eugene, OR: Wipf & Stock, 2010.

*Grayson, Kenneth, *The Gospel of John*. London: Epworth, 1990.

*Green, Joel B., ed. *Hearing the New Testament: Strategies for Interpretation*. 2nd ed. Grand Rapids: Eerdmans, 2010.

Griffiths, Leslie J. *The Far Side of the Cross: The Spirituality of R. S. Thomas*. Exeter: Methodist Sacramental Fellowship, 1996.

*Grigor, Jean C. *Grow to Love: A Resource Book for Groups*. Edinburgh: Saint Andrew, 1977.

*Grosz, Stephen. *The Examined Life: How We Lose and Find Ourselves*. London: Chatto and Windus, 2013.

Guite, Malcolm. *Sounding the Seasons: Seventy Sonnets for the Christian Year*. Norwich: Canterbury, 2012.

Gunn, Giles B., ed. *Literature and Religion*. London: SCM, 1971.

Guntrip, Harry. *Psychoanalytic Theory, Therapy and the Self*. London: Karnak, 1991.

Hägerland, Tobias. "John's Gospel: A Two-Level Drama?" *JSNT* 25:3 (March 2003) 309–22.

Handley, Paul, et al. *The English Spirit: The Little Gidding Book of English Spirituality*. London: Darton, Longman & Todd, 1987.

Hanson, A. T. *The Prophetic Gospel*. Edinburgh: T. & T. Clark, 1991.

Hengel, Martin. *The Johannine Question*. London: SCM, 1989.

Hildebrandt, Franz. *Christianity According to the Wesleys*. London: Epworth, 1956.

Hildebrandt, Franz, and Oliver A. Beckerlegge, eds. *The Works of John Wesley*, vol. 7: *A Collection of Hymns for the Use of the People Called Methodist*. Oxford: Clarendon, 1983.

Hindmarsh, D. Bruce. *The Evangelical Conversion Narrative: Spiritual Autobiography in Early Modern England*. Oxford: Oxford University Press, 2005.

*Hobson Robert F. *Forms of Feeling: The Heart of Psychotherapy*. London: Tavistock, 1985.

Hodgson, Peter C. *Theology in the Fiction of George Eliot*. London: SCM, 2001.

*Holland, Norman N. *Holland's Guide to Psychoanalytic Psychology and Literature-and-Psychology*. Oxford: Oxford University Press, 1990.

Holloway, Richard. "Preaching." *Theology* 82:690 (November 1979) 404–12.

Hoskyns, Edwyn, *The Fourth Gospel*. Edited by Noel Davey. 2nd ed. London: Faber, 1947.

Hoskyns, Edwyn, and Noel Davey. *The Riddle of the New Testament*. London: Faber, 1958.

*Howard, Susan. *Psychodynamic Counselling in a Nutshell*. 2nd ed. London: Sage, 2011.

Hurst, J. S. "An Awkward Blessing: The Poetry of Jack Clemo." *Expository Times* 103:9 (June 1992) 268–71.

Hymns and Psalms: A Methodist and Ecumenical Hymn Book. London: Methodist Publishing House, 1983.

*Jacobs, Michael. *D. W. Winnicott*. London: Sage, 1995.

———. *Psychodynamic Counselling in Action*. London: Sage, 1988.

*————. *Swift to Hear: Facilitating Skills in Listening and Responding*. London: SPCK, 1985.

Jenson, Alexander S. "Martin Luther's 'Sin Boldly' Revisited: A Fresh Look at a controversial Concept in the Light of Modern Pastoral Psychology." *Contact* 137 (2002) 2–13.

Jeremias, Joachim. *Jerusalem in the Time of Jesus*. London: SCM, 1969.

John, Jeffrey. *The Meaning in the Miracles*. Norwich: Canterbury, 2001.

Jones, Ernest. *Sigmund Freud: Life and Work*. 3 vols. London: Hogarth, 1953–1957.

Jones, J. Morgan. *The New Testament in Modern Education*. London: Hodder and Stoughton, 1922.

Jones, Larry Paul. *The Symbol of Water in the Gospel of John*. JSNT Supplement Series 145. Sheffield: Sheffield Academic, 1997.

Jud, Gerald J., and Elizabeth Jud. *Training in the Art of Loving: The Church and the Human Potential Movement*. Philadelphia: Pilgrim, 1972.

Jung, Carl. *Selected Letters of Carl Jung, 1909–1961*. Edited by Gerhard Adler, translated by R. F. C. Hull. Princeton, NJ: Princeton University Press, 1984.

*Kalsched, Donald. *The Inner World of Trauma: Archetypal Defences of the Personal Spirit*. London: Routledge, 1996.

————. *Trauma and the Soul: A Psycho-Spiritual Approach to Human Development and Its Interruption*. London: Routledge, 2013.

Kitzberger, Ingrid. "Mary of Bethany and Mary of Magdala—The Female Characters in the Johannine Passion Narrative." *NTS* 41:4 (1995) 564–86.

Knights, Ben. *The Listening Reader: Fiction and Poetry for Counsellors and Psychotherapists*. London: Jessica Kingsley, 1995.

Koester, Craig R. "Messianic Exegesis and the Call of Nathanael (John 1.45–51)." *JSNT* 12:39 (1990) 23–34.

————. "Rethinking the Ethics of John: A Review Article." *JSNT* 36:1 (2013) 83–98.

————. "The Savior of the World (John 4.42)." *JBL* 109:4 (1990) 665–80.

————. *Symbolism in the Fourth Gospel: Meaning, Mystery and Community*. Minneapolis: Fortress, 1995.

*Lake, Frank. *Clinical Theology: A Theological and Psychiatric Basis to Clinical Pastoral Care*. London: Darton, Longman & Todd, 1966.

*————. *Clinical Theology: A Theological and Psychiatric Basis to Clinical Pastoral Care*. Abridged by Martin H. Yeomans. London: Darton, Longman & Todd, 1986.

————. *Tight Corners in Pastoral Counselling*. London: Darton, Longman & Todd, 1981.

————. *Transference in Pastoral Care*. Lingdale Paper 9. Church Westcote, Oxford: Clinical Theological Association, 1989.

Lear, Jonathan. *Therapeutic Action: An Earnest Plea for Irony*. London: Karnac, 2003.

Lebrecht, Norman. *Why Mahler?: How One Man and Ten Symphonies Changed the World*. London: Faber, 2010.

Lee, Dorothy. *The Symbolic Narratives of the Fourth Gospel*. Sheffield: Sheffield Academic, 1994.

Lehrer, Jonah. *Proust Was a Neuroscientist*. New York: Houghton Mifflin, 2008.

*Leslie, Robert C. *Sharing Groups in the Church: An Invitation to Involvement*. Nashville: Abingdon, 1970.

Levine, Stephen K. *Poiesis: The Language of Psychology and the Speech of the Soul*. London: Kingsley, 1997.

Lieu, Judith. "Blindness in the Johannine Tradition." *New Testament Studies* 34:1 (1988) 83–95.

———. "Temple and Synagogue in John." *NTS* 45:1 (1999) 51–69.

———. *The Theology of the Johannine Epistles*. Cambridge: Cambridge University Press, 1991.

Lindars, Barnabas. *The Gospel of John*. Grand Rapids: Eerdmans, 1972.

———. *The Johannine Literature*. Sheffield: Sheffield Academic, 2000.

*———. *John: New Testament Guides*. Sheffield: Sheffield Academic, 1990.

Loader, William. *The Christology of the Fourth Gospel*. 2nd ed. Frankfurt: Peter Lang, 1992.

Lynch, Gordon, ed. *Clinical Counselling in Pastoral Settings*. London: Routledge, 1999.

Maccini, Robert Gordon. "A Reassessment of the Woman at the Well in John 4 in Light of the Samaritan Context." *JSNT* 16:53 (April 1994) 35–46.

Mace, Chris, ed. *Heart and Soul: The Therapeutic Face of Philosophy*. London: Routledge, 1999.

Mack, Phyllis. *Heart Religion in the British Enlightenment: Gender and Emotion in Early Methodism*. Cambridge: Cambridge University Press, 2008.

Mallison, John. *Christian Lifestyle: Discovery Through Small Groups*. West Ryde, Australia: Renewal, 1977.

*Marsh, John. *Saint John*. London: Penguin, 1968.

Martyn, J. Louis. *History and Theology in the Fourth Gospel*. 2nd ed. Nashville: Abingdon, 1979.

Maury, Philippe, ed. "Life for the World." *Student World* 51:3 (1958).

May, Rollo. *Paulus*. London: Collins, 1973.

Mayeski, Marie Ann. "Women and Their Mothers: Rejecting and Proclaiming the Tradition of the Saints." *Anglican Theological Review* 83:2 (Spring 2001) 223–38.

Meeks, Wayne. "The Man from Heaven in Johannine Sectarianism." *JBL* 91 (1972) 44–72.

Miller, Gavin. "Crossing the Border: Pastoral Theology and Psychotherapy." *Expository Times* 124:4 (January 2013) 157–65.

*Moloney, Francis J. *Belief in the Word: Reading John 1–4*. Minneapolis: Augsburg Fortress, 1993.

———. "The Fourth Gospel and the Jesus of History." *NTS* 46:1 (2000) 42–58.

*———. *Glory Not Dishonor: Reading John 13–21*. Minneapolis: Augsburg Fortress, 1998.

*———. *Signs and Shadows: Reading John 5–12*. Minneapolis: Augsburg Fortress, 1996.

Moltmann-Wendel, Elizabeth. *The Women Around Jesus*. Translated by John Bowden. London: SCM, 1982.

Moore, Stephen D. "Are There Impurities in the Living Water that the Johannine Jesus Dispenses?" *Biblical Interpretation* 1:2 (1993) 207–27. Also found in Moore, *The Bible in Theory*, 81–97.

———. *The Bible in Theory: Critical and Postcritical Essays*. Atlanta: Society of Biblical Literature, 2010.

*Moran, Frances M. *Listening: A Pastoral Style*. Alexandria, Australia: Dwyer, 1996.

Motyer, Steve. "Method in Fourth Gospel Studies: A Way Out of the Impasse?" *JSNT* 66:2 (1997) 27–44.

Moule, C. F. D. *An Idiom-Book of New Testament Greek*. 2nd ed. Cambridge: Cambridge University Press, 1959.

Need, Stephen W. "Re-Reading the Prologue: Incarnation and Creation in John 1.1–18." *Theology* 106:834 (November/December 2003) 397–404.

Newheart, Michael Willett. *Word and Soul: A Psychological, Literary, and Cultural Reading of the Fourth Gospel.* Collegeville, MN: Liturgical, 2001.

Neyrey, Jerome H. *The Gospel of John.* Cambridge: Cambridge University Press, 2007.

———. *The Gospel of John in Cultural and Rhetorical Perspective.* Grand Rapids: Eerdmans, 2009.

Nolan, Greg, and William West, eds. *Extending Horizons in Helping and Caring Therapies.* London: Routledge, 2020.

Northridge, W. L. *Disorders of the Emotional and Spiritual Life.* London: Epworth, 1960.

O'Day, Gail R. "Towards a Narrative-Critical Study of John." *Interpretation* 49:4 (October 1995) 341–46.

*Oden, Thomas C. *The Intensive Group Experience: The New Pietism.* Philadelphia: Westminster, 1972.

Paddison, Angus. "Engaging Scripture: incarnation and the Gospel of John." *Scottish Journal of Theology* 60.2 (2007) 144–60.

Painter, John. *The Quest for the Messiah.* Edinburgh: T. & T. Clark, 1993.

Pearson, Jenny, ed. *Analyst of the Imagination: The Life and Work of Charles Rycroft.* London: Karnac, 2004.

Pembroke, Neil. *The Art of Listening: Dialogue, Shame, and Pastoral Care.* Edinburgh: T. & T. Clark, 2002.

Phillips, Thomas E. "'The Third Fifth Day?' John 2.1 in Context." *Expository Times* 115.10 (July 2004) 328–31.

Quiost, Michel. *Prayers of Life.* Dublin: Gill & Son, 1963.

Ramsey, Ian T. *Religious Language: An Empirical Placing of Theological Phrases.* London: SCM, 1957.

Rensberger, David. *Overcoming the World: Politics and Community in the Gospel of John.* London: SPCK, 1989.

Richardson, Alan, and John Bowden, eds. *A New Dictionary of Christian Theology.* London: SCM, 1983

Ridderbos, Herman N. *The Gospel of John: A Theological Commentary.* Translated by John Vriend. London: Eerdmans, 1997.

Rizutto, A. M. *The Birth of the Living God.* Chicago: University of Chicago Press, 1979.

Roberts, Vaughan S. "Water as an Implicit Metaphor for Organisational Change Within the Church." *Implicit Religion* 5.1 (2002) 29.

Robinson, John A. T. *The Priority of John.* London: SCM, 1985.

Robinson, Marilynne. *Gilead.* London: Virago, 2005.

———. *Lila.* London: Virago, 2014.

Rollins, Wayne G. *Soul and Psyche: The Bible in Psychological Perspective.* Mineapolis: Augsburg, Fortress, 1999.

Rollins, Wayne G., and D. Andrew Kille, eds. *Psychological Insight into the Bible.* Grand Rapids: Eerdmans, 2007.

Routley, Eric. *The Gift of Conversion,* London: Lutterworth, 1957.

Rupp, Gordon. *The Righteousness of God: A Reconsideration of the Character and Work of Martin Luther.* London: Hodder and Stoughton, 1953.

Rycroft, Charles. *Psychoanalysis and Beyond.* London: Hogarth, 1991.

———, ed. *Psychoanalysis Observed.* New York: Coward-McCann, 1966.

*St. Clair, Michael. *Object Relations and Self Psychology: An Introduction.* Monterey, CA: Brooks, 1986.

Samuels, Andrew. *Jung and the Post Jungians*. London: Routledge, Kegan & Paul, 1985.

Samuels, Andrew, Bani Shorter, and Fred Plaut. *A Critical Dictionary of Jungian Analysis*. London: Routledge, 1991.

Sanford, John A. *Mystical Christianity: A Psychological Commentary on the Gospel of John*. New York: Crossroad, 1994.

Schnackenburg, Rudolf. *The Gospel According to St. John*. Translated by Kevin Smith. 3 vols. Tunbridge Wells, Kent: Burns & Oates, 1980.

Schüssler Fiorenza, Elisabeth. *In Memory of Her: A Feminist Theological Reconstruction of Early Christian Beginnings*. London: SCM, 1983.

Scott, Martin. *Sophia and the Johannine Jesus*. JSNT Supplement Series 71. Sheffield: Sheffield Academic, 1992.

Segal, Julia. *Melanie Klein*. London: Sage, 1992.

Segovia, Fernando F. "The Significance of Social Location in Reading John's Story." *Interpretation* 49:4 (October 1995) 370–78.

Singing the Faith. Trustees for Methodist Church Purposes. London: Hymns Ancient & Modern, 2011.

*Sloyan, Gerard S. *John*. Interpretation. Atlanta: John Knox, 1988.

*———. *What Are They Saying About John?* New York: Paulist, 1991.

Smail, David. *Illusion and Reality: The Meaning of Anxiety*. London: Dent, 1984.

Smith, David L. *Approaching Psychoanalysis: An Introductory Course*. London: Karnac, 1999.

Smith, Dwight Moody. *The Theology of the Gospel of John*. Cambridge: Cambridge University Press, 1995.

Sobornost/ECR Vol. 12, issue 1, 20–39; Vol. 12, issue 2, 145–156. Oxford: Fellowship of St. Alban and St. Sergius, 1990

Solignac, Pierre. *The Christian Neurosis*. Translated by John Bowden. London: SCM, 1982.

Sparks. H. F. D. *A Synopsis of the Gospels. Part II: The Gospel according to St John with the Synoptic Parallels*. London: A. & C. Black, 1974.

*Stead, Tim. *Mindfulness and Christian Spirituality: Making Space for God*. London: SPCK, 2016.

Stewart, Columba. "Radical Honesty about the Self: The Practice of the Desert Fathers." *Sobornost*, incorporating *Eastern Churches Review*, 12.1 (1990) 25–39.

———. "Radical Honesty about the Self: The Tradition of the Desert Fathers and Its Heirs." *Sobornost*, incorporating *Eastern Churches Review*, 12.2 (1990) 143–55.

Stibbe, Mark W. G., ed. *The Gospel of John as Literature: An Anthology of Twentieth Century Perspectives*. Leiden: Brill, 1993.

*———. *John*. Readings: A New Biblical Commentary. Sheffield: Sheffield Academic, 1996.

———. *John as Storyteller*. Cambridge: Cambridge University Press, 1992.

———. *John's Gospel*. London: Routledge, 1994.

Stroup, George W. *The Promise of Narrative Theology*. London: SCM, 1984.

Stubbs, John. *Donne: The Reformed Soul*. London: Penguin, 2007.

Sutcliffe, Joseph. *The Mutual Communion of Saints: Showing the Necessity and Advantages of the Weekly Meetings for a Communication of Experience*. 1797.

Taylor, Charles. *Sources of the Self: The Making of the Modern Identity*. Cambridge: Cambridge University Press, 1989.

Taylor, John V. *The Go-Between God: The Holy Spirit and the Christian Mission*. London: SCM, 1972.

Temple, William. *Readings in St. John's Gospel*. London: Macmillan, 1947.

Theissen, Gerd. *Psychological Aspects of Pauline Theology*. Translated by John P. Galvin. Edinburgh: T. & T. Clark, 1987.

Thiselton, Anthony C. "Biblical Theology and Hermeneutics." In *The Modern Theologians*, edited by David Ford. 2nd ed. Oxford: Blackwell, 1997.

———. "Language and Meaning in Religion." In *Dictionary of Pastoral Care and Counselling*, edited by Rodney J. Hunter, 1123–43. Nashville: Abingdon, 1990.

———. "Truth." In *The Dictionary of New Testament Theology*, edited by Colin Brown, 3:874–902. Grand Rapids: Zondervan, 1986.

Thomas, R. S. *Collected Poems 1945–1990*. London: Pheonix, 2000.

———. *Later Poems: 1972–1982*. London: Macmillan, 1983.

———. *Selected Poems, 1946–1968*. Newcastle: Bloodaxe, 1986.

Thorne, Brian. *The Counsellor as Prophet*. 1994 Frank Lake Memorial Lecture. Lingdale Paper 21. Oxford: Clinical Theology Association, 1996.

Thurneysen, Eduard. *Theology of Pastoral Care*. Richmond: John Knox, 1962.

Tillich, Paul. *The Courage to Be*. London: Collins, Fontana, 1962.

———. *The Shaking of the Foundations*. London: Penguin, 1962.

Time to Talk of God: Recovering Christian Conversation as a Way of Nurturing Discipleship. A report of the [UK] Methodist Conference 2005, with questions for group conversation. London: Methodist Church, 2005.

Todd, Andrew J. "The Interaction of Talk and Text: Re-Contextualizing Biblical Interpretation." *Practical Theology* 6.1 (2013) 69–85.

Tolmie, D. Francois. "The Characterisation of God in the Fourth Gospel." *JSNT* 20:69 (1998) 57–75.

Tompkins. Jane P., ed. *Reader Response Criticism: From Formalism to Post-Structuralism*. Baltimore: John Hopkins University Press, 1980.

Tucker, Paul Hayes. *Monet in the '90s: The Series Paintings*. Edited by Stephen Robert Frankel. Boston: Museum of Fine Arts; New Haven, CT: Yale University Press; London, Royal Academy, 1990.

Ulanov, Ann, and Barry Ulanov. *The Healing Imagination: The Meaning of Psyche and Soul*. Einsiedein, Switzerland: Daimon, 1999.

Ulanov, Ann Belford. *Finding Space: Winnicott, God, and Psychic Reality*. Louisville: Westminster John Knox, 2001.

———. *The Functioning Transcendent: A Study in Analytical Psychology*. Wilmette, IL: Chiron, 1996.

———. *Picturing God*. Einsiedein, Switzerland: Daimon, 2002.

Vanier, Jean. *Drawn into the Mystery of Jesus through the Gospel of John*. London: Darton, Longman & Todd, 2012.

Van Deusen Hunsinger, Deborah. *Bearing the Unbearable: Trauma, Gospel, and Pastoral Care*. Grand Rapids: Eerdmans, 2015.

Van Tilborg, Sjef. *Imaginative Love in John*. Leiden: Brill, 1993.

Verhagen, Peter J., John L. Cox, et al., eds. *Psychiatry and Religion: Beyond Boundaries*. Oxford: Blackwell, 2010.

Verney, Stephen. *Water into Wine: An Introduction to John's Gospel*. London: Darton, Longman and Todd, 1995.

Waddell, Margot. *Inside Lives: Psychoanalysis and the Growth of Personality*. Tavistock Clinic Series. London: Karnac, 2002.

Wahide, Urban C. von. "Community in Conflict: The History and Social Context of the Johannine Community." *Interpretation* 49:4 (October 1995) 379–89.

Wakefield, Gordon S., ed. *A Dictionary of Spirituality*. London: SCM, 1983.

Watson, Richard. "Charles Wesley and Eighteenth-Century Poetry." *Proceedings of the Wesley Historical Society* 60:6 (October 2016) 279–92.

*Watts, Fraser, et al. *Psychology for Christian Ministry*. London: Routledge, 2002.

Wesley, John. *Great Thoughts from Wesley*. Edited by Hilda Noel Schroetter. London: Collins, 1968.

———. "A Plain Account of the People Called Methodists." 1749. Reprinted in *A History of the Methodist Church in Great Britain*, edited by Rupert Davies, A. Raymond George, and E. Gordon Rupp, 92–102. London: Epworth, 1983.

———. *Preface to a Collection of Psalms and Hymns*. 1739.

Wessels, Anton. *A Kind of Bible: Vincent van Gogh as Evangelist*. Translated by John Bowden. London: SCM, 2000.

Whitfield, Richard. *Mastering E-Motions: Feeling Our Way Intelligently in Relationships*. Ropley, Hants: Hunt, 2005.

Wilber, Ken. *The Marriage of Sense and Soul: Integrating Science and Religion*. Dublin: Gateway, 2001.

Williams, H. A. *The True Wilderness*. London: Constable, 1965.

Williams, Rowan. *Being Disciples*. London: SPCK, 2016.

———. *Meeting God in Mark*. London: SPCK, 2014.

———. "Reformed Characters: Rediscovering a Common Tradition." Address to the Joint Synod of the Methodist Church in Wales, September 16, 1995.

*———. *The Wound of Knowledge: Christian Spirituality from the New Testament to St. John of the Cross*. London: Darton, Longman & Todd, 1979.

Wilson, Linda. "Conversion among Female Methodists, 1825–75." *Proceedings of the Wesley Historical Society* 51:6 (October 1998) 217–25.

Winnicott, Donald W. *Playing and Reality*. Abingdon: Routledge, 2005.

Wolmar, Christian. *The Subterranean Railway*. London: Atlantic, 2012.

Wood, James. *Directions and Cautions Addressed to the Class Leaders*. 1803.

Woodman, Marion. *The Pregnant Virgin: A Process of Psychological Transformation*. Studies in Jungian Psychology Series. Toronto: Inner City, 1985.

Wright, Elizabeth. *Psychoanalytic Criticism: Theory in Practice*. London: Routledge, 1984.

Wright, N. T. *John for Everyone: Chapters 1–10*. London: SPCK, 2002.

Young, Frances M. *Construing the Cross: Type, Sign, Symbol, Word, Action*. London: SPCK, 2016.

Further Reading: Group Work

There are many books on group work with a psychodynamic base! As well as reading, the best way to learn is to get into a growth group or group therapy experience oneself!

Beetham, P. A., ed. *Members One of Another*. Christ and the Cosmos Series. Oxford, 1996.

Bion, W. R. *Experiences in Groups*. London: Tavistock, 1961.

Brown, Dennis, and Louis Zinkin, eds. *The Psyche and the Social World: Developments in Group-Analytical Theory*. London: Routedge, 1994.

*Egan, Gerard. *Face to Face: The Small Group Experience and Interpersonal Growth*. Monterey, CA: Brooks-Cole, 1973.

Foulkes, S. H., and E. J. Anthony. *Group Psychotherapy: The Psychoanalytical Approach*. London: Penguin, 1973.

Hinshelwood, R. D. *What Happens in Groups: Psychoanalysis, the Individual and the Community*. London: Free Association, 1987.

Jacoby, Mario. *The Analytic Encounter: Transference and Human Relationships*. Toronto: Inner City, 1984.

Lawrence, W. Gordon. *Tongued with Fire: Groups in Experience*. London: Karnac, 2000.

Rogers, Carl R. *Encounter Groups*. London: Penguin, 1969.

*Thorne, Brian. *Person Centred Counselling: Therapeutic and Spiritual Dimensions*. London: Whurr, 1991.

Walton, Henry, ed. *Small Group Psychotherapy*. London: 1971.

*Watson, David Lowes. *Covenant Discipleship: Christian Formation Through Mutual Responsibility*. Nashville: Discipleship Resources, 1996.

Wolmar, Christian. *The Subterranean Railway*. London: Atlantic, 2012.

Wright, Harry. *Groupwork Perspectives and Practice*. Middlesex: Scutari, 1989.

Yalom, Irvin D. *The Theory and Practice of Group Psychotherapy*. 5th ed. New York: Basic Books, 1995.

Further Reading: Psychodynamic Approaches to Texts

On psychodynamic criticism and literary theory there are, for example, the writings of Linda Anderson, Marie Bridge, Maud Ellman, Terry Eagleton (see *Literary Theory: An Introduction* (Oxford: Blackwell, 1983), 131–68), Shoshana Felman, Norman Holland, Ingrid Kitzberger, David Lodge, Jane Tompkins, Paul Williams and Glen Gabbard, and Elizabeth Wright.